Victorian Critics of Democracy

Victorian Critics of Democracy

CARLYLE · RUSKIN · ARNOLD
STEPHEN · MAINE · LECKY

By

Benjamin Evans Lippincott

1964
OCTAGON BOOKS, INC.
NEW YORK

Reprinted 1964
by special arrangement with the University of Minnesota Press

OCTAGON BOOKS, INC.

175 FIFTH AVENUE
NEW YORK, N. Y. 10010

LIBRARY OF CONGRESS CATALOG CARD NUMBER: 64-24850

Printed in U.S.A. by
NOBLE OFFSET PRINTERS, INC.
NEW YORK 3, N. Y.

To

HAROLD J. LASKI

*who knows, as so few do, that the
secret of great teaching
lies in friendship*

PREFACE

CARLYLE, Ruskin, and Arnold have been written about many times before, but they have been written about mainly by publicists or professors of English literature. Ruskin alone has been fully treated by a social scientist; J. A. Hobson's *John Ruskin* is a definitive work. The essay on Ruskin in this volume obviously does not pretend to any such complete treatment as Hobson gives; yet it may be of some use as a brief analysis, written at a later time. Stephen's political ideas have been dealt with only in summary form, Maine's as incidental to his legal thought, and Lecky's not at all.

The aim of this book is not to write history but to present, to explain, and to evaluate the intellectual protest made against democracy in England in the nineteenth century. The chief critics, Carlyle, Ruskin, Arnold, Stephen, Maine, and Lecky, brought forward all the main criticisms of democracy that can be brought forward, except the Marxian. In a fundamental way their criticism is more relevant today than when they wrote, for though their criticism could be ignored in the last century, it can be ignored today only at democracy's peril.

Never has it been more urgent to dissect anti-democratic thought into its elements. Never has it been more necessary to evaluate the ideas of the critics of democracy. Never has it been more urgent to attempt to discover why men support or oppose the institutions of their day; why, in the case of our study, such outstanding intellectuals came to take issue with democracy.

Preface

Nor is it less worth while to see the nineteenth-century writers in the thought and life of their time. And it is well to see what impression they made on their contemporaries; to attempt, especially, to explain the surprising fact that though Carlyle exercised an extraordinary moral influence, he hardly touched the mind of his generation; and to explain why the prophets' criticism of democracy and their charge of materialism fell upon deaf ears.

A word may not be out of the way with regard to the particular form I have given the essays of this volume. It will be noticed that each essay is divided into five sections; such a division best permits an answer to what I believe are essential questions confronting the critic in a study of this kind: What are the distinctive characteristics of the writer, and, in virtue of these, what place does he hold in the thought of his time? What are the influences that go to shape the writer's thought? What are the writer's basic assumptions and how do they affect the structure of his thought? What is his criticism of democracy, and his criticism of the ideas and institutions in which it works? Finally, is his criticism of democracy valid?

I wish to thank Professors Harold J. Laski and H. L. Beales of the London School of Economics and Political Science for the interest they have taken in this book in its different stages, for their kindness in reading it in its final form, and for giving me the benefit of their suggestions. Evron M. Kirkpatrick of the University of Minnesota kindly read the manuscript and gave me helpful comments on a number of passages. I also want to thank J. S. Fulton, fellow of Balliol College, Oxford, for reading the essay on Maine and for his helpful observations. I am indebted to F. M. Atkinson, Esq., of Harrup and Company, London, for suggestions as to matters of style.

The chapter on Stephen has previously appeared, in a more condensed and a somewhat different form, in *Economica* for August, 1931.

B. E. L.

University of Minnesota

CONTENTS

INTRODUCTION

CARLYLE, Ruskin, Arnold, Stephen, Maine, and Lecky were perhaps the most vigorous and distinguished critics of democracy in England in the nineteenth century. These men attacked, in varying degree, the liberal tradition which was at its zenith in the Victorian age; above all, they attacked middle-class democracy.

When they first began to write, the middle class had established its claim to power; by the franchise act of 1832 the aristocracy had abdicated in favor of the men of industry and commerce. Henceforth the chief concern of the state was to maintain the rules not of a feudal economy but of capitalism. In its rise to power the middle class had exploited the wage earner; by the thirties the poverty and suffering and the miserable conditions in which the working class lived had made an impression on the more responsible leaders of the community.

If men like Owen and writers like John Stuart Mill helped to persuade the new rulers that the plight of the workingman must be ameliorated, so also did Carlyle. In fact, the prophet of Chelsea, with a literary power unrivaled in his time, made the educated public conscious of social distress. More than anyone else he made his generation aware of the fact that the workingman was a human being, who suffered gross injustice, who was exploited as if he were no more than a mere instrument to be used, worn out, and discarded.

So degrading and chaotic for Carlyle was the lot of the mass

I

of men under the factory system driven by the profit motive that he found middle-class democracy completely impotent to solve the social problem. Rejecting democracy, he argued for a benevolent dictatorship, whose leaders would be drawn from the best British stock; such a dictatorship, he thought, would put things straight by reigning in the military fashion.

Ruskin, Carlyle's disciple, was no less confident that the program of middle-class liberalism had brought about and perpetuated economic, social, and political disorder. Ruskin probed the economic and intellectual foundations of the industrial system that made possible the Victorian age with more acuteness than any writer in the century save Marx. He insisted that capitalism must be abandoned and cooperation replace competition, and that industry must be made honest and responsible; and, like Carlyle, he insisted that a decent standard of life should be provided for the worker, that the worker should be educated and made secure. Again, like Carlyle, he placed his faith in autocracy and looked to English aristocrats to manage his ideal state. Unlike Carlyle, however, he did not urge the aristocracy to grab the reins of power, but beseeched them to usher in a new day by reforming themselves. In spite of the reactionary political remedy that Carlyle and Ruskin advocated for the ills of their time, these men fathered the socialist movement in England.

Still another prophet attacked the "do-nothing" state; Matthew Arnold joined Carlyle and Ruskin in the assault on laissez faire and maintained that English society, dedicated to inequality of property and conditions of life, was failing in education. So long, he argued, as English society remained in the hands of the aristocracy, it must remain uncivilized. In order to break down the materialism of the upper class, the vulgarity of the middle class, and the brutality of the lower, Arnold recommended a national system of public education and the reduction of inequality; to this same end, he also proposed that the state democratize the municipal system and establish a national church. Unlike Carlyle and Ruskin, Arnold did not turn

Introduction

to feudalism to find a means of transforming the raw and unlovely civilization of his age; while he would give authority a larger place than the liberals and would expand the services and connections of the state, he would do these things under democracy. Though he favored extending the suffrage to the lower classes, he placed his confidence in the leadership of the middle class, educated by the state for service in government and the professions.

In varying degree Carlyle, Ruskin, and Arnold opposed the capitalist system and the laissez-faire state of liberalism; and in varying degree they sought a solution in authority and in expanded social services—above all, in education. Arnold parted company from Carlyle and Ruskin in that he refused to see these things imposed upon the nation by an "enlightened" despotism; yet he feared that the masses were not quite ready for power. Where Carlyle and Ruskin were certain that democracy would lead to anarchy, Arnold thought only that democracy might bring it about.

Stephen, Maine, and Lecky, so far from taking issue with middle-class democracy because it failed to deal with the social evils of capitalism, opposed the extension of the suffrage to the lower classes. Where Stephen believed that the ideals of liberty, equality, and fraternity, as propounded by advanced liberal thought, would loosen all social bonds, Maine and Lecky insisted that universal suffrage would most likely destroy private property. Stephen and Maine had no remedy for what they believed was the disease of democracy save authority, restricted very largely to law and order, and the introduction of institutional checks upon the popular will. Stephen, Maine, and Lecky both supported and challenged the liberal tradition. They stood for economic individualism and free competition, yet they distrusted democratic government, even as it was managed by the middle class. Like Carlyle and Ruskin and, to some extent, Arnold, their ideal government was one ruled by the wisdom of the few, which they easily discovered in the aristocracy or in the middle class.

3

Introduction

As the problems of democracy and capitalism are today essentially what they were in the Victorian age, the criticism of these intellectuals is as pertinent now as then. In a sense their criticism is even more pertinent at the present time, for, unlike the situation in the Victorian period, the liberal tradition is under fire on many fronts; both democracy and capitalism are on the defensive.

The Victorian critics are, indeed, modern. Carlyle had to wait until the third and fourth decades of the twentieth century before his message found considerable fulfillment. Hitler and Mussolini are his heroes in action, ruling the dull millions. Hitler and Mussolini made Carlyle's fight; they attacked the anarchy of liberalism and are enforcing order, without stint, in the military manner. The fascist states are an application of Ruskin's ideal of autocracy no less than of Carlyle's; in a sense Ruskin was more of a National Socialist than the present Nazi leaders, for he stood for the abolition of capitalism. Ruskin's analysis of capitalism, moreover, is as applicable today as when he wrote; and his advocacy of a professional view of industry anticipates in part the Guild Socialism of R. H. Tawney in *The Acquisitive Society*. Arnold lives in the present as much as Carlyle and Ruskin. His argument for democracy comes as a refreshing analysis, full of insight, at a time when there is a widespread belief in the efficacy of force, especially among the reactionaries of the right. Arnold's brilliant discussion of equality anticipates the Fabian Socialists and shows the profound inadequacy of the liberal view of the state.

The conservative who refuses to reconstruct the political and social institutions of our time, institutions whose basic ideas were shaped in the seventeenth and eighteenth centuries, to go back no further, will find that, apart from Burke, no writers have stated his case more forcefully than Stephen and Maine. And Lecky is the perfect illustration of the dilemma of the middle-class liberal, which is to say, of most liberals at the present time. Trained in the traditional freedom of his class, Lecky did not see that there could be no genuine freedom for

Introduction

the mass until economic and also full political democracy had been attained. As there are elements of fascist thought in Stephen and Maine, in their insistence on the difficulty and inefficiency of democracy, so are there elements in Lecky — in his preference for capitalism to democracy.

None of these intellectual critics were political philosophers like T. H. Green, nor political thinkers like John Stuart Mill; theoretical and systematic thinking was not characteristic of their minds. Carlyle, Ruskin, and Arnold were men of letters, perhaps the most eminent of the Victorian period. Stephen, Maine, and Lecky, who are little known outside academic circles, were what may be called technical writers. Stephen is best known for his *History of English Criminal Law,* which is still the authoritative work on that subject; and Maine, in his celebrated *Ancient Law,* founded the historical school of juris-prudence in the English-speaking world. Lecky, who first at-tracted notice by his *History of Rationalism,* established his reputation with *A History of England in the Eighteenth Cen-tury*. These critics were intellectuals or professional men; none of them were men of practical affairs.

All these men turned away from their intellectual pursuits to criticize the political and social ideas of their time; all these men, except Arnold, turned to challenge the democratic move-ment. Their opposition to democracy was essentially Platonic; they opposed democracy fundamentally for the same reason as Plato — that democracy led to disorder. Though as a critic none of these men equalled Plato, who, as Bryce well saw, is the greatest critic of all, they nevertheless made a contribution. Their significance is to be found in a criticism of democracy under modern conditions and especially in a criticism of de-mocracy as it was working in an industrial society organized on the profit motive, in short, under capitalism. Where Plato opposed democracy above all on the ground that it produced spiritual anarchy in men, the nineteenth-century critics op-posed democracy above all on the ground that it led to social anarchy.

THOMAS CARLYLE

I

Save for Rousseau, Marx, and Voltaire, Carlyle is perhaps unsurpassed in modern times as a political and social critic. Unlike Marx, he was not the chief intellectual source of a great change; nor was he, like Voltaire or Rousseau, a great leader in a great movement. He was not even, like Bentham, the founder of a school; if he had in his time what is known as a following, he had, apart from Ruskin, no important disciples. He contributed no new ideas to political and social reform; yet no political writer in nineteenth-century England was as widely read as he. He did not exert an influence in the world of ideas comparable to that of Bentham or John Stuart Mill, yet he was more widely discussed than either; he reached circles in the aristocracy and in the lower classes that these men could not touch. Carlyle was such a power in his day primarily because he appealed not to men's minds but to their emotions. And here his strength lay above all in his extraordinary ability to stir the moral feelings — he was nothing so much as a prophet.

Almost all of the prominent figures in Victorian life testify to Carlyle's influence as a prophet. Charles Darwin said of him, "he has been all-powerful in impressing some grand moral truths on the minds of men."[1] Leslie Stephen said, "such men as Carlyle and Emerson, vague and even contradictory as was their teaching, did more to rouse lofty aspirations and to moral-

[1] Francis Darwin, *Life and Letters of Charles Darwin* (2 vols., New York, 1899), I, 77.

6

ize political creeds than the teaching of the Utilitarians." [2] Miss Martineau remarked, "if I am warranted in believing that the society I am bidding farewell to is a vast improvement upon that which I was born into, I am confident that the blessed change is attributable to Carlyle more than to any single influence besides." [3] Writers in recent years have also pointed out that Carlyle was an important moral force in the nineteenth century; J. G. Robertson speaks of him as the greatest moral force in his day. [4]

In view of his unusual influence, it is curious that his age should have accepted so few of his ideas. His championing of the spiritual view of life as against materialism, one of his greatest efforts, met with little success. The mechanical view of life did not lose but, on the whole, gained throughout the period in which Carlyle wrote. It is true that as a writer with a strong religious sense, and as an exponent of what may be called Calvinistic theism, he undoubtedly strengthened in many the "will to believe." True, also, that as a critic of theology and of organized religion he promoted skepticism. But his plea for "renunciation" was all but in vain. No one could say that Carlyle significantly affected religious thought as did F. D. Maurice and Cardinal Newman.

Nor did Carlyle exercise any great influence over men's minds in the social sphere. Some of his ideas, to be sure, left their mark. His doctrine of work, which he was never tired of urging as an antidote to skepticism, seems to have made a deep impression on many in his generation. His insistence on morality probably strengthened the belief in puritanism. His intense individualism, with its emphasis on "heroics," and his belief in inequality were apparently well received. And his belief in the humanity of ordinary men, which so frequently

[2] Leslie Stephen, *The English Utilitarians* (3 vols., London, 1900), III, 477.

[3] Harriet Martineau, *Autobiography* (Maria W. Chapman, editor, 2d ed., 2 vols., London, 1877), I, 387.

[4] *Cambridge History of English Literature*, XIII, 24. For Carlyle's influence in New England see Van Wyck Brooks, *The Flowering of New England* (New York, 1936), pages 193–95.

found expression in his writings in his earlier years, seems to have exerted considerable influence. Apart from his doctrine of work, no idea that Carlyle advocated seems to have been so influential as the idea of state interference; there seems to be no doubt that he took considerable toll of laissez faire as a principle of governmental policy.

His attack, however, on the economic order was hardly better than a splendid failure. If he was partly responsible for making a breach in the outer defenses of the profit-gain system, he did not penetrate to the citadel itself. He did not diminish the prestige of what R. H. Tawney has called the acquisitive instinct, the profit motive, which is the mainspring of economic individualism. And selfishness, the by-product of the system that prompted each to take what he could, was hardly if at all mitigated by his criticism. After Carlyle wrote men were not less preoccupied with Mammon; on the contrary, by the eighties they were more concerned with Mammon than ever before. Neither was Carlyle very successful in his criticism of the utilitarian philosophy, though it was the intellectual foundation of laissez-faire individualism.

He convinced very few that the proper system of government for combating "anarchy" was a strong aristocracy of hero-kings, of captains of industry. Not many were willing to side with him in the case he made out for authority and the attack he made on democracy. His insistence that Parliament should be nothing more than an adviser to the executive, that the administrative branch of the government should assimilate most of the power into its hands, gained no support. In *Latter-Day Pamphlets* Carlyle made one of the most impressive pleas for administrative reform ever penned; but the book was hardly read by his generation, still less by those that followed.

Carlyle's solution for the industrial problem, that workers should be induced to emigrate, that industry should be planned, and that part of it should be owned and run by the government in competition with private enterprise, made no headway. Nor did his proposal that workers should be organized in industry after the military model, that they should be regimented like so many soldiers. His strictures on humanitarianism and his defense of negro slavery provoked only ridicule and disgust. His enthusiasm for the Anglo-Saxon race and for empire attracted little notice, though he may have prepared the ground to some extent for the imperialism of Disraeli and Chamberlain.

That Carlyle's age did not accept the burden of his message, that it was positively repelled by not a few of his ideas, while it permitted him, in spite of this, a sway over men's moral feelings unequaled in the nineteenth century, only testifies to the nature of the prophet. The secret of a prophet's influence, so far as he himself is concerned, lies essentially not in ideas, but in qualities other than ideas. This does not mean that ideas play no part, for they most certainly do, only that they do not generally play a major part. Perhaps the chief source of a prophet's influence is his capacity for deep moral feeling—his feeling for injustice, his sense of right and wrong, his grasp of moral realities. But moral feeling can be of no influence by itself, but only in so far as it is able to operate successfully with other factors such as ideas, and only in so far as the age is in a mood for prophets.

To explain either fully or precisely how Carlyle's moral feeling operated successfully with certain other of his qualities, and how his age, being in a mood for prophets, was affected by them is, of course, out of the question. All that can be done with a problem so intricate and so complex is to hint at a solution; yet it is important that this be attempted, for the problem of a prophet's influence is the chief problem concerning him.

Carlyle attained to a position of power through the sheer force of personality more perhaps than anyone else in his age. Nevertheless, contrary to his "great man" theory of history, he was largely dependent upon his time for the influence he exerted. When Carlyle appeared, the industrial system was running roughshod over society; the lot of the mass of men was poverty and misery, not a decent life. Carlyle appeared also when some men were becoming dimly aware, and a few keenly aware, of the injustice of the social and economic system under which they lived. That Evangelicals like Wilberforce and Shaftesbury, Philosophical Radicals like Brougham and Romilly, men of letters like Dickens and Kingsley, interested themselves in reform, is proof enough of a growing sense of moral concern. With evil and suffering on the one hand, and an awakening moral conscience on the other, the times were ripe for a prophet. Carlyle appeared to champion right against wrong; in him more than in anyone else there was crystallized the moral protest against the industrial civilization of the nineteenth century. No one pointed out the wrongs of the age with such passion and force as he, nor did anyone express indignation against injustice with such intensity.

Carlyle's spiritual attitude, which was closely related to his moral feeling, made for not a little influence. By his spiritual attitude we mean the feeling and, so far as it can be rationalized, the point of view that life is of spiritual significance. Perhaps nowhere in Carlyle's writings is such an attitude better illustrated than in the following passage:

Thus, like a God-created, fire-breathing-Spirit host, we emerge from the Inane, haste stormfully across the astonished Earth, then plunge again into the Inane. . . . Can the Earth, which is but dead and a vision, resist Spirits which have reality and are alive? On the hardest adamant some footprint of us is stamped in. The last Rear of the host will read traces of the earliest Van. But whence?—Oh, Heaven! whither? Sense knows not; Faith knows not, only that it is through Mystery to Mystery, from God and to God.[5]

No one in modern times, says Ernest Barker, has had so vivid a sense of the spiritual reality of the universe; and it is because of this that Carlyle is of modern thinkers the most akin to Plato.[6] The times were indeed favorable to the reception of Carlyle's spiritual attitude. Religious dogma was suffering more than ever from a loss of prestige, owing to the increasing at-

[5] *Sartor Resartus* (Centenary Edition, London, 1907), p. 212. Hereafter all references to Carlyle's work will be to the Centenary Edition.

[6] Ernest Barker, *Political Thought in England, 1848 to 1914: From Herbert Spencer to the Present Day* (rev. ed., London, 1928), p. 189.

tacks of science, especially the new biology, and to the corrosive effect of the higher criticism; at the same time, however, there was a revival of religious feeling. Carlyle appealed to those who had parted with dogma but who still longed to satisfy the religious impulse, just as he appealed to those who had respect for science but who still felt that life was something more than a phase of mechanics. His affirmation of the spiritual significance of life tended to satisfy both the reason and the spirit. That Carlyle's spiritual attitude was permeated with a strong factual as well as a deep mystical element could only augment its power. Few things appeal more strongly to the English mind, especially to the English mind of the nineteenth century, than a happy marriage of the nonrational with respect for fact.[7]

The attitude Carlyle expressed toward his age enhanced his moral and spiritual appeal. This attitude was distinguished, on the one hand, by relentless opposition to his time and, on the other, by a desire to reform it. Inspired, like most prophets, with the idea of the divinity of the universe and with the idea of its essential justice, Carlyle found the world about him in all but direct contradiction. There was no alternative for him but to attempt to purge English civilization of what he believed was its evil and corruption. The missionary zeal when found in gifted hands must always in England, the modern home of the evangelical, the home of Wesley, command admiration. Perhaps this is especially true when it is combined with the spirit of implacable opposition, the spirit so well exemplified by Cromwell. Calling upon almost every weapon known to the armory of invective and satire, Carlyle lampooned and reviled his epoch. Never has a prophet more bitterly assailed an age for its shortcomings; in this respect Carlyle well holds a place with Isaiah, Juvenal, and Swift. When opposition is so tenaciously persisted in as it was with Carlyle, above all when that

[7] See Wilhelm Dibelius' illuminating work, *England: Its Character and Genius* (London, 1930). The above analysis is especially indebted to his chapter "National Characteristics," pages 147–81. See also Taine's suggestive remarks in his essay on Carlyle in *History of English Literature* (rev. ed., 3 vols., New York, 1900), III, 319–24 and 335.

opposition is in many respects justified, as it was also with Carlyle, it tends to become an argument in itself.

This brings us to Carlyle's ideas. It may be observed that in general they acted as a kind of framework in and through which his moral feeling, his spiritual attitude, and his attitude toward his age, could be expressed. What concerns us is, how were certain of his ideas able to exert the influence they did? Carlyle's doctrine of work, that work was man's chief duty, that only by turning to work could man hope for a victory over skepticism, was a doctrine that appealed to many who had been unsettled by the religious problem. It was a doctrine that was in harmony with a distinctive trait of the Englishman, his flair for the practical. It fitted in with a civilization that devoted so much of its energy to industry and trade. It must needs be congenial to the middle class, which administered the industrial system; the middle class believed that men got on in the world through work and was certain that the function of the laborer was to work; everyone, in the eyes of the middle class, must make sacrifices. And puritanism, the dominant religion, preached the gospel of work and paid homage to worldly success. In such an atmosphere the doctrine of "do" could not be unpopular.

When Carlyle took his stand for state interference, a reaction had already set in against laissez faire. Social legislation such as the factory acts and the reform of municipal corporations signaled the coming of a new era. Religious thought in the form of the Evangelical, the High Church, and the Christian Socialist movements, protested that the state could not remain indifferent to the social and economic distress that was everywhere in evidence. The workers refused to remain defenseless against laissez faire; many of their number organized themselves into trade-unions and cooperatives, and insisted on collective bargaining. Nor did the employers fail to turn to some extent against laissez faire; prosperity had arrived, and this, along with the growing power of labor, the tendency of the older trades-unions to conservatism, and the fact that strikes interfered with profits, changed their hearts. Besides, to stand for some social amelioration not only helped to eliminate the small competitor but was balm to the conscience.

Again, the characteristics of modern commerce, the growth of corporate trade, suggested monopoly and in turn state interference. The operation of the party system itself acted as something of a curb on laissez faire; the see-saw struggle for power meant concessions to the workers.[8] The reaction against laissez faire must not be overemphasized, for it touched little more than the periphery, not the center. Yet, such as it was, it provided a fertile soil in which Carlyle's advocacy of collectivism could flourish. Attacking laissez faire with a destructive power given to no other individual in his age, he was more responsible than any other writer, more responsible than such critics as Dickens, Reade, Mrs. Gaskell, and Ruskin, for its loss of prestige.[9]

Carlyle's insistence on the humanity of the ordinary man was supported by more than one tendency of the age. It was supported, clearly, by the humanitarian movement, which among other things focused attention on the common man through social legislation. It was supported by democracy with its emphasis on equality—the equal right of all to the franchise, and the equal right of all to happiness. And it was supported by utilitarianism, which helped to explain democracy's demands. It was supported, too, by Christianity with its emphasis on individual worth; and by science with its emphasis on man in this world. Again, it was supported by the very fact of the rise of the common man to greater recognition and power in the community.

If we take the less influential of Carlyle's ideas, we find that they, too, were such as to find favor with his age. It goes with-

[8] In the above analysis I am indebted for a number of ideas to Werner Sombart's *Socialism and the Social Movement* (New York, 1898), pages 151–54.

[9] It must not be thought that the attack by intellectuals on laissez faire was a major factor in bringing about its decline. See Sombart's convincing analysis, pointing out that Carlyle and the Christian Socialists played rather a minor part in the development of the social movement between 1850 and 1880. *Ibid.*, pp. 149–54.

out saying that any individualism must find a sympathetic response in the breast of the Englishman, for individualism is the very stuff of which he is made. But Carlyle's individualism was particularly well suited to find a response during the time in which he wrote. It involved "heroics," that is, it made the individual feel that he was important, it encouraged him to strive for the unattainable, it persuaded him that his dreams might come true if he would but reach; in a word, it exalted his "will." Carlyle's individualism made for self-assertion and for the realization of power, and it acted as a kind of sanction for the tiger ethic. In a real sense, indeed, Carlyle's individualism vindicated the very system against which he waged so uncompromising a war. The doctrine of self-assertion for power is part and parcel of the psychology of a competitive society, especially in its earlier stages; it is the very rationale of action of the captain of industry.

Little need be said to show that Carlyle's belief in inequality, which was closely associated with his idea of individualism, was in accord with the views of many to whom he spoke. A liberal like Gladstone could say that equality was unattractive to the English people, that inequality was dear to their hearts.

Anyone attempting to account for Carlyle's influence can hardly overestimate the importance of the mode of expression he imposed upon his thought and feeling, the importance, that is, of his style. Emerson said, "the greatest power of Carlyle, like that of Burke, seems to me to reside rather in the form . . . each has a splendid rhetoric to clothe the truth." [10] And Carlyle's sharpest critic has held that his style, along with his moral fervor, was the main source of his influence.[11] We should say rather that as a source of influence Carlyle's style was second in importance only to his moral feeling. The question is, how was his style able to exercise the influence it did?

Almost every commentator on Carlyle points out that his style created something of a sensation in his day. We suggest

[10] James E. Cabot, *A Memoir of Ralph Waldo Emerson* (2 vols., Boston, 1887), I, 198.

[11] John M. Robertson, *Modern Humanists Reconsidered* (London, 1927), p. 24.

that this was due to no small extent to the fact that the more general qualities of his style were romantic in character and answered the basic literary demand of his age. If by the eighteen thirties some men still admired the classical style of Pope and Dr. Johnson, most men had ceased to be vitally interested in it. They had tired of the balanced sentence and the polished phrase. They wanted expression of thought and feeling regardless of niceties of form. They had become sated with a style that was fitted to deal with conventionalities and with respectable subjects. They wanted a style that was capable of a broad range, that could deal with whatever the writer considered was important, not with what polite society believed was important for him to consider. Nor did they relish a style that asked for the self-effacement of the writer. They wanted a style that gave scope to the writer's personal thought and feeling, that brought them in touch with his personality. They wanted, too, a style that contained color, that appealed to the senses. All these qualities marked Carlyle's style.

But as important as these romantic qualities were in attracting and influencing readers, it cannot be said that they were any more important than the peculiarly personal qualities of his style. As is well recognized, Carlyle's style is one of the most, if not the most, individualistic in English literature.[12] Possessing an imaginative power that has led one critic to speak of him as the greatest prose-poet of the English language, Carlyle developed a style that for vividness and force is perhaps unsurpassed.[13] No one who remembers his picture of the flight to Varenne in *The French Revolution* or his phrase "Robespierre sea green and incorruptible" will doubt his genius for

[12] Saintsbury, in one of his estimates of Carlyle's writing, has said that it is the most brilliant, the most stimulating, the most varied, the most original in English literature. George Saintsbury, *A History of Nineteenth Century Literature* (London, 1896), p. 238.

[13] George Saintsbury, *Corrected Impressions: Essays on Victorian Writers* (New York, 1895), p. 58, and *A History of Nineteenth Century Literature*, p. 239. See also Hugh Walker, *The Literature of the Victorian Era* (Cambridge University Press, 1910), p. 33, and Emile Legouis and Louis Cazamian, *A History of English Literature* (2 vols., London, 1927), II, 349.

vividness. Nor will anyone who recalls his attack in *Past and Present* on the typical businessman of the day, Plugson of Undershot, or his description in the same work of the poor Irish widow who was forced to prove her sisterhood by typhus fever, dispute that Carlyle is a master of force. Though vividness and force are qualities usually found in romantic styles, it is abundantly clear that with Carlyle they took a unique form. Perhaps their most distinctive characteristic is a certain nervous quality, which frequently produces in the reader a galvanic effect. That Carlyle had an almost unerring eye for the sharp, concrete image, an extraordinary aptitude for the representation of ideas and facts so that they could be seen if not touched, accounts for much of the vividness he achieved. So, too, does it account for much of the force he attained. But other qualities were hardly less important, especially in making for force. Directness, the use of the apostrophe, the imperative, exhortation — in a word, "the manner of a revivalist preacher" — increased the power of his writing. He could command in speech both the lightning and the thunder.

His writing undoubtedly gained strength by the mood of self-confession in which he so often cast it; he could reveal the reader to himself and give him the feeling that no one understood his "inner" life so well as Carlyle. And its forcefulness was further increased by an irony and a satire that were frequently as piercing dead as Swift's; and by a humor which, as G. K. Chesterton has said, was distinguished by a "sense of the sarcasm of eternity." Because Carlyle's humor was essentially serious, it was well adapted to the temper of his age. No one has better explained how well adapted it was than Carlyle himself when he defined humor as springing from the well of laughter which lies near the well of tears. We may see the effect of Carlyle's style upon a Victorian mind in Saintsbury's description of it; he says it was "full of lights and colours, full of voices covering the whole gamut from storm to whisper." [14]

We may say, then, that Carlyle could never have exerted the

[14] George Saintsbury, *Corrected Impressions*, p. 58.

power he did had it not been for an unusual combination of factors. It is apparent that he would have been a prophet of a lesser order if the conditions of the times had not been favorable to the chief characteristic of the prophet, to his moral feeling and to his spiritual attitude; Carlyle is inconceivable in the eighteenth century. His seed was sown in the ground prepared by Wesley, Rousseau, and Goethe. And it goes without saying that he could not have exerted the same influence if his moral feeling and his spiritual attitude had been less intense than they were, or if his attitude toward his age had been less unyielding, or less inspired by missionary zeal. And, to have made the impression he did, it was necessary that some of his ideas should be pertinent to the issues of the day. He could not have stirred men so deeply if his style had not shocked the mind as often as it fired the imagination.

Though Carlyle's age did not really grasp the meaning of what he had to say, it was shaken from its complacency by the way he said it. M. Cazamian has said that Carlyle infused into a society threatened with decadence the necessary psychological energy for its survival.[15] To claim for Carlyle something of a national salvation is to claim too much. But few will disagree with M. Cazamian that Carlyle's outstanding contribution as a prophet was to evangelize a small élite, and to awaken a large number of minds that might not otherwise have been awakened.[16] Surely, to stimulate men to think must rank next to the act of creative thought itself.

Carlyle's political and social thought, as has doubtless been discerned, cannot be identified with any one movement of his time. It was at once radical and reactionary. G. K. Chesterton described it aptly when he said that Carlyle was "something of a Tory, something of a Sans-culotte, something of a Puritan, something of an Imperialist, something of a Socialist; but he was never, even for a single moment, a Liberal."[17] As Ernest

[15] Emile Legouis and Louis Cazamian, *A History of English Literature*, Vol. II (by Cazamian), pp. 348–49.
[16] *Ibid.*, p. 349.
[17] G. K. Chesterton, *Thomas Carlyle* (London, 1902), p. 22.

Thomas Carlyle

Barker has pointed out, it is with Plato that Carlyle has most in common.[18] With Plato he believed that life was meaningless except as it had spiritual and moral significance. With Plato he believed that the measure of the value of social institutions was their approximation to the ethically ideal; and here justice and morality were the criteria ever to be applied. Again, he was with Plato in maintaining that order was second in importance only to justice and morality; and with Plato he urged that there was always a qualification to be added, that it was worth while at times to pluck up society by the roots and plant it anew. With Carlyle, as with Plato, the canon of order condemned democracy and exalted the authoritarian state. And, finally, Carlyle held with Plato that the ordinary man was not intelligent enough to be trusted with political power, that the only suitable government was an aristocracy of gifted men — for Carlyle hero-kings, for Plato philosopher-kings.

The significance of Carlyle's thought, however, is not to be found in a comparison with Plato's, but in the criticism it presents of an industrial civilization whose dominant impulse was the profit motive. It is Carlyle's distinction that in England in the nineteenth century he is unequaled as a critic of the social effects of individualism, of the profit-gain system. Nor is this his only significance. The authoritarian state fashioned on the military pattern, which he advocated, and the strong leader who does not hesitate to use force, whom he admired, are today a commonplace of Europe. Mussolini and Hitler above all have put into practice ideas for which Carlyle stood; fascism is to a great extent Carlyle's creed brought up to date. Little did liberal England of the nineteenth century dream that ideas which they dismissed as the aberrations of an eccentric would so soon be used to govern nations where democracy had once existed.

II

Born in Ecclefechan, a small village in Scotland, in 1795, Carlyle was molded by the basic characteristics of the people from

[18] Ernest Barker, *Political Thought in England, 1848 to 1914*, pp. 188–90.

which he sprang more than by any other influence. Brought up among peasants of straitened circumstances, he learned from his earliest years the importance of work. His father, who struggled hard to make a living as a farmer and stonemason, stood out as an example that work was man's first calling. Through the hardship endured in his early years, Carlyle was fully acquainted with suffering and privation; "man is born," he said later, "unto trouble, unto toil, as the sparks fly upwards." That his father rose above trouble and was a strong personality showed him that character could emerge from hardship. To have been brought up in poverty and to have struggled against it must have strengthened the combative streak that was in him. Carlyle's peasant surroundings not only instilled in him a deep sympathy for the laborer but also encouraged his radical temper.

Carlyle was very much like his father. He inherited his parent's earnestness, his sharp temper, his capacity for antagonism and for absolute statements, his confidence that others were wrong; he inherited his father's style of speech — his turn for a striking phrase, his competence in abusive language; and he inherited his humor, which was "of a most grim and Scandinavian sort." Carlyle learned from his father respect for truth and hatred of sham, and he learned from him the worth of man. Carlyle's combination of harshness and sympathy was exhibited in his early years by a readiness to strike and to weep.

Carlyle's father so imbued him with Calvinism as to make it the dominant force of his life, determining to a great extent his political ideas. From an early age the Old Testament was impressed upon him; from an early age he was given to understand that God was sovereign and that righteousness was the greatest truth for man. He learned that law, not the Gospel, was the bond between God and man. And he came to see that physical suffering was trivial compared with injustice and error, for puritanism placed great emphasis on the need of struggle and considered austerity an ideal. So powerful was God and so weak was man, that there was ever present for Carlyle, as there must be for the puritan, a consciousness of human depravity. Not a little of Carlyle's gloom came from the conviction that man was a sinful creature; and his strong belief in work, in action, and in energy, in all the practical means of exhibiting moral strenuousness and of thrusting out sin, derived in part from the same conviction. And his belief in these things was undoubtedly strengthened by the puritan notion that man's moral capacity represents the divine in him; it must be exalted by action.

Puritanism taught Carlyle to place great value on the concrete and to reverence facts. God was indeed great in his transcendence, but he was also present in his immanence; events were the mysterious will of "Him that walketh on the wings of the wind." God was present even in the evaporation of a raindrop or the rotting of a leaf. That Carlyle saw things in sharp contrast, that an act was indisputably right or indisputably wrong, may be traced in part to his puritanism: puritanism demands a forcible relation to life; it must divide light from darkness, distinguish friends from enemies. It must not be a flickering ray in the midst of gloom, but a steady, unquenchable light—a permanent star to every wandering bark.

Carlyle's mysticism seems to have come not only from his temperament but also from the puritan view of God's transcendence; so great was He in comparison with all other things that life itself could be little more than a trifling episode of appearances. So significant was the sovereignty of God for Carlyle that worldly titles were mere wrappings, just "clothes." The things that were most tangible — work, action, morality — these were the only certainties for him. He learned these puritan certainties not only from the preaching of his father but also from the application his father made of them; Carlyle lived in a household in which there was discipline, obedience, and abstinence from pleasure.

Believing that it was sinful to leave high talents unused, Carlyle's father in 1809 sent him to Edinburgh University. Here contact with physical science and with materialist philosophy, which was reigning at Edinburgh, undermined the lad's belief in the foundations of Christianity. He was no longer able to consider the ministry as a career — the traditional one in Scotland for an intellectual boy. French literature, even more, Hume's *Essays,* which he read while teaching mathematics at Annan Academy in 1814, shattered his early beliefs. The final blow was dealt by Gibbon's *Decline and Fall,* which he read while schoolmastering in Kirkcaldy in 1818. About this time Carlyle went through a period of spiritual doubt. The old dogmatic creed of the Kirk no longer satisfied; the collapse of his beliefs seemed to leave him no escape from a gloomy and degrading materialism. Teaching had become intolerable and law was unsatisfactory. He was beginning to suffer from the dyspepsia that tormented him throughout life, and the world about him appeared in a wretched state. The misery of the lower classes left an indelible impression on him, and he sympathized with the general discontent.

Carlyle soon emerged from the depths of his spiritual disillusionment, which he vividly described in *Sartor Resartus.* To assert his spiritual "new birth," as he called it, with "grim, fire-eyed Defiance," he declared, in 1821, war on materialism. Carlyle, says Leslie Stephen, won not peace, but a change of misery. He remained a Calvinist, but one who had lost his creed. Carlyle's "new birth" was an affirmation of confidence in himself, the resolution of his doubts concerning a career. He would take up literature as a profession. In 1817 he read Madame de Staël's *Allemagne,* which opened up a new world to him. For Carlyle German literature was second in importance only to the influence of his father: it helped to cure him of uncertainty; it was a source of inspiration that confirmed the moral and spiritual nature of his puritan faith.[19]

Carlyle was attracted by Goethe more than by any other German writer; Goethe was superficially for him what Wordsworth was for Mill, a harmonizer of life. Though Carlyle never assimi-

[19] For the analysis that follows I am very much indebted to Charles F. Harrold's able study, *Carlyle and German Thought* (Yale University Press, 1934).

lated Goethe's attitude toward life, which was the classical ideal of the development of all the individual's powers, he found in him, in spite of his avowed paganism, a champion of the essential truth and spirit of Christianity. Goethe was for Carlyle the hero of modern times. Goethe provided Carlyle with a new form for his conviction that happiness is not the aim of life and supported him in his view that duty, reverence, and self-renunciation are more important ideals than happiness. Goethe supported his belief in action; Goethe said, as Aristotle had said, that the end of man is an action, not a thought. Goethe strengthened Carlyle's belief in work; he held that man could only come to know himself through active, daily tasks. And Goethe, by holding that whatever survives the test of history is good, provided a German background for Carlyle's doctrine that might makes right.

If Goethe helped to give Carlyle faith in himself, Fichte supplied him with ideas that implemented his puritan view. Fichte stood, as did Goethe, for the spiritual nature of all existence; Carlyle drew from Fichte the doctrine that history is the revelation of God, and that the man of perception may see right triumphing as might. Carlyle could take from Fichte the idea of the alternation of periods of belief and unbelief. He found in Fichte the main elements of his doctrine of the hero, which was probably Fichte's chief contribution to his thought.

It may be well to point out here that before Carlyle became acquainted with German literature, his chief interest in history was biographical; before he read Fichte he was already prepared to exalt the leader above the mass. Carlyle was indebted to Fichte for the view that the hero reveals the Divine Idea, and that the hero is a champion of order whose aim is to establish right and justice. Carlyle could find support in Goethe and Fichte for the belief that the many need rulers rather than liberty, and in Goethe and Novalis for the conviction that the mass of men owe nothing but obedience and reverence to their rulers. All three German writers taught Carlyle that society is "organic," that all men are closely united in spiritual bonds,

Thomas Carlyle

that all men make up society. If Goethe, Fichte, and Novalis did not add any fundamental conceptions to his thought, they refreshed his beliefs and gave him new terms in which to express them; and they encouraged him to make war upon his time.

In turning to literature as a career, as he had always set his heart on doing, Carlyle occupied himself at the outset with German literature, translating *Wilhelm Meister* (1824) and writing a life of Schiller (1825). A visit to London proving uncongenial to his puritan spirit, he followed the example of Southey and Wordsworth and "retired from the din of this monstrous city." While in retirement Carlyle, in a letter to Jane Welsh, to whom he had just become engaged, alluded to a passage in Schiller, which he said expressed his very creed.[20] The passage, which is undoubtedly the following, indicates his future career as a prophet: "The artist, it is true, is the son of his age; but pity for him if he is its pupil, or even its favourite! Let some beneficent Divinity snatch him when a suckling from the breast of his mother, and nurse him with the milk of a better time; that he may ripen to his full stature. And having grown to manhood, let him return, a foreign shape, into his century; not, however, to delight it by his presence; but terrible, to purify it. The Matter of his works he will take from the present; but their Form from the Absolute unchanging Unity of his own nature."

Carlyle's first social writings of significance, "Signs of the Times" (1829) and "Characteristics" (1831), which appeared later in *Critical and Miscellaneous Essays* (1841), were notable for their attack on materialism. *Sartor Resartus,* which appeared serially in 1833 and 1834, was a product of German romanticism. Among other things, it criticized social conditions, universal suffrage, and the aristocracy in what were for him restrained terms, and it advocated hero worship. In *Sartor,* says Froude, Carlyle came into the outer world like his hero,

[20] *Love Letters of Thomas Carlyle and Jane Welsh* (Alexander Carlyle, editor, 2 vols., London, 1909), II, 93.

Teufelsdröckh, as a "Baptist living on locusts and wild honey," and occasionally presented himself to others as a dyspeptic polar bear.

In 1834 Carlyle settled in London and began work "in tolerable spirits" on *The French Revolution,* a theme to which he had been directed by his correspondence with Mill. He said that he would not have known what to make of this world had it not been for the French Revolution. He looked upon it as the vindication of the ways of God to man; it was a sermon on the text that "whatsoever a man soweth, that shall he also reap." It was for him a judgment, a proclamation of the bankruptcy of imposture; and he looked upon it as part of the revolt of the oppressed classes of Europe against their oppressors. Though he could say that it was the stern end of much, he also held that it was the fearful but sternly beneficent beginning of much. At the same time, he believed that the "rights of man" theories, which he thought demanded that the reins of government be thrown on the necks of the governed, could only lead to chaos. Carlyle's *French Revolution* was not only a prose epic but a tract for the times; it was a profound warning to England to avoid the catastrophe that he feared all his life long was imminent. The book, said Lord Acton, delivered the English mind from the thraldom of Burke, who could see in the French Revolution nothing but destruction. In the thirties a number of young men began to gather round Carlyle; Charles Buller visited him and took him to radical meetings, where the popular wrath gave him a grim satisfaction.

Carlyle was a thorough radical in so far as the word implies a profound dissent from the existing order; he represented in an extreme form the discontent that had accumulated during the first quarter of the century against existing institutions. He welcomed the Reform Bill agitation as the first movement toward the destruction of the old order. He looked forward, indeed, to a reconstruction of principles and institutions which was entirely opposed to the views of the Mills and their associates. Though he held that the "Whigs were amateurs, the

Thomas Carlyle

Radicals guild-brethren,"[21] he believed that the Whigs and Radicals were genuine as far as they went. Mill's respect and sympathy touched him, and he was prepared to form a temporary alliance with the Philosophical Radicals. But it was not long before his relations with Mill began to cool. Mill's friends repelled him, and though he thought Mill infinitely too good for his associates, he was to him "a friend frozen in ice." Their many differences of opinion and Mill's gradual withdrawal from society widened the gulf to complete separation.

In 1839, while he was gathering material for *Cromwell,* Carlyle wrote his first important political pamphlet, *Chartism;* it was the first writing of a series calling attention in unforgettable words to the "Condition-of-England Question," the condition of poverty and unemployment. This writing shows, as *Past and Present* and *Latter-Day Pamphlets* were to show, that what prompted Carlyle to take pen in hand and deliver a withering indictment of his age was the fact that men, whose end, he thought, is work, were without work and rotting in idleness. *Past and Present* is an attack on industrialism; it is a call to action against unemployment; and it is a denunciation of the aristocracy, the churches, democracy, Parliament, radicalism, and political economy as impotent in face of the problem. Carlyle strongly hinted at his chief remedy for a disordered society in his lectures *On Heroes, Hero-Worship, and the Heroic in History,* published in 1841. His theory that history is the record of the thoughts and actions of great men, that the "Hero as King" is the greatest of heroes, showed that he was ready to find the savior of society in the great leader.

In *Past and Present* (1843) Carlyle repeated in more picturesque form and in stronger terms the criticisms made in *Chartism.* In this work on the new "feudalism," he is vehement against laissez faire, and he is more scornful than ever of democracy. He appeals to the captains of industry to act as heroes, pointing out that the Horse Guards show that government can

[21] James A. Froude, *Thomas Carlyle: A History of the First Forty Years of His Life, 1795–1835* (2 vols. in 1, New York, 1882), II, 73.

govern, and he insists that despotism is essential to most enter-prises. At the same time, he asks the aristocracy to believe in their own erosion, and suggests that they aid the captains of industry. *Past and Present* is in a real sense an essay on fascism. In spite of its reactionary elements, *Past and Present* exercised a wide influence; its social teachings can be seen in Disraeli's *Sybil* (1845), Kingsley's *Alton Locke* (1850), Charlotte Brontë's *Shirley* (1849), and in the early poetry of Clough and Tenny-son. *Past and Present,* more than any other book of Carlyle's, was the source of Ruskin's inspiration.

Cromwell appeared in 1845 and was received with general applause. It was a picture of Carlyle's ideal hero, the autocrat by divine appointment, who attempted to bring the Divine Law of the Bible into actual practice in men's affairs on earth. Carlyle's position in the world of letters was now established, and his home became more and more the meeting place of eminent people. Tennyson, John Forster, Dickens, and Thackeray were among his visitors, and refugees such as Mazzini and Cavaignac came to see him.

Carlyle's turn to reaction was still more marked in his "Oc-casional Discourse on the Nigger Question," which appeared in 1849. It was a vitriolic denunciation of humanitarianism, which, he insisted, emancipated the West Indian negroes only to sink them into barbarism. This essay showed that Carlyle no longer had any pity for the unemployed needlewomen; they were now mutinous maidservants who, instead of learning to work and to obey, had learned to give warning. Carlyle ex-hibited an imperialism that must follow naturally from his doc-trines; he who can triumph, he says, by the fortunes of war or get the most out of the West Indian islands is the nobler.

Carlyle wrote to Emerson that the revolutions of 1848 on the continent gave him a deep-seated satisfaction, showing once again that the righteous gods yet live and reign. *Latter-Day Pamphlets,* which appeared in 1850, was partly a reflex of these revolutions. In this book Carlyle brought his doctrines sharply to focus on the social disorder in England. It was an impas sioned plea for state action, a great plea for the administrative reform of English government. It contained both his most friendly and his most scathing criticism of democracy and Parliament. As the most savage assertion of his principles, it flouted ruthlessly the cherished ideas of Victorian liberalism. His excitement carried him away "in a torrent of sulphurous denunciation," with an astonishing display of grotesque humor and vivid imagination. His hearers listened in silence or were overpowered by his rhetoric. The pamphlets gave general offense, and Froude tells us that the outcry stopped the sale for months and even for years. They were neglected, says Leslie Stephen, "as stupendous growls from a misanthropic recluse."

Carlyle supported his political theories with a monumental history of Frederick the Great, which was published between 1858 and 1865. Frederick was for him the one heroic figure in the most unheroic of centuries, the incarnation of fact and efficiency, and another example of the virtues of one-man rule. Carlyle was awarded a medal by Bismarck for his study; the two men recognized each other's qualities. Carlyle had his last say on contemporary politics in 1867 in *Shooting Niagara,* which was a tirade against democracy and the Reform Bill of that year. Believing that England was on the verge of disaster, he urged the aristocracy to recover their leadership. Noble heads, he declared, were in danger of hoofs and hobnails. That Carlyle could turn to the aristocracy for his heroes because he found its womenfolk charming is eloquent testimony to the hospitality he enjoyed after he had risen to eminence.

We can see that as Carlyle grew older he became less and less sympathetic to the working masses and more insistent on the worth of the few and the need of strong measures. J. M. Robertson has said that after his German period Carlyle had a gradual resurgence of the dominant qualities of temperament inherited from his father.[22] The mysticism of the studious period was abandoned, and a stand gradually taken on a few powerful prepossessions — resentment of human feebleness and

---

[22] John M. Robertson, *Modern Humanists* (London, 1891), p. 50.

faultiness, of all incompetence, of anarchy, of candid atheism; and admiration of masterfulness. He turned, too, against the saner radicals and developed theoretic Caesarism.

That Carlyle was, on the one hand, a radical of radicals and, on the other, one of the most reactionary of conservatives was due not merely to dyspepsia, to an irritable temper, and to insomnia, but also to a temperament that was at bottom in deep and irreconcilable conflict. That he could speak in one breath of the divinity of the common man and in the next of the millions mostly fools, that he could draw, as Henry James said, inspiration from despair, reflected a disposition that was fundamentally at war with itself.

III

Carlyle's deep conviction that God's will, that His Law, is destined to triumph in the world, that right (morality, justice, and truth) will prosper, led him to a view of progress; and in the perspective of this view he looked at history and his own time. He did not exclude periods of retrogression; he held only that mankind in the long run went forward:

Find mankind where thou wilt, thou findest it in living movement, in progress faster or slower: the Phoenix soars aloft, hovers with outstretched wings, filling Earth with her music; or, as now, she sinks, and with spheral swan-song immolates herself in flame, that she may soar the higher and sing the clearer. . . . Thus likewise, I note, the English Whig has, in the second generation, become an English Radical; who, in the third again, it is to be hoped, will become an English Rebuilder.[23]

This theory of progress shows why Carlyle was concerned not with the superficial forces of history, but with the elemental.[24] It shows why he was attracted to the revolutionary periods, when the underlying forces come to the surface and the foundations of the great deep are broken up, when all conventions are summarily swept aside and attention is given to the

[23] *Sartor Resartus*, p. 197.
[24] I owe much of the following analysis to Leslie Stephen's illuminating essay "Carlyle's Ethics," *Hours in a Library* (4 vols., New York, [1899]), Vol. IV.

great principles of social life. Carlyle sees modern history beginning with Luther, as a gigantic revolt against shams; Cromwell represents the second, the French Revolution the third, great revolt against untruth. His theory of progress explains his interest not only in the French Revolution and the period of Civil War in England, but also in the Germany of Frederick the Great. It explains why he was led to study and to idealize Cromwell and Frederick; these two men were heroes not only because they were great leaders, but also because they summed up in their careers the significant forces of an epoch.

As we have said, Carlyle's theory did not exclude periods of regression; he found the nineteenth century just such an epoch, an epoch of dissolution. This partly explains why he saw so little of value in the civilization of his day. It partly explains his opposition to his age, why he could denounce its conventions as "red tape" formulas, and its institutions as ineffectual machinery. Again, it partly explains why he insisted that his age must be purged of its disease — of its misery, its squalor, and its viciousness — if it was to recover its health. And it helps to explain his enthusiasm for the French Revolution of 1848, which he looked upon as one of the steps in the purging process through which society must go in order to attain to a creative era, to a greater realization of the right.

That God is the indisputable ruler of the universe, who governs in the name of justice, must have inspired in Carlyle a love of order and a hatred of anarchy. That man's chief duty is, in his view, to work, that man cannot fulfill his duty if there is disorder, must have strengthened his belief in order. That God is for Carlyle the great sovereign of the universe, who imposes the Law, which it is man's firm duty to obey, must have led Carlyle not only to an emphasis on authority and obedience in general, but also to an emphasis on these things as vested in His representatives. The injunction that Carlyle ever makes, that it is man's duty to obey God's Law (the law of right), that only by so obeying can he lead a just life and attain freedom, raises the question, how are men to know God's Law?

Carlyle's answer is, by intuition or conscience. But Carlyle is too much of a realist and too much of a puritan to leave conscience unaided. The Law is to be discerned in history; it is to be seen in the great movements and in the lives of great men:

God did make this world, and does for ever govern it; the loud roaring loom of time, with all its French revolutions, Jewish revelations, "weaves the vesture that thou seest Him by." There is no biography of a man, much less any history or biography of a nation, but wraps in it a message out of heaven.[25]

As Leslie Stephen has said, this is the special doctrine of Carlyle, embodied in all his works; a doctrine which possesses him rather than is possessed by him. Though the general run of mankind, according to Carlyle, possess conscience and are more or less aware of right and wrong, they are profoundly ignorant and have little understanding. The Law is to be imparted to them through the heaven-sent few who are endowed with insight. Thus we have Carlyle's famous doctrine of heroes. It is a new version of the old puritan formula; instead of God revealing himself through the Bible, he reveals himself through the inspired guide. The hero transmits God's Law through governance.

The hero must have unquestioning obedience from the mass of men, for he, not the multitude, has seen into the course of things. Carlyle's doctrine of the hero, of the inspired guide, seems partly to explain the contempt in which he so very frequently held ordinary human beings. To exalt the stature of your hero, you must diminish his fellows; if Gulliver is to be a giant, he must go to Lilliput. Nor is this the only source of Carlyle's contempt; the Puritan view that a vast chasm divides the elect from the unelect is equally a source. His doctrine of the hero and his view of the common man, as well as his admiration for authority and obedience, made Carlyle an implacable opponent of democracy.

Not only heroes, however, but also important movements in history embody God's Law. How are we to know an important

[25] *Latter-Day Pamphlets,* pp. 325–26.

movement? Carlyle's answer is that an important movement is one which persists over a long period of time; a successful movement is a right movement.

Puritanism . . . was a genuine thing, for Nature has adopted it, and it has grown and grows. I say sometimes, that everything goes by wager of battle in this world; that *strength,* well understood, is the measure of all worth. Give a thing time; if it can succeed it is a right thing.[26]

This doctrine leads Carlyle to exalt force and at times to argue that might makes right. It is not surprising that the two heroes to whom he devoted long studies, Cromwell and Frederick the Great, are warriors.

The puritan view of life, with its stress on authority, order, and control, could only make Carlyle hostile to laissez faire. This was no less true of his organic conception of society; its stress on the ties that bind man to man could only make him hostile to the "let alone" philosophy. Again, Carlyle's deep belief in morality and his conviction of the great need of its authoritative imposition were probably the chief reasons why he was scornful of organized religion in his time. And his belief in a law of right divinely inspired accounts for his violent opposition to hedonism, to the pleasure philosophy of the utilitarians, which he thought reduced ethics to a mere question of individual taste. His feeling for justice, which he drew in such large measure from puritanism, explains to a great extent his reaction against the inhuman social conditions of his age.

IV

Carlyle, as we have seen, came like the prophet of old to deliver his generation; for, like the prophet of old, he was convinced that his age was the victim of such tyrannies as must destroy the very purpose and meaning of life. Of these none was a greater tyranny for Carlyle than materialism. Mechanism, he says, has struck its roots deep into man's most intimate feelings; it has destroyed man's religious convictions.

[26] *Heroes and Hero-Worship,* p. 143.

Religion . . . is not what it was, and should be, — a thousand-voiced psalm from the heart of Man to his invisible Father . . . but for the most part, a wise prudential feeling grounded on mere calculation; a matter, as all others now are, of Expediency and Utility; whereby some smaller quantum of earthly enjoyment may be exchanged for a far larger quantum of celestial enjoyment. Thus Religion too is Profit, a working for wages.[27]

Morality, likewise, has been reduced to a materialistic basis, to a mere calculation of pleasure and pain. And we worship and follow after power: "What morality we have takes the shape of Ambition, of 'Honour'; beyond money and money's worth, our only rational blessedness is Popularity. It were but a fool's trick to die for conscience." By arguing, he remarks, on the "force of circumstances" we have argued away all force from ourselves and stand leashed together, uniform in dress and movement, like the rowers of some boundless galley. Thus while our civil liberty is more and more secured to us, our moral liberty is all but lost. Practically considered, our creed is fatalism; though free in hand and foot, we are shackled in heart and soul far straiter than by feudal chains.[28]

Carlyle admits that undue cultivation of the inward province leads to idle, visionary, impracticable courses and, in rude eras, to superstition and fanaticism. Yet, he says, undue cultivation of the outward, though less immediately prejudicial, and even for a time productive of many palpable benefits, must, in the long run, prove hopelessly pernicious by destroying moral force, which is the parent of all other force. By our skill in mechanism we excel all other ages in the management of external things; while in respect of the pure moral nature, in true dignity of soul and character, we are perhaps inferior to most civilized ages.[29]

Materialism, according to Carlyle, has had a destructive effect not only on religion and morality but also on intellect. We have given up, he says, knowing and believing, and have given ourselves over to logic, to the mere power of arranging and

[27] "Signs of the Times," *Critical and Miscellaneous Essays*, II, 76–77.
[28] *Ibid.*, p. 79.   [29] *Ibid.*, p. 73.

communicating. Cause and effect is the only category under which we look at Nature; our first question is not, what is the object? but, how is it? An Order of Ignatius Loyola, a Wycliffe, or a Henry VIII, are simply so many mechanical phenomena, caused or causing.[30] Carlyle argues that mechanism with its penchant for rational inquiry has made men self-conscious as they never were before. And our whole relations, he declares, to the universe and to our fellowman have became an inquiry, a doubt.[31] This defeats the end of man; man was sent hither not to question, but to work — "the end of man," it was long ago written, "is an Action, not a Thought." The thought conducts not to the deed, but to paralyzing bewilderment.[32]

Nowhere, Carlyle points out, is faith in mechanism more visible than in politics. Government is the "Machine of Society," and it is now assumed that if we change it we change man. The philosopher of this age is not a Socrates or a Plato, who inculcates the great truths that moral goodness and happiness depend upon the mind within us; but a Smith, a De Lolme, a Bentham, who chiefly inculcates the reverse — that our happiness depends entirely on external circumstances.[33] It is no longer the spiritual, the religious, and moral condition of the people that is our concern, but their physical, practical, economic condition, as regulated by public laws. Though mechanism, wisely contrived, has done much for man from a social and moral point of view, it cannot be the chief source of his worth or happiness.[34]

When Carlyle turned to consider social life he found a still greater deterioration of human values. Industrialism, he maintained, with its worship of Mammon, had created an inhuman and materialistic society:

. . . men go about as if by galvanism, with meaningless glaring eyes, and have no soul. . . . The haggard despair of Cotton-factory,

[30] *Ibid.*, pp. 74–75.
[31] "Characteristics," *Critical and Miscellaneous Essays,* III, 19.
[32] *Ibid.*, pp. 27–28.
[33] "Signs of the Times," *Critical and Miscellaneous Essays,* II, 67.
[34] *Ibid.*, p. 69.

Coal-mine operatives, Chandos Farm-labourers, in these days, is painful to behold; but not so painful, hideous to the inner sense, as that brutish godforgetting Profit-and-Loss Philosophy and Life-Theory, which we hear jangled on all hands of us, in senate-houses, spouting-clubs, leading-articles, pulpits and platforms, everywhere as the Ultimate Gospel.[35]

Industrialism, he held, was the parent of anarchy; it threw men out of work and into pauperism: "Two million shirtless sit enchanted in Workhouse Bastilles, five million more (according to some) in hunger-cellars." Industrialism disorganized the lives of the workers; it made them the victims of uncertainty. English commerce, he says, changes its shape like a very Proteus and infallibly, at every change of shape, oversets whole multitudes of workmen, hurling them asunder, this way and that, so that the wisest no longer knows his whereabouts.[36] English commerce turns the life of the worker into a gambler's existence; today prosperity, tomorrow "short-time"; now luxurious superfluity, now starvation.[37]

Carlyle, however, sees some merit in industrialism; it is valuable as a half-result. Though it is successful in production, it fails in distribution. The beaver intellect, he says, contrives to accumulate capital, but it fails in the guidance of what it has accumulated; though Plugson of St. Dolly Undershot, the buccaneer, has conquered disobedient cotton fiber and made shirts, he has not covered backs. He has hung up scalps in his wigwam, the hundred thousand at his banker's, but his own host is all in mutiny. Cotton is conquered, but the "bare backs" are worse covered than ever![38] In the midst of plenty the people perish.[39]

Nothing, Carlyle declared, contributed so much to the social anarchy born of industrialism as the policy of laissez faire. Laissez faire, he said, meant not mutual helpfulness, but mutual hostility, cloaked under due laws of war, named "fair com-

[35] *Past and Present*, p. 187.
[36] *Chartism* (*Critical and Miscellaneous Essays*, Vol. IV), pp. 141-42.
[37] *Ibid.*, p. 143.
[38] *Past and Present*, p. 193.   [39] *Ibid.*, pp. 6, 204.

petition." [40] Society, he thought, was so dominated by laissez faire that it was well nigh extinct. The "let alone" philosophy set man against man; it left the poor to perish from poverty and, what was worse, the rich from idleness:

Call ye that a Society where there is no longer any Social Idea extant; not so much as the Idea of a common Home, but only of a common over-crowded Lodging-house? Where each, isolated, regardless of his neighbour, turned against his neighbour, clutches what he can get. . . . Thus, too, does an observant eye discern everywhere that saddest spectacle: The Poor perishing, like neglected, foundered Draught-Cattle, of Hunger and Overwork; the Rich, still more wretchedly, of Idleness, Satiety, and Over-growth. [41]

In the face of the "Condition-of-England Question," in the face of "thirty-thousand outcast Needlewomen working themselves swiftly to death, three-million paupers rotting in forced idleness, *helping* said Needlewomen to die," we are told that the complex social recipe for our condition is to button our pockets and stand still. [42] There is not a horse willing to work but can get food and shelter in requital — a thing this two-footed worker has to seek for. [43] Not only does laissez faire, in Carlyle's view, mean freedom to die of starvation, it also means isolation; to be cut off, he says, to be left solitary, to have a world alien, not your world — that is wretchedness for man: "To have neither superior, nor inferior, nor equal, united man-like to you. Without father, without child, without brother. Man knows no sadder destiny. . . . Encased each as in his transparent 'ice-palace'; our brother visible in his, making signals and gesticulations to us; — visible, but forever unattainable." [44]

Carlyle insists that the suffering of the working class must affect the whole of society. The misery, he says, of the great universal underclass cannot be isolated from the untoiling class; by infallible contagion it spreads upward until it reaches the highest, till all has grown miserable, palpably false, and wrong;

[40] *Ibid.*, p. 146.
[41] *Sartor Resartus*, p. 185.   [42] *Chartism*, p. 131.   [43] *Ibid.*, p. 135.
[44] *Past and Present*, pp. 274-75.

and poor drudges hungering on meal-husks and boiled grass do by circuitous but sure methods bring kings' heads to the block. He sees the condition of the working class driving them to radicalism and revolt; Chartism with its five points born aloft on pikeheads and torchlight meetings is the reflection of smoldering discontent. He declares that it is not mere physical suffering that drives men to a sullen and revengeful humor; nakedness, hunger, distress of all kinds have been cheerfully suffered when the heart was right. It is, he says, that their condition is unjust, that they are unfairly dealt with, that their lot in this world is not founded on right.[45]

In Carlyle's view spiritual and social disruption had gone so far that nothing short of a drastic remedy could achieve the task of reconstruction. Democracy, he held, so far from being equal to the task, itself led to anarchy. Democracy, he asserted, is a regulated method of rebellion and abrogation; it abrogates the old arrangement of things and leaves zero and vacuity.[46] It is the consummation of laissez faire. You say democracy means freedom. True, the workers have freedom to go without work, a greater slavery than before. The self-government of a multitude, moreover, is an impossibility; how in conjunction with democracy is sovereignty to exist?[47]

Democracy's cardinal tenet of equality is for Carlyle scarcely less objectionable than that of liberty. Any man, he asks, equal to any other? Quashee Nigger to Socrates or Shakespeare, Judas Iscariot to Jesus Christ?[48] Democracy runs counter to the laws of the universe. The universe is a monarchy,[49] a man has his superiors, a regular hierarchy above him, extending up, degree above degree, to Heaven itself and God the Maker.[50] Democracy for Carlyle is also contradictory to what he calls the most fundamental right of man; the "right of the ignorant man to be guided by the wiser, to be, gently or forcibly, held in the true course by him, is the indisputablest."[51]

[45] *Chartism*, pp. 144–45, 148–49.   [46] *Ibid.*, pp. 158–59.
[47] *Past and Present*, p. 251.
[48] "Shooting Niagara," *Critical and Miscellaneous Essays*, V, 4.
[49] *Latter-Day Pamphlets*, pp. 21–22.   [50] *Chartism*, p. 189.   [51] *Ibid.*, p. 157.

Thomas Carlyle

Yet Carlyle believes there is some merit in democracy. The votes of men, he says, are worth collecting not for their wisdom, but for their instincts, because where these can be deciphered, they are wise and human; know well what the people inarticulately feel, for the Law of Heaven itself is dimly written there.[52] He values, however, the suffrage, parliaments, public opinion, and the like rather for a negative reason: to inform the governors at what pitch the widespread folly of the nation now stands, to inform them of what can be safely attempted and what not.

Beyond all doubt it will be useful, will be indispensable, for the King or Governor to know what the mass of men think upon public questions legislative and administrative; what they will assent to willingly, what unwillingly. . . . No Governor otherwise can go along with clear illumination on his path, however plain the loadstar and ulterior goal be to him; but at every step he must be liable to fall into a ditch; to awaken he knows not what nests of hornets.[53]

There is, he says, no foolishest man but knows one and the other thing more clearly than the wisest man does, something which even the intelligence of a Newton, not present in that exact juncture of circumstances, would otherwise have failed to discern. Nay, on certain points I even ask my horse's opinion: as to whether beans will suit at this juncture, or a truss of tares, and unhesitatingly follow his candid opinion.[54] As what prudent rider would not? But in regard to the choice of roads, my horse has no competency whatsoever.

It follows for Carlyle that parliaments, admirable as advising bodies, are useless as ruling and sovereign bodies; parliaments, he affirms, should only be advisers to the sovereign,[55] for by express appointment they are nothing more than a talking apparatus.[56] A sovereign with six hundred and fifty-eight heads, all set to talk against each other, and to consult about "business" with twenty-seven millions, mostly fools, assiduously listening in, cannot do the work of sovereignty at all, but is

[52] *Latter-Day Pamphlets*, p. 240.
[53] *Ibid.*   [54] *Ibid.*, p. 244.
[55] *Ibid.*, p. 232.   [56] *Ibid.*, p. 194.

smitten with eternal incompetence.[57] The only ability, he declares, that Parliament recognizes is ability to talk: "what a high-soaring, helplessly floundering, ever babbling yet inarticulate dark dumb Eternity it is . . . Alas, it is our fatalest misery just now . . . that no British man can attain to be a Statesman, or Chief of *Workers,* till he has first proved himself a Chief of *Talkers*." [58]

Carlyle, however, insists that it is preposterous to believe that universal suffrage can solve the central problem of politics, which is to find the best men.[59] Though, he says, the very essence of democracy is that the able may be chosen, in whatever rank he is found, that he be searched for as hidden treasure is,[60] how can the ballot box achieve this? If of ten men nine are recognizable as fools, which is a common calculation, how, in the name of wonder, will you ever get a ballot box to grind you out a wisdom from the votes of these ten men? [61] Never by any conceivable ballot box nor by all the machinery in Bromwicham or out of it will you attain such a result. The crux of the problem is to recognize true worth, a thing most difficult to do. How can you expect the multitude to recognize true worth?

. . . can it be proved that, since the beginning of the world, there was ever given a universal vote in favour of the worthiest man or thing? . . . the worthiest, if he appealed to universal suffrage, would have but a poor chance. John Milton, inquiring of universal England what the worth of *Paradise Lost* was, received for answer, Five Pounds Sterling. George Hudson, inquiring in like manner what his services on the railways might be worth, received for answer (prompt temporary), Fifteen Hundred Thousand ditto. Alas, Jesus Christ asking the Jews what *he* deserved, was not the answer, Death on the gallows! [62]

The mass of men consulted at hustings, upon any high matter whatsoever, is as ugly an exhibition of human stupidity as this world sees.[63] And no division-list or Parliamentary majority was ever yet known to yield a leader; [64] Dame Dubarry's pet-

[57] *Ibid.*, pp. 225–27.   [58] *Ibid.*, pp. 194–95.   [59] *Ibid.*, pp. 108–09.
[60] *Ibid.*, pp. 119–20.   [61] *Ibid.*, p. 238.   [62] *Ibid.*, p. 242.   [63] *Ibid.*
[64] *Past and Present*, p. 260.

ticoat was a better seine-net for fishing out premiers than that.[65]

What, he asks, is the verdict of history in regard to democracy? Past experience testifies against it; the work of ruling men has always been done by the intelligent few, and they have frequently resorted to force without stint.[66] In Rome and Athens the work of ruling was done not by the loud voting and debating of many, but by the wise insight and ordering of a few; and it was no less true of the French Convention, which was a parliament elected "by the five points," with ballot boxes and universal suffrage. Moreover it had to guillotine into extinction all that gainsaid it, and rule and work literally by the sternest despotism ever seen in Europe before it could rule at all. Napoleon was not president of a republic; Cromwell tried hard to rule in that way but found that he could not. If we take America as an example of democracy in modern times, Carlyle observes, we cannot predict success from its record:

Hitherto she but ploughs and hammers, in a very successful manner. She has roast goose with applesauce for the poorest working-man; well, surely that is something; but that is not enough. . . . What great human soul, what great thought, what great noble thing that one could worship, or loyally admire, has yet been produced there? What have they done? They have doubled their population every twenty years. They have begotten, with a rapidity beyond recorded example, Eighteen Millions of the greatest bores ever seen in this world before, that hitherto is their feat in History.[67]

If democracy was for Carlyle incapable of achieving reform, humanitarianism was still more so. The sugary philanthropists, he said, of the new reign of love and fraternity believe in paradise to all and sundry, not to the well-deserving: "Such pilots, being sorely admonished by the Iceberg and other dumb councillors — instead of taking their sextants and asking What are the laws of wind and water, of Heaven and Earth — decide that in these new circumstances, they will, to the worthy and unworthy, serve out a double allowance of grog." [68]

[65] *Latter-Day Pamphlets*, p. 134. [66] *Chartism*, pp. 158–59.
[67] *Latter-Day Pamphlets*, p. 21. [68] *Ibid.*, p. 50.

Thomas Carlyle

Carlyle was especially incensed at the humanitarian treatment of criminals; instead, he declared, of providing palaces and schoolmasters for them, we should sweep them into the dust bin — hate, not love, for scoundrels, enmity to the enemies of God.[69] Worship of mud-serpents! This is the rotten carcass of Christianity, this malodorous phosphorescence of postmortem sentimentalism. Though Carlyle believed that there was a fraction of sense in humanitarianism, which should be laid hold of, it was repugnant not only to his sense of right and wrong but also to his view of reform. He insisted that the philanthropists do not aim at the real, the supreme scoundrel but at the lowest, who robs shop tills and puts the skin of mankind in danger.[70] The supreme scoundrel, he declared, sits well cushioned in high places; instead of sinking him in a peat bog, we mount the brazen image of him on high columns.[71]

Carlyle could see no hope of dispelling the deep sickness of his age except through the leadership of great men of action; he appealed for hero-kings, who would act and inspire. He was convinced, until the latter part of his life, that the hero-kings could not be found among the aristocracy. For the aristocracy, he said, no longer governed nor guided;[72] to the "Condition-of-England Question" it had nothing whatever to say. It went gracefully idle in Mayfair, it handsomely consumed the rents of England, shooting its partridges, and dilettante-ing in Parliament and Quarter Sessions. Its gospel was far worse than that of Mammonism; it stood for idleness, and idleness alone was without hope.[73]

Carlyle looked to the captains of industry for his hero-kings; to him they were the most promising saviors of modern society. He hailed them as the new aristocracy, the true fighters; and he looked to them to create a "noble just Industrialism and Government by the Wisest."[74] The key to the policy Carlyle advocated for his industrial aristocracy is summed up in his two passages: "Wheresoever thou findest Disorder, there is thy

[69] *Ibid.*, pp. 58, 62–70. [70] *Ibid.*, p. 85. [71] *Ibid.*, p. 84.
[72] *Past and Present*, p. 150. [73] *Ibid.*, pp. 146, 150, 178. [74] *Ibid.*, p. 271.

eternal enemy; attack him swiftly, subdue him; make Order of him, the subject not of Chaos, but of Intelligence, Divinity";[75] and "Let no man despair of Governments who looks on these two sentries at the Horse-Guards."[76]

Reform, Carlyle declares, must begin with the problem of pauperism, for "pauperism is the general leakage through every joint of the ship that is rotten":[77]

Pauperism is the poisonous dripping from all the sins, and putrid unveracities and god-forgetting greedinesses and devil-serving cants and jesuitisms, that exist among us. Not one idle Sham lounging about Creation upon false pretenses, upon means which he has not earned, . . . but yields his share of Pauperism somewhere or other.[78]

Carlyle warns that if Mammonism is to continue, it is idle to solicit remedial measures from any government, the disease being insusceptible of remedy.[79]

The crux, he holds, of the problem of reform is the organization of labor — "Giant Labour, truest emblem there is of God the World-Worker."[80] The state, he asserts, must become as it is actually bound to be, the keystone of a most real "Organization of Labour."[81] However, he believes that organization must come from within, from those who themselves work and preside over work.[82] No principle of organization is more important for Carlyle than that of permanent contract,[83] for in his view the great defect of industrialism, apart from the poverty and injustice it creates, is its failure to establish any bond between employer and employee save that of the cash nexus. Workers, he insists, must be bound by deeper ties than mere wages.[84] The system of freedom of contract and laissez faire cuts the ligature of society and leads to dissolution;[85] unorganized labor becomes the victim of an unjust industrial system. Except by "Mastership and Servantship" there is no conceivable

[75] *Ibid.*, p. 201.   [76] *Ibid.*, p. 262.
[77] *Latter-Day Pamphlets*, p. 158.   [78] *Ibid.*, pp. 158–59.
[79] *Past and Present*, p. 270.   [80] *Ibid.*, p. 170.
[81] *Latter-Day Pamphlets*, p. 159.
[82] *Past and Present*, p. 270.
[83] *Ibid.*, p. 277.   [84] *Ibid.*, p. 274.
[85] "The Nigger Question," *Critical and Miscellaneous Essays*, IV, 380.

deliverance from nomadism, from tyranny and slavery.[86] Carlyle demands that men shall be hired for life with a just wage and under just conditions, determined by experience.[87] He believes that a code of laws should be drawn up for their maintenance; no working world, he says, can be led on without a noble chivalry of work, and laws and fixed rules which follow out of that.[88]

His code for labor would presumably lay down the basic principle that he who will not work, neither shall he eat.[89] And he doubtless would demand here, as he does in the case of government, that there be full opportunity for talent to rise to the top, however humble its origin; that it be within the reach of every laborer to rise, by ability and industry, to mastership.[90] For, as he says, the alpha and omega of social questions is what methods the society has of summoning aloft into the high places, for its help and government, the wisdom that is born to it in all places, and of course is born chiefly in the more populous or lower places.[91] Carlyle thinks that it may be well in the not distant future for the captain of industry to grant his workers permanent economic interest in his enterprise and theirs. "So that it become in practical result, what in essential fact and justice it ever is, a joint enterprise; all men, from the Chief Master down to the lowest Overseer and Operative, economically as well as loyally concerned for it." [92]

The method Carlyle advocates for organizing labor is one of industrial regimentation, to be carried out along military lines. It is his fundamental belief that "wise obedience and wise command" is under most conditions the inviolable principle of good government.[93] He says that the regimentation of pauper banditti into soldiers of industry is but the beginning of this

[86] *Ibid.*, p. 362.
[87] *Ibid.*, p. 368.
[88] *Past and Present*, p. 273.
[89] "The Nigger Question," *Critical and Miscellaneous Essays*, IV, 355.
[90] *Latter-Day Pamphlets*, pp. 130–33; cf. *Chartism*, p. 127.
[91] *Latter-Day Pamphlets*, p. 183.
[92] *Past and Present*, p. 282.
[93] *Latter-Day Pamphlets*, pp. 166–67; *Chartism*, p. 189.

blessed process, which will extend to the topmost heights of our society. He adds that all kinds of industry will be found capable of regimenting.[94] And he recommends that the state compete with private industry in regimentation, until once more there be a "Governed Commonwealth and Civitas Dei":

> . . . all manner of free operatives, as yet unregimented, nomadic under private masters, seeing the example of the State will say: "Masters, you must regiment us a little, make our interests with you permanent a little, instead of temporary and nomadic; we will enlist with the State otherwise!" . . . This will go on, on the one hand, while State-operation goes on, on the other: thus will all Masters of Workmen, private Captains of Industry, be forced to incessantly cooperate with the State and its public Captains . . . till their fields *meet* (so to speak) and coalesce, and there be no unregimented worker.[95]

In addition to his scheme of organizing economic and social conditions in England, Carlyle strongly urges many practical measures of immediate reform. He insists, to begin with, that the country cannot be saved by reforming the reformed Parliament. The one method, he says, of staving off virtual anarchy lies not in reforming Parliament but in reforming Downing Street; there must be a "Reformed Executive," a reformed administrative system. Clean out all the dead pedantries![96] How is your ship to be steered by a pilot with no eyes but a pair of glass ones got from the constitutional optician?[97] Great state action, Herculean scavengerism, is indispensable, else that tremendous cloaca of pauperism will choke the world.[98]

He demands first and foremost a drastic reform in education; nothing, he says, is so urgent for bringing order and arrangement out of chaos as to irradiate by intelligence.[99] To impart the gift of thinking to those who cannot think and yet could, with education, think is the first function of a government.[1] Carlyle asks for an education bill, for the establishment

[94] *Latter-Day Pamphlets*, p. 166.
[95] *Ibid.*   [96] *Ibid.*, pp. 92–93.
[97] *Ibid.*, p. 109.   [98] *Ibid.*, pp. 163–64.
[99] *Past and Present*, p. 266; *Chartism*, p. 194.
[1] *Chartism*, p. 192.

of a Ministry of Education and an effective "Teaching Service."[2]

Hardly less important, he believes, is the setting up of an "Emigration Service," so that every honest workman who finds England "too strait" may find a bridge built to carry him to new lands.[3] And the state must embark upon other social legislation; there must be sanitary regulations[4] and improvements for bettering the health of the community, especially the health of workers. He recommends that

> . . . the Legislature order all dingy Manufacturing Towns to cease from their soot and darkness; to let in the blessed sunlight, the blue of Heaven, and become clear and clean; . . . Baths, free air, a wholesome temperature, ceilings twenty feet high, might be ordained, by Act of Parliament, in all establishments licensed as Mills. . . . Every toiling Manchester should have a hundred acres or so of free greenfield . . . for its all-conquering workers to take a breath of twilight air in.[5]

Carlyle remarks that if in the face of this program vested interests say, "I shall lose profits," the state will answer, "Yes, but my sons and daughters will gain health, and life, and a soul."[6]

Among his practical suggestions of reform, Carlyle has one or two of a scientific nature. It is most necessary, he believes, that we should discover how many are unemployed and the average rate of wages.[7] Statistics, he says, in its present unguided condition cannot ascertain the average rate of day's wages for any portion of the country, any more than it can tell us what it was in the past. Besides finding this out, we must know also the constancy of unemployment, the difficulty of finding employment, the fluctuation from season to season, from year to year. The simple fundamental question, can the laboring man find work, and subsistence by his work? is as yet a matter of pure conjecture. And still Parliament passes its new poor law.

Toward the end of his life, Carlyle looked to the aristocracy

---

[2] *Past and Present*, p. 265; *Latter-Day Pamphlets*, pp. 148, 167.
[3] *Past and Present*, pp. 266–67.   [4] *Ibid.*, p. 264.   [5] *Ibid.*, p. 265.   [6] *Ibid.*
[7] *Chartism*, p. 127.

for his hero-kings. He confessed that their possibilities lay in a most abstruse, and as yet uninvestigated, condition. Nevertheless, he declared, "a body of brave men, and of beautiful and polite women, furnished *gratis* as they are . . . ought to be good for something, in a society fallen vulgar and chaotic like ours." [8] He believed that the English nobleman had still left in him, after sorrowful erosions, something considerable of chivalry and magnanimity, qualities which no king could be without.[9] Though Carlyle thought that the captains of industry should unite with the aristocratic leaders,[10] he appealed to the latter to take the initiative.[11] And he warned the aristocrat that if he thought he could hang by the bridle of the wild horse of Plebs any longer, he had better go yachting to Algeria and shoot lions for an existence, or stay at home and hunt rats. He reproached the aristocrat for his docile submission; to run panting, he said, by Pleb's side, patting its stupid neck — that was no existence for a man of honor.[12]

V

Carlyle called attention to the "Condition-of-England Question" with a dramatic power unequaled in his time; more than any other he impressed upon Victorians the fact of unemployment and the fact of pauperism. He showed that uncurbed industrialism, which admitted little interest in the worker save the payment of his wage, was socially irresponsible. He showed that unbridled laissez faire brought about the demoralization of those who had no property save their labor. Opposing the "let alone" doctrine with the idea of state action, he was a factor in limiting the power of the industrial buccaneer, making him less able to oppress the unfortunate. That the state has embarked upon social services in the sphere of education, health, and sanitation is in some measure due to the fact that he wrote. And no one saw more clearly that administration is the great problem of modern government.

[8] "Shooting Niagara," *Critical and Miscellaneous Essays*, V, 16.
[9] *Ibid.*, p. 19.   [10] *Ibid.*, p. 31.   [11] *Ibid.*, pp. 19, 21, 48.   [12] *Ibid.*, p. 48.

Thomas Carlyle

By holding that "through every living soul the glory of a present God still beams," that the veriest human scarecrow holds his title of manhood, he did something to promote the idea of equality. By his championship of the worker's cause, by pointing out the need of work and of decent conditions of work, he did something to educate his generation to the worth and dignity of labor. Few things were more refreshing than his view that workingmen do not possess a natural fondness for discontent; and few were more enlightening than his view that injustice, not mere physical discomfort, drives men to revolt. He argued persuasively that disaffection in a great part of society becomes disaffection in the whole of it.

No one has pointed out with more force that a society dominated by Mammon is a society of oppression that invites disorder. Scarcely less effective was his argument that a class whose chief contribution to the national welfare is to live by owning can never provide leadership. Carlyle performed a service by pointing out that an industrial society tends to look at life with mechanical ideas, just as an industrial system whose chief incentive is profit tends to look upon wealth as the goal of effort. His assertion of a spiritual quality in life, his insistence on moral values over and above expediency, his denunciation of pleasure and happiness as the end of existence, provided a healthy antidote to materialistic views, not least to the crude philosophy of the Utilitarians and to the ideal of comfort which a machine civilization engenders. By flashes of insight he made more vital almost every idea that he touched.

In spite of his contribution to the social thought of the Victorian period, Carlyle belongs to the twentieth rather than to the nineteenth century. His criticism of an industrial system that gives birth to unemployment is as pertinent today as when he wrote. If the poverty he denounced has been somewhat mitigated, it still stalks the streets. It is true that some education is within reach of the worker, and it is true that there are healthier and safer conditions of work, but the attack on these problems has only just begun. State intervention has made considerable headway, but the laissez-faire philosophy is still predominant. State action in the economic sphere is more necessary than ever before.

Carlyle is of the twentieth century above all because the remedy he urged as a cure for the disorder of the liberal middle-class state is the remedy practised in Italy and Germany. Carlyle stood for fascist ideas fifty years before their advent. He advocated rule by the hero, by the man of action who must not hesitate to use force; Il Duce rules Italy and Der Führer rules Germany, and both act and use force ruthlessly. Carlyle demanded the regimentation of society; he recommended a "universal system of drill in all things human." Mussolini and Hitler have regimented their nations and rule by a government of the military pattern. Hitler has said that the "renascence of the German people has been crowned by the creation of a great and powerful army consisting of the entire people."[13]

Carlyle and the fascists are reactions against capitalistic democracy, against economic liberalism and parliamentary government. Though both criticize the materialism of the profit motive, neither abolishes the capitalist system of industry; though both subject the capitalist to greater restrictions than is the case under political democracy, they increase his power over the worker. By their destruction of free associations, they destroy trade-unions and the ability of the worker to protect himself; they enhance the power of the captains of industry in proportion as they destroy the power of the workers. In the drive to power Carlyle and the fascists enlist the services of the capitalists and make use of the aristocracy. Both emphasize society as against the individual and make order an end in itself; both insist on the great value of sacrifice and on blind obedience to the leader whom they exalt. Carlyle and the fascists attack reason: Carlyle insists that reason is an instrument of disintegration and that man's function is to act, not to think; Hitler declares that he does not want truth, but action. Both, however, make a concession to democracy: the leader, in theory,

[13] *Paris Herald Tribune*, September 18, 1936.

is responsible to the people; he must strive to satisfy their wants; he must strive to solve unemployment and to establish social services. In view of the similarity between Carlyle's ideas and those of the fascists, it is not surprising that editions of translated excerpts from Carlyle appeared in Italy from 1920 through 1922, and that 300,000 copies of selections were sold in Germany between 1926 and 1932.[14] Nor is it surprising that Carlyle's lectures on heroes are prescribed reading in many schools in Germany.

Carlyle argues for an aristocracy of hero-kings; in view of the great power he would place in their hands and in view of his frequent justification of force, his rulers would in practice be an aristocracy of autocrats with noble intentions. Such an aristocracy, however, could hardly exist for long; no strong man can tolerate competitors. Mussolini degrades Grandi and Balbo when they threaten to become important, Hitler sends Roehm to the firing squad because his lieutenant is a threat to his position, and Stalin executes Zinoviev for the same reason. If Carlyle would have been satisfied with a one-man rule, this would not greatly improve his case for autocracy, for the trouble with one strong man is that he is not strong enough. If he is not destroyed from within, he is generally destroyed from without; if his fate is not that of Caesar, it is generally that of Napoleon. And if he is destroyed neither from within nor from without, he finds it extremely difficult, as Cromwell illustrates, to perpetuate his strength. Strong men generally do not beget strong men; Marcus Aurelius, who is perhaps the most benevolent autocrat in history, begot Commodus. One reason for the advent of democracy is that men have tired of the instability to which autocracy, however benevolent in rare instances, gives rise. No type of government has been tried more often in history and no type has so frequently failed to secure its purpose.

Assuming, however, that a benevolent autocracy assures order and security, the final argument against autocracy is that it is always autocratic and seldom benevolent. The final argument

[14] Emery Neff, *Carlyle* (New York, 1932), pp. 268–69.

against Carlyle's remedy is the kind of life it would produce; an autocracy produces arrogance in the autocrat and servility in the people. It instills fear and a sense of inferiority in its citizens because the autocrat must continually assert his superiority and because he must frequently use force to maintain what he asserts. He must frequently use force because his claim to superiority breaks down; he makes mistakes and is found to be human like everyone else. Since he exacts blind obedience from his subjects as a condition of his rule, he is prevented from securing his power by an appeal to reason. He must appeal to the emotions of men, above all, to their fears and to their hatreds, and no principle is so successful in these realms as the principle of force. Because the autocrat stands for force and flaunts it in the face of his people, and because he frequently uses it against them, he brutalizes his people.

Carlyle wanted to construct a society that would give men full opportunity of developing the best that was in them; but because he believed that the mass did not have very much in them to develop, he constructed a society that was calculated to stunt the growth of its citizens. His insistence on blind obedience and regimentation meant that the people of his state could not hope to discover their best selves. Unless men have some real responsibility for directing their own lives, they must remain as children. Men develop their faculties very largely not by being told what to do with them, but by exercising them. A student becomes proficient in mathematics not by being told how to work the problem, but by being thrown upon his own and by making mistakes, by doing the problem himself. If men are not to remain as children, one of the first steps necessary to bring them out of adolescence is to assume their maturity. Carlyle's denial of democracy and liberty is a denial of a fundamental condition for the achievement of a healthy society, to which he looked forward.

Carlyle desired to establish a just state but, by advocating the principle of autocracy, he made such a state impossible of attainment. In an autocracy not justice but the interest of the stronger generally prevails. A minimum requirement of a just state is an appeal beyond the ruler, because men are fallible, because they make errors and commit wrongs, though they may have the best of intentions. Justice, then, requires a means of correcting errors and righting wrongs by an appeal beyond the ruler. An autocracy cannot satisfy this minimum requirement because there is no appeal beyond the autocrat except to violence. Democracy, on the other hand, satisfies this requirement, for it affords an appeal beyond the government to the community; it permits of a change of governments without a resort to force.

Justice requires that certain acts and decisions of a ruler shall be open to inspection and possibly invalidated by a disinterested party; justice requires that certain acts and decisions of the executive shall be open to judicial review (in the general sense) by the courts. But an autocrat cannot permit a review of his decisions, for to permit a review implies that the autocrat is not supreme, which is incompatible with the principle of autocracy. An autocrat cannot tolerate a disinterested party; the courts must believe, so far as fundamentals are concerned, as the autocrat believes, else his power may be undermined. It is not unsignificant that the emblem of the swastika has now been affixed to the robes of Nazi judges. A fundamental condition of a just state is a rule of law; in an autocracy there is, so far as important matters are concerned, only a rule of men. There can be no vital rule of law, for the autocrat is not subject to, but is above, the law. The law can always be set aside by the arbitrary wish or fancy of the autocrat.

Carlyle, like Plato, never told us how to choose the aristocracy of the best; both repudiated democracy, which is so far the only rational method of discovering them. Carlyle never really understood democratic institutions. To be sure, he saw that the vote and parliaments were useful in finding out the wants of men; and his wish that Parliament in England would become nothing more than an adviser to the sovereign has to some extent been realized. But if the executive was made all-powerful, as he desired, Parliament would cease to advise and would become, as in Germany at the present time, a rubber stamp. Carlyle never saw that democratic institutions were a means of making rulers responsible to the community; he never saw, for example, that Parliament with its discussion, criticism, and debate was a method of testing character and ability, and a method of bringing into public view the acts of ministers. Though Carlyle denounced Parliament as an institution mainly devoted to talk, Mussolini and Hitler, whom he would unquestionably have admired, indulge in far more talk than an English prime minister or an American president. What is worse, they indulge in fanatical talk; they bully their own people, and they threaten their neighbors; they talk, as they think, not with their brain, but with their blood.

Carlyle's objection to democracy on the ground that it must lead to ignorant government is based on the assumption that the ordinary man is too stupid to discern ability and character. The history of democratic government would seem to show that humble men are not incapable of discovering ability and character; it does not require genius, as Lincoln and Gladstone show, to detect genius. A greater difficulty for democracy is the discovery by men of ability and character of the humble man. Assume, however, that there is a great deal of ignorance in the electorate, as there most certainly is, it by no means follows that ignorant representatives will therefore be chosen. Nor even if there should be a considerable amount of ignorance among the elected legislators, does it follow that ignorant government will result. For the actual working of the party system in an atmosphere of discussion, criticism, and debate tends to confer leadership on the able. The same conditions, along with the impact of the expert, tend to purge away ignorance. Political democracy may produce unjust, but not generally ignorant, laws.

The truth is that though Carlyle could speak of the common man in terms of lofty commiseration, he did not respect him, at least when he dealt with the problem of government. Carlyle was impatient with him; in his eyes the common man was not capable of uprooting the great evils with which society was afflicted. The hero alone, as history showed Carlyle, was competent to deal with such things. Though Carlyle insisted on the community of the race and poured scorn on the man who said "Am I my brother's keeper?" he was a strong individualist. Just as Nietzsche's reverence for personality led him to believe in the superman as the hope of mankind, Carlyle's led him to believe in the hero. As an egoist, it was not unnatural that Carlyle should look to the heroic individual for a solution of the political problem and have little appreciation for, and less knowledge of, the part played by the broad mass of men, by institutions, and by accident in history.

Carlyle's egoism inclined him to authority, and his egoism in combination with his autocratic temper led him to exalt it; such a temperament as his was attracted by the idea of force. With a mind that was hostile to speculation and that placed reliance upon intuition, it was difficult for him to detach himself from his puritan conviction that what was right was strong. So intent was he on seeing right prevail that it was incredible to him that what was right was not necessarily either strong or weak. And it was easy for one who had a domineering temperament and little faith in reason to confuse at times right with might.

Carlyle denounced democracy's doctrine of equality, though he frequently stood for this very doctrine himself. Democracy does not deny individual differences; in fact, it recognizes their importance, for it sponsors the principle of *la carrière ouverte aux talents*. What it upholds is that the things men have in common are far more important than the things in which they differ; it emphasizes, as Carlyle so frequently did, man's humanity, and insists that men are equal in regard to their common characteristics.[15]

The source of Carlyle's uncompromising hostility to democracy was his deep conviction that it brought about the dissolu-

[15] For further discussion of the meaning of equality, see the chapter on Stephen, pages 161–62.

tion of society. Though there is an anarchical element in the individualism that democracy stands for, it is an unavoidable element if men are to have the opportunity of developing their powers. There can be no genuine freedom in a community unless the risk is taken of some men abusing their freedom. If people are to exercise their faculties, they are bound to make mistakes, and some mistakes will have disintegrative effects. The price of a free community is that some men are not able to take advantage of it. The charge that democracy leads to disintegration is the severest criticism that can be made of democracy; but, as Plato showed, this charge is more pertinent to the moral and spiritual aspects of men's lives than to the social. The answer to Plato is that it is better that some men lose their standards than that the community be put in a strait jacket, which is the alternative to democracy.

Carlyle, it should be observed, was able to look upon democracy as making for the rupture of all social relations because he identified it with laissez faire, with a policy of government pursued by the middle class of the nineteenth century, which permitted social "anarchy." Democracy, obviously, is by no means identical with laissez faire, as its collectivist tendencies have shown.

JOHN RUSKIN

I

IF CARLYLE was the chief critic of the social effects of capitalism, Ruskin next to Marx was the chief critic of its principles. Unlike Marx, he did not use Hegelian dialectic as a weapon of assault; he had no Marxist conception of history; his criticism was seldom historical but almost always analytical, moral, and psychological. Nor did he use, as Marx did, a theory of the class struggle, though he thought that the exploited might one day rise against the tyranny of their masters. For him, as for Marx, the labor theory of value was the base on which he rested his charge that capitalism was unjust; both insisted that capitalism exploited the worker and denied him the fruits of his labor. Where Marx supported this charge with a great wealth of historical fact, Ruskin supported it with a few simple analogies and numerous illustrations.

If Marx made a more convincing indictment of capitalism on the ground of the unfair distribution of reward, Ruskin was unequaled in showing the moral defects of capitalism in general. No one could match him in showing the materializing effect of the profit motive or the degrading effect of the assumption of self-interest. He declared that a system that made profit, not excellence of work, the chief incentive of production must encourage poor workmanship, foster greed, and generally degrade those who took part in the industrial process. And he pointed out that the emphasis on profit meant the worship of the "Goddess of Getting-On," and made dishonesty popular.

John Ruskin

Ruskin argued with no less vigor that a system that was indifferent to ultimate ends, that produced regardless of whether its products satisfied moral desires, stood self-condemned. He argued, too, that capitalism through excessive specialization dehumanized the worker. Nor did his indictment stop here. He insisted that a system that made money the chief relation between master and men, that paid little heed to the conditions under which men worked, that was indifferent to the social life of the workers, vitiated its own purpose as it wasted their energies. He pointed out incisively the connection between capitalism and war. In fine, Ruskin analyzed both the moral and the social effects of capitalism with far greater precision than any other writer; and this is true even though he did not carry his message to as many minds as did Carlyle.

Ruskin's attack did not end with his analysis of the moral and social defects of capitalism. He invaded the domain of political economy, and launched an offensive on the concepts that he believed gave support to capitalism. He was anxious to destroy its intellectual foundations; to change the mind was to change the system. His criticism of orthodox political economy was not as profound as Marx's; he did not show as fundamental a contradiction between capitalist assumptions and the result in practice; nor did he ever bring to the support of his case so formidable a weight of irresistible fact. He insisted that political economy was not only open to error on its own ground, but also that it was unreal; few charges were more important for him, as few were more important for Marx. Where Marx found orthodox economics impaired by a failure to take account of history, Ruskin found it impaired by a failure to take account of human nature; in his eyes political economy took account only of the selfish side of man, not of the whole of man. And he maintained that it emphasized production and ignored distribution, that its conception of value was a monetary not a moral one, and that it was not concerned with the question of what should and what should not be produced, any more than it was with the social conditions under which production took place.

John Ruskin

As against the self-interest philosophy, Ruskin appealed to a professional view of industrial and commercial incentive. He asked the businessmen of his day to consider themselves as professional men; he asked them to perform their tasks for the sake of a task well performed, not for the sake of profit; he asked them to make the quality of work, not reward, their primary concern. In seeking a remedy for an industrial system that brought out man's worst side, and for the materialism to which it gave birth, Ruskin appealed to the conscience of men. He asked the upper classes above all to transform themselves, to change their hearts, and to seek justice not profits. Unlike Carlyle, he did not combine this appeal with the recommendation to the aristocracy to seize power. He brought forward, however, a plan for the initiation of a new order. He suggested that the government should set up workshops in which principles of good work and decent working conditions would become the standard for the community. The government would be a model employer, attracting into its organization workers and employers alike, until industry was based on the principle of cooperation and service for the common good instead of competition and self-interest.

The state to which he eventually looked forward was a combination of Plato's *Republic* and Carlyle's *Past and Present*. In his ideal state each man would perform to the best of his ability the function for which he was best fitted. As he followed Carlyle in looking upon the worker as a soldier, he also sought officers for the soldiers in the more cultivated classes. Though he believed in the principle of the tools to him who can use them, he was prepared to take for his rulers the upper classes as they were constituted in his own day. Like Carlyle, he found extraordinary virtue in the aristocracy, though he, too, condemned them unsparingly for their frivolity, for their idleness, and for their materialism; and, like Carlyle, he found ample virtue in the captains of industry in spite of their worship of Mammon.

Ruskin's remedy for a disordered society, like Plato's and Carlyle's, was authoritarian; like them, he sought a solution of the anarchy of individualism in a government of wide authority, as well as in an "organic" view of society. Not only did he propose a social service state and suggest that government should enter into the field of manufacturing, operate public utilities, and provide land for those who could use it, but he also proposed that the state be given power over the smallest details of men's lives. Unlike Carlyle, he made room for religious functionaries; he would have bishops and clergymen acting as the custodians of men's conduct. In his ideal state he made obedience and order leading principles, as Plato and Carlyle did in theirs; and, like these writers, he looked upon democracy with its liberty and equality as a system of government that made for the disintegration of society.

Ruskin had great difficulty at first in obtaining a hearing for his ideas; he was in deeper conflict with his age than Carlyle. He attacked the industrial system root and branch, scandalizing those who ruled it, those who lived by it, and those who spoke for it. So bitter was the protest against his articles, which appeared in the *Cornhill Magazine* and *Fraser's,* that their publication was suspended. The intolerance of his own class broke his spirit. To be sure, he continued to write, but discursively; though he had planned a systematic treatise on political economy, his failure to obtain a hearing in those crucial years disheartened him and he never attempted a thorough study.

Even after he had created his public, which he began to do some ten years later, he was never able to exercise as strong an influence as Carlyle. He was not as great a personality as Carlyle, and he could not equal Carlyle's moral and spiritual appeal, though he, too, was a prophet and was, as Carlyle said, "born in the clouds and struck by lightning." [1] Nor could his style, though it possessed great beauty, engage men's interest as successfully as Carlyle's; it was less romantic and less prophetic; it was clear and never mystical; it was logical and in

---

[1] Leslie Stephen points out that Carlyle exercised a greater influence than Ruskin because his puritanism made a stronger appeal. Stephen also remarks that Carlyle was the more potent influence on the thoughtful young men of his day. *Studies of a Biographer* (4 vols., London, 1898–1907), III, 102.

many respects classical. Ruskin's thought was analytical; Mazzini said of him that he had the most analytical mind in Europe. While Carlyle constantly appealed to emotional symbols, Ruskin generally appealed to ideas. Another factor may help to explain why Carlyle exercised a greater influence than Ruskin. Carlyle offered men of industry and commerce greater compensation for the sacrifices he asked them to make. In return for social services, Carlyle conferred heroship upon the middle class; in exchange for the amelioration of social conditions, he consecrated its individualism. Ruskin did not permit the middle class to ransom their self-respect so easily. Ruskin asked the men of industry and commerce not only to adopt measures of socialization, but also to give up profit as a chief incentive; though he promised them the top places in his new society, they were to find their life by losing it.

If Ruskin was not the power that Carlyle was, if he did not stir the moral feelings as effectively as Carlyle, he did more to influence the thinking of a few minds than did the prophet of Chelsea. He taught many to criticize the abstract "economic man"; he persuaded many to consider the use as well as the accumulation of wealth.[2] His teaching, according to Ernest Barker, influenced the teaching of pure economics.[3] Ruskin's advocacy, he says, of the economic ideas of Plato, Aristotle, and Xenophon has helped to turn economists since the days of Jevons from the theory of production to the theory of consumption; it has helped to correct the old emphasis laid on saving, and to give more weight to spending; it has helped to modify the old conception of value as mainly determined by cost of production, and to give more consideration to utility as a factor in its creation.

Ruskin's attack on the middle-class liberal state and the system of capitalism it sheltered helped to diminish the authority of both. His criticism, like Carlyle's, helped to undermine

[2] Ernest Barker, *Political Thought in England, 1848 to 1914* (rev. ed., London, 1928), p. 195.
[3] *Ibid.*

John Ruskin

laissez faire both in principle and in application; at the same time, he did not a little to accustom men's thoughts to a social service state. Though Ruskin was not a socialist, and Carlyle still less, these men did more than any other writers to prepare the way for socialist ideas.[4] If Ruskin was not the begettèr of English socialism, he was a foster father to many English socialists.[5] And through William Morris, his greatest disciple, he inspired the Arts and Crafts and the Guild Socialist movements. It was only a fitting recognition of his interest in educating those without opportunity that a college at Oxford for teaching workingmen was founded in his name.

II

Born in 1819 to parents of Scotch origin, Ruskin, unlike Carlyle, was brought up in a family of ample means. His religious education began in his infancy; his mother, a strict evangelical puritan, made certain that her young son was fully acquainted with the Bible; she would begin with the first chapter of Genesis, go straight through to the last verse of the Apocalypse, and begin again at Genesis the next day.[6] The night before he was three, Ruskin repeated the whole of the one hundred and nineteenth Psalm. Ruskin's mother, who was the chief influence of his life, implanted in him a puritan view of things which was the chief source of his political ideas. His mother's teaching, he says, gave him a perfect understanding of the nature of obedience and of faith.[7] His mother carried her puritanism into the smallest details of ordinary life; she held strong views on the sinfulness even of toys. Ruskin's early education was entirely within his family; he was educated in the "monastic severities and aristocratic dignities" of a sheltered household where there were few playthings and no playmates.[8]

[4] *Ibid.*, p. 202.
[5] *Ibid.*, p. 196. Ruskin's *Unto This Last* influenced the Labour members of the Parliament of 1906 more than any other book. See Edward T. Cook, *The Life of John Ruskin* (2 vols., London, 1911), II, 14.
[6] Edward T. Cook, *The Life of John Ruskin*, I, 13.   [7] *Ibid.*
[8] Frederick W. Roe, *The Social Philosophy of Carlyle and Ruskin* (New York, 1921), p. 130.

John Ruskin

If he owed puritanism to his mother, Ruskin owed his interest in literature to his father, who read to him from the classics, Shakespeare, Don Quixote, Scott, and Byron. "I am," he says, "and my father was before me, a violent Tory of the old school: — Walter Scott's school, that is to say, and Homer's; these two were my own two masters." [9] He remarks that their effect was tempered on Sunday by *Robinson Crusoe* and *The Pilgrim's Progress* — his mother's aim being to make an evangelical clergyman of him.

Ruskin's instinct for beauty was given full encouragement in the journeys he took with his father during the summer. The elder Ruskin, who was a wine merchant, traveled by coach in the English countryside during the warm months, taking orders for sherry from aristocratic patrons. While visiting the great houses, Ruskin's father would insist on seeing the paintings and would not leave until he and his son had made a thorough study. [10] His artistic gifts were further developed in later years by frequent trips to the Continent to visit the art centers of the world.

Ruskin graduated from Christ Church, Oxford, in 1842. In speaking of the books he read there, he said that he loved Plato from the first line. [11] He remarked in 1843 that he thinks himself wrong if he does not read Plato every day; [12] the study of the *Republic* and the *Laws* exercised a strong influence on him in later years. He was to follow Plato's conception of justice: each man fulfilling the function for which he was best fitted, and each man in his place. Plato's emphasis on the wisdom of the few and the unwisdom of the mass, as well as his emphasis on authority, supported attitudes, if not ideas, in which Ruskin had been trained and to which his temperament naturally inclined him. Xenophon's *Economist,* long a favorite with Ruskin, was the foundation of his studies in political economy. [13] Plato, Xenophon, and Aristotle all taught him that economics cannot be separated from other social studies, that it is a sub-

[9] Edward T. Cook, *The Life of John Ruskin,* I, 14.
[10] *Ibid.,* p. 18.   [11] *Ibid.,* p. 62.   [12] *Ibid.,* p. 158.   [13] *Ibid.,* II, 373.

ordinate branch of the great art of politics, which is concerned with the moral betterment of society.[14] As he later said, he wanted to recall to modern minds the wisdom of Plato and Xenophon.[15]

With the publication of the first volume of *Modern Painters* in 1843, he began a career in art which was his main occupation until 1860. His *Modern Painters* (1843–60), *The Seven Lamps of Architecture* (1849), and *The Stones of Venice* (1851–53) made Victorians aware of a sense of beauty; William Morris and Burne-Jones declared him a "Luther of the Arts." Oxford recognized him in 1869 by making him the first Slade Professor of Fine Arts. It had been clear for some time that religion would never become a leading interest with Ruskin. He found Carlyle's doctrine of work an aid in putting away any further doubts about religion; in the last volume of *Modern Painters* (1860) he declared that "in resolving to work well is the only sound foundation of any religion whatsoever."

Ruskin spoke of 1860 as the beginning of his days of reprobation;[16] in the valley of Chamounix he decided to give up his art work and deal with a world that made art all but impossible. It was not a sudden break, for he had been aware of the social problem for some time; many years earlier when his father's Spanish partner, Señor Domecq, came to visit his family, Ruskin was shocked to hear the Spanish laborers and French tenantry referred to as mere cumberers of the ground. It was the talk of Señor Domecq and his family that gave him the first clue to the real sources of wrong in the social laws of modern Europe and led him, he says, "necessarily into the political work which has been the most earnest of my life." Ruskin could see no justice in a system that gave the graceful, gay Andalusian peasants, who played guitars, danced boleros, and fought bulls,

[14] Ernest Barker, *Political Thought in England, 1848 to 1914,* p. 191.

[15] Edward T. Cook, *The Life of John Ruskin,* II, 361–62.

[16] *Lectures on Landscape: Michaelangelo and Tintoret* (Library Edition of the complete works, Edward T. Cook and Alexander Wedderburn, editors, 39 vols., London, 1903–12, Vol. XXII), p. 512. All future references to the works of Ruskin will be to this edition; each work will be identified in the series by a volume number in parentheses after the title.

nothing but the bunch of grapes or stalk of garlic they frugally dined on; and those for whom they worked Danish gardens with milk and honey, and fine noble houses in Paris.[17]

His change from the criticism of art to the criticism of society arose naturally from his principles of art. He held that fine painting consisted in the representation of beautiful objects, pursued in a spirit of delight;[18] and he held that architecture was the reflection of national character[19] and that its beauty depended on the happiness of the worker.[20] He was convinced that in an ugly, materialistic world, where there was so much misery and injustice, true art was impossible. "It is the vainest of affectations," he afterwards wrote, "to try and put beauty into shadows, while all real things that cast them are in deformity and pain."[21] With the triumph of the moralist over the artist, Ruskin devoted his energies to reconstructing man's political and social ways as a first necessity of vital art.

By 1851 Ruskin's political ideas were beginning to take definite shape. He was a republican as against institutions or laws which oppressed the poor, and a conservative as against theories and reforms which were based on doctrines of liberty and equality.[22] Ruskin had come to favor a graduated income tax and a supertax on large incomes. His radical tendency disturbed his father. He attempted to pacify his parent by pointing out what they had in common; he wrote, "I am just as far from universal suffrage as you are — and by my measure, one man of parts and rank would outweigh in voting a whole shoal of the mob."[23]

If he was a learner from Plato and Xenophon, he was a disciple of Carlyle.[24] Next to his mother, Carlyle was the

[17] *Praeterita and Dilecta* (Vol. XXXV), p. 409.
[18] *The Elements of Drawing* (Vol. XV), p. 354; *Lectures on Art* (Vol. XX), p. 121.
[19] "The Nature of Gothic," *The Stones of Venice* (Vol. X); *Sesame and Lilies* (Vol. XVIII), p. 443.
[20] *Fors Clavigera* (Vol. XXIX), p. 137.
[21] Edward T. Cook, *The Life of John Ruskin*, II, 4.
[22] *Ibid.*, I, 273.   [23] *Ibid.*, p. 276.
[24] *Lectures on Architecture and Painting* (Vol. XII), p. 577.

strongest influence of his life. As early as 1854 Ruskin acknowledged in a public lecture that he owed more to Carlyle than to any other writer.[25] The message of *Sartor* and *Heroes* aroused him, he says, "to *do* something, to be something useful." Of all Carlyle's writings, *Past and Present* and *Latter-Day Pamphlets* influenced him most; he sent a much-scored copy of the former to a friend, with the words, "I have sent you a book which I read no more because it has become a part of myself, and my old marks in it are now useless, because in my heart I mark it all." [26] Carlyle's denunciations swept Ruskin's heart with a passionate storm of sympathy.[27] Carlyle's deep sympathy — at first deeper than his contempt — for the blind multitude, who were miserable for the lack of a heaven-born feudal ruler, found an echo in Ruskin; so did his derision of all the remedies of all the liberal freethinkers. Though Ruskin already held many of the social, authoritarian, and aristocratic ideas that Carlyle advocated, Carlyle, it seems, strengthened his belief in them, added to them, and made them more articulate. Carlyle above all reinforced his puritanism, which his mother had bred in him. That Ruskin could say that his teachings were expressed in a single phrase "soldiers of the Ploughshare as well as soldiers of the Sword" shows the nature of his debt to Carlyle.

Ruskin's political philosophy began to appear in his writings on art. In *The Seven Lamps of Architecture,* written in the stirring year of 1848, the year of Chartism at home and revolution abroad, he denounced liberty as the most treacherous of phantoms, and he praised obedience.[28] And he remarked that idleness was the chief cause of the evils of Europe — of the recklessness of demagogues, of the immorality of the middle class, and of the effeminacy and treachery of the nobles. He said that occupation was the chief need. In the closing pages of *The Stones of Venice* (1851–53) he again attacked liberty; he argued that it permitted multitudes to be sent like fuel to

[25] *Ibid.*, p. 507.
[26] *Fors Clavigera* (Vol. XXVII), p. 179n.
[27] John A. Hobson, *John Ruskin, Social Reformer* (3d ed., London, 1904), p. 39.
[28] *The Seven Lamps of Architecture* (Vol. VIII), p. 248.

feed the factory smoke.[29] He pointed out that never had the upper classes done so much for the lower, yet never were the lower so antagonistic to the upper; he believed that this was due to the great inequality that separated them.[30] *The Stones of Venice* showed him in rebellion against excessive division of labor.[31] In the last volume of *Modern Painters* (1860) he spoke in favor of military asceticism as against a religious or monetary one; the latter, he thought, stood for the refusal of pleasure and knowledge for the sake of money.[32] He held that all men should perform useful work so that no man need work more than was good for him;[33] and he insisted that the best of the world's work was done for nothing, not for pay.[34]

Not a few of Ruskin's cardinal tenets appeared in a series of lectures delivered in Manchester in 1857. These were first printed as *The Political Economy of Art* and afterward as *A Joy Forever*. In the citadel of economic orthodoxy, he proposed that the sacred principle of economic competition be replaced by cooperation, and the policeman's state by a paternalistic state. In *Unto This Last,* the most powerful book he ever wrote on social matters, he attacked the assumptions of political economy and of the industrial and commercial system; he criticized incisively the character of the profit order. And he came out unequivocally for a state that should set itself up as a model employer, manufacturing products of quality and providing fully for the physical welfare of the worker. His succeeding works added little that was fundamental to the views expressed in *Unto This Last;* his later writings were concerned rather with elaborating its principles. *Unto This Last* appeared originally in *Cornhill,* but the essays brought down such a storm of protest that Thackeray, the editor, was compelled to stop further publication. The *Manchester Examiner and Times* said of Ruskin, "he is not worth our powder and shot . . . yet

[29] *The Stones of Venice* (Vol. X), p. 193.
[30] *Ibid.*, p. 194.   [31] *Ibid.*, pp. 196–97.
[32] *Modern Painters* (Vol. VII), p. 424.
[33] *Ibid.*, pp. 427–28.   [34] *Ibid.*, p. 449.

if we do not crush him, his wild words will touch the springs of action in some hearts, and ere we are aware a moral floodgate will open and drown us all." [35]

Though Ruskin continued to attack orthodox political economy in *Munera Pulveris* (1863), he was mainly concerned in this book with setting forth his own ideas on the subject. Not the least striking feature of *Munera Pulveris* was Ruskin's analysis of the origin of wealth, especially of capitalist wealth. *Time and Tide* appeared in the year of the Reform Bill of 1867, and admonished workingmen to see if they could obey a good law before attempting to change bad ones. In *Time and Tide* Ruskin presented a blueprint of his ideal state and suggested the means of its attainment.

The most popular of Ruskin's books, *Sesame and Lilies,* which appeared in 1865, was an attempt to teach the educated classes the moral principles he thought essential to a life well lived. With the publication in the same year of *The Crown of Wild Olive,* which was well received, Ruskin was established as a popular writer. This book, which deals with the nature of work and holds that the end of work is not profits but "wealth," contains Ruskin's most devastating attack on profit as the motive of industry.

In 1865 Ruskin joined Carlyle, Tennyson, Kingsley, and Dickens to form a defense committee on behalf of Governor Eyre, who had taken stern repressive measures in Jamaica.[36] In supporting Governor Eyre, Ruskin stood for authority even to the extent of justifying a gross abuse of power.

Ruskin, in 1869, defined his politics clearly. In commenting on the two great parties, the radical and the conservative, as he called them, he remarked that they have two opposite watchwords, which are both right and only right together — "Radical, everyman his chance; Tory, everyman in his rank." [37] *Fors Clavigera* (1871–78), which appeared, like *Time and Tide,* in

[35] *Manchester Examiner and Times,* October 2, 1860.
[36] Edward T. Cook, *The Life of John Ruskin,* II, 111. See below, page 140, for Stephen's part in the affair.
[37] *Ibid.,* p. 167.

the form of letters. to workingmen, was a vehement criticism of conditions of the times. It added further details to his scheme of social reconstruction, and set forth his venture into Utopia — St. George's Guild. *Fors,* Frederick Harrison said, was Ruskin's *Hamlet* and his Apocalypse; *Fors* showed Ruskin to be isolated from the world, it showed him in loneliness, and it showed that the more he lost touch with people round him the more license he gave to his pen. *Fors,* says his biographer, was a ransom to win peace.[38]

St. George's Guild, which was founded during this period, was an attempt to establish the principle that a sound society was one in which everybody worked for his living, and that the healthiest work of all was work done on the land.[39] Ruskin speaks of this scheme as following Carlyle's grander exhortation in *Past and Present.* The Guild, with eight vows for its members and Ruskin for its master, and with the practical policy of acquiring land for settlement by laborers who should enjoy fixed rents and decent conditions of life, was to come under the control of a landed aristocracy enforcing a beneficent military rule. There was almost no response to Ruskin's scheme. St. George's farms produced very little except disappointment; his ideal settlements, described with such charm in the pages of *Fors,* were too often in practice grim or grotesque, and sometimes they were both.[40]

In the writing of *Fors,* Ruskin frequently fell into a state of anger, aggravated by overwork; in the later letters he was constantly struggling against excitement, but in vain.[41] The men, he says, capable of the highest imaginative passion are tossed on the fiery waves by it. Toward the end of his life he frequently sank into moods of despair, broken now and then by the opposite mood of optimism. As the clouds were descending, he was more and more surrounded by uncritical adulation, which helped to accentuate his strong tendency to absolutism. When conditions were suitable he worked at a feverish pitch; after numerous attacks of brain fever, he died in 1900.

[38] *Ibid.,* p. 320.   [39] *Ibid.,* p. 336.   [40] *Ibid.,* p. 343.   [41] *Ibid.,* I, 396.

John Ruskin

Ruskin's thought did not spring from a religious base, as did Carlyle's. Though morality was fundamental to his view, righteousness was not for him the aim of man, as it was for Carlyle. Ruskin believed in right conduct, but also in happiness; in fact, he held that happiness was the ideal at which man should aim. This accounts for the great importance he attached to the view that the end of art is to delight as well as to ennoble. This also accounts for his view that there can be no true industrial and commercial order, any more than there can be a true educational or social system, that does not take full account of the desire for beauty. It helps to explain his conception of work, which was revolutionary for his time; in his view work, under proper conditions, was not painful but good. It helps to explain his demand that the working conditions in factories and elsewhere be made as healthful and as pleasant as possible.

For Ruskin, as for Plato and Carlyle, the mass of men were inferior beings, who were not fitted to rule themselves but to obey the wise and intelligent few. It followed for Ruskin, as it did for Plato and Carlyle, that his ideal state would be authoritarian; great power must be exercised by the rulers if the lives of the many are to be ruled. An authoritarian state such as Ruskin's must be hostile to democracy and to the policy of laissez faire, and it must favor the government's performing social services.

Ruskin, like Plato, looked upon man as he did upon society—as "organic." His view that man was a creature of affection as well as of self-interest enabled him to attack capitalism and orthodox political economy. That man was capable of disinterested action, and of delight, and of a sense of beauty, as well as of selfishness, meant that Ruskin was able to indict industrialism on the ground of ugliness; in his eyes satisfaction of man's aesthetic sense was essential to a sound society. That Ruskin looked upon society as "organic," as did Plato and Carlyle, explains his view that disease in any part of society is disease in the whole of it, and that a social remedy is necessary to cure a social ill. His "organic" view accounts for his conviction that a solution of the social problem is dependent on a solution of the economic problem, just as it does for his conviction that man's sense of beauty can never develop in the midst of materialism.

In view of his "organic" conception of man and society, it was fitting that he made use of Plato's idea of justice. Plato's conception lies behind the organization of Ruskin's ideal society — his organization of classes, his division of labor and assignment of functions between and in different classes, and his professional view of industry. The Platonic idea of justice, which requires that each man should do the job for which he is best fitted, was in his mind opposed to the democratic view of equality, and supported his contention that the few should rule and that the many should obey, and that the many should perform the degrading tasks of civilization. Finally, his labor theory of value, which holds that a man should receive in exchange for his product an equivalent of the amount of labor he himself has expended, lay behind his attack on the exploitation of labor by capitalism, his denunciation of speculation, and his criticism of profit, rent, and interest.

IV

Ruskin, like Carlyle, attacked the materialism of his age; like his master, he insisted that a machine civilization degrades the nature of man. In Ruskin's eyes, the machine civilization of his day was a blight upon man's spirit; the unspeakable ugliness of the factories and the factory towns left their inhabitants blind to a sense of beauty: "to the general people, trained in the midst of the ugliest objects that vice can design, in houses, mills, and machinery, *all* beautiful form and colour is as invisible as the seventh heaven. . . . think what ruin it is for men of any sensitive faculty to live in such a city as London is now!" [42] Humanity, he said, is "sunk in mechanism numbered with its wheels and weighed with its hammer strokes." Division of

[42] *Fors Clavigera* (Vol. XXVIII), p. 267.

labor divides the man:[43] "Labour is divided into mere segments of men; so that all the little piece of intelligence that is left in a man is not enough to make a pin, or a nail, but exhausts itself in making the point of a pin, or the head of a nail."[44]

Ruskin declared that the first of all English games was making money, and that more were knocked down in this game than in any other.[45] He remarked that Christianity was used to justify the results of this game: you knock, he remarked, a man into the ditch and tell him to remain content in the "position in which Providence has placed him."[46] Ruskin maintained that the money game was irrational.[47] Ask, he said, a great money-maker what he wants to do with his money. He never knows; he gets it only that he may get it. Nor do men pay for things of worth; people as a rule pay for being amused or being cheated, not for being served:

Five thousand a year to your talker, and a shilling a day to your fighter, digger, and thinker, is the rule. None of the best head work in art, literature, or science, is ever paid for. How much do you think Homer got for his *Iliad?* or Dante for his *Paradise?* Only bitter bread and salt, and going up and down other people's stairs.[48]

In his view there is no stronger indictment of the worship of wealth than the mockery it has made of Christianity: "Modern society is as willing as ever to crucify its Christ in the persons of His poor; but by no means now to crucify its thieves beside Him! It elevates its thieves after another fashion; sets them upon a hill that their light may shine before men."[49]

Ruskin insists that the wealth and luxury enjoyed by the few in capitalist society is the result of the exploitation of labor. No man, he says, can become largely rich by his personal toil.[50] The work of his own hands, wisely directed, will indeed always maintain himself and his family and make fitting provisions

[43] *The Stones of Venice* (Vol. X), pp. 194–95.   [44] *Ibid.*, p. 196.
[45] *The Crown of Wild Olive* (Vol. XVIII), p. 405.
[46] *Ibid.*, p. 422.   [47] *Ibid.*, p. 405.   [48] *Ibid.*, p. 422.
[49] *Time and Tide* (Vol. XVII), p. 392.
[50] *Munera Pulveris* (Vol. XVII), p. 264.

John Ruskin

for his age. But it is only by discovering some method of taxing the labor of others that he can become opulent. Stated in its simplest terms, wealth is accumulated as follows: [51] A provident person works much and lays by a store; a number of persons, through either improvidence or misfortune, produce little and lay by no store. Accident, such as sickness, interrupts the daily work and the provident person has the poor ones at his mercy. He agrees to provide for them on the condition that they shall work hard and surrender to him all their surplus.

The provident person, says Ruskin, can now improve his estate. He leaves the poor ones only as much ground as will maintain their numbers; as the population increases, he takes the extra hands, who cannot be maintained on the narrowed estates, for his own servants. Some cultivate his own ground, some serve him in his household, and some become workmen, whom he educates in ornamental arts; these decorate his mansion. Thus without any abuse of right, we find established all the phenomena of poverty and riches which accompany modern civilization. In one part of the district we have unhealthy land, miserable dwellings, and half-starved poor; in another a well-ordered estate, well-fed servants, and refined conditions of highly educated and luxurious life.

Ruskin points out that the exploitation of the laborer under capitalism is mitigated to some extent by competition.[52] The power, he says, of the rich person over the poor is checked only by some well-off neighbor who will say to the laborer, "I will give you a little more than the other provident person, come and work for me." Thus the power of the well-to-do over the laborer depends primarily on the relative numbers of the adverse parties, secondarily on the modes of agreement between the two. The accidental level of wages is a variable function of the number of well-to-do and poor persons in the world, of the enmity between them as classes, and of the agreement between those of the same classes.

[51] *Ibid.*, pp. 262–68. Cf. *Unto This Last* (Vol. XVII), pp. 45–52.
[52] *Munera Pulveris* (Vol. XVII), p. 263.

John Ruskin

Ruskin says that the antagonism created by the exploitation of workingmen is modified by kind persons among the rich and by wise persons among the poor.[53] The efforts, he remarks, made to raise and relieve on the one side, and the success of honest toil on the other, bind and blend the orders of society into the confused tissue of half-felt obligation, sullenly rendered obedience, and variously directed, or misdirected, toil which forms the warp of daily life. But this great law rules all the wild design: that success (while society is guided by laws of competition) signifies always so much victory over your neighbor as to obtain the direction of his work and to take the profits of it. This is the real source of all great riches.

Ruskin insists that what is really desired under the name of riches is power over men — in its simplest sense, the power to obtain for our own advantage the labor of servant, tradesman, and artist; in its wider sense, authority to direct large masses of the nation to various ends (good, trivial, or hurtful, according to the mind of the rich person).[54] He declares that the art of becoming rich is not absolutely the art of accumulating money, but also of contriving that our neighbors shall have less. It is, he says, the art of establishing the maximum of inequality in our own favor.[55] Riches are a power, like that of electricity, acting only through inequalities or a negation of itself.

The force of the guinea you have in your pocket depends wholly on the default of a guinea in your neighbour's pocket. If he did not want it, it would be of no use to you; the degree of power it possesses depends accurately upon the need or desire he has for it, — and the art of making yourself rich, in the ordinary mercantile economist's sense, is therefore equally and necessarily the art of keeping your neighbour poor.[56]

The power of wealth is greater or less in direct proportion to the poverty of those over whom it is exercised, and in inverse proportion to the number of persons who are as rich as ourselves, and who are ready to give the same price for an article of which the supply is limited.

[53] *Ibid.*, p. 264.
[54] *Unto This Last* (Vol. XVII), p. 46.   [55] *Ibid.*   [56] *Ibid.*, p. 44.

John Ruskin

It follows for Ruskin that under competitive capitalism there is no just wage; what determines a worker's wages is the economic strength of the two parties; robbing the poor because he is poor is the underlying principle of exchange.[57] Ruskin condemns capitalism not only because it permits exploitation of the worker but also because it makes profit, not excellence of work, the end of production.[58] He points out that because the merchant is presumed to act selfishly, society holds him in low esteem; it places him below the soldier, the clergyman, the doctor, and the lawyer.[59]

The merchant's first object in all his dealings must be (the public believe) to get as much for himself, and leave as little to his neighbour (or customer) as possible. Enforcing this upon him, by political statute, as the necessary principle of his action . . . the public, nevertheless, involuntarily condemn the man of commerce for his compliance with their own statement, and stamp him for ever as belonging to an inferior grade of human personality.[60]

Ruskin declares that the capitalist's insatiable desire for gain is the cause of war. Capitalists, he says, persuade peasants in various countries that they want guns to shoot each other with. The peasants shoot until they get tired, and burn each other's homes down; then they put the guns back in towers in ornamental patterns (and the victorious party put also some ragged flags in churches). The capitalists tax both parties to pay interest on the loans of the guns and gunpowder; and that is what they call "knowing what to do with your money."[61] Again Ruskin argues the connection between capitalism and war and makes his indictment still more specific. He says that the capitalists are the real thieves of Europe, and that their interest in theft is the real cause of all deadly war in it.[62] He remarks that when children ask for firecrackers, you think twice before you give them money to buy, for you have an idea that the money is wasted when it flies off in fireworks, even though no mis-

[57] Ibid., p. 58. Cf. The Two Paths (Vol. XVI), pp. 401ff.
[58] Unto This Last (Vol. XVII), pp. 29ff; Time and Tide (Vol. XVII), p. 427.
[59] Unto This Last (Vol. XVII), pp. 36–39.　[60] Ibid., p. 38.
[61] Munera Pulveris (Vol. XVII), p. 142.
[62] Fors Clavigera (Vol. XXVII), p. 127.

chief is done.[63] But, he says, the Russian children and the Austrian children come to borrow money to buy cartridges and bayonets to attack you in India with and to keep down all noble life in Italy with, and to murder Polish women and children with; and that you will give at once because they pay you interest for it. Now, in order to pay you that interest, they must tax every working peasant in their dominions, and on that work you live. You therefore at once rob the Austrian peasant, assassinate or banish the Polish peasant, and live on the produce of the theft and the bribe for the assassination! That is the practical meaning of your foreign loans.

Not only does Ruskin affirm that capitalism makes for war, he also insists that it makes for inferior products.[64] Such dishonesty, he says, is not objected to; you have fair play in games, but not fair work in toil: "Your prize-merchant gains his match by foul selling, and no one cries out against that! You drive a gambler out of the gambling room who loads the dice." [65]

Ruskin charges capitalism with subjecting the worker to much useless toil; when, he says, work comes to nothing, when our bees' business turns to spiders', and for honeycomb we have only cobweb, blown away by the next breeze — that is the cruel thing.[66] Of all wastes the greatest is the waste of labor:

If you put him to base labour, if you bind his thoughts, if you blind his eyes, if you blunt his hopes, if you steal his joys, if you stunt his body, and blast his soul, and at last leave him not so much strength to reap the poor fruits of his degradation, but gather that for yourself, and dismiss him to the grave, when you have done with him . . . this you think is no waste and no sin! [67]

Capitalism in Ruskin's view exploits the worker, debases the function of commerce and industry in society, makes for war, makes for inferior products, and wastes human labor, because its principle of profit is a principle of theft. It is a principle of

[63] *The Crown of Wild Olive* (Vol. XVIII), p. 416.
[64] See *The Two Paths* (Vol. XVI), pp. 401ff; *Unto This Last* (Vol. XVII), p. 84; *Time and Tide* (Vol. XVII), p. 383.
[65] *The Crown of Wild Olive* (Vol. XVIII), p. 425.
[66] *Ibid.*, p. 426.   [67] *Ibid.*, p. 427.

theft because capitalists are people who live by percentages on the labor of others, instead of by fair wages of their own.[68] He argues that the theft of capitalism is not of the ordinary variety; the highwayman robbed the rich, but the capitalist robs the poor. Still more important, the theft of capitalism is occult theft; because, he says, it is legal and respectable, it corrupts the body and soul of man to the last fiber.

In Ruskin's view no criticism of the economic arrangements of his day could be adequate which did not take account of orthodox political economy. It was his conviction that this science lent support to competitive industry. He was not opposed to economic theory as such; what he opposed was the false application of theory to practice. He held that the economists were entirely within their rights in excluding certain factors for the purpose of theoretical analysis, but that they had no right to neglect the excluded factors when they applied their theory to practice. In theory they made the fundamental assumption that man is motivated by self-interest; in practice they failed to take account of the fact that he is very often motivated by the affections.[69]

Political economy, he says, assumes, as do those who manage industry, that the greatest material gain will result if men act in self-interest. Suppose the master of a household desires to get as much work out of his servants as he can, at the rate of wages he gives. He never allows them to be idle, feeds them as poorly and lodges them as ill as they will endure, and in all things pushes his requirements to the exact point beyond which he cannot go without forcing his servants to leave him. According to the politico-economic view of the case, this procedure will result in the greatest average of work, and therefore the greatest benefit to the community, and through the community, by reversion, to the servants themselves.[70]

That, Ruskin argues, is not so; it would be so only if the servant were an engine. The largest quantity of work will be

[68] *Fors Clavigera* (Vol. XXVII), p. 127.
[69] *Unto This Last* (Vol. XVII), pp. 25ff.   [70] *Ibid.*, p. 29.

John Ruskin

done only if the will or spirit of the creature is brought to its greatest strength by the affections: [71]

Treat the servant kindly, with the idea of turning his gratitude to account, and you will get, as you deserve, no gratitude, nor any value for your kindness; but treat him kindly without any economical purpose, and all economical purposes will be answered; in this, as in all other matters, whosoever will save his life shall lose it, whoso loses it shall find it.[72]

Ruskin points out that there is no enthusiastic affection among cotton spinners for the proprietor of a mill; yet, he says, a body of men associated for the purposes of robbery (as a Highland clan in ancient times) is animated by affection, and every member ready to lay down his life for the life of the chief.[73] A band of men associated for purposes of legal production and accumulation is usually animated by no such emotion, and none of them is willing to lay down his life for the life of his chief. This is so because no action of the affections can take place. The workman's employment is contingent on the risks of the trade; his work and wages are variable according to the demand for labor, and at any time he may be thrown out of his position by chance of trade.[74] Only an explosive action of disaffection can take place in his case.

Ruskin criticized political economy not only for supporting industrialism by its doctrine of selfishness, but also for supporting inequality. To accept inequality irrespective of its origin and the conditions of its maintenance and the purposes to which it was applied was repugnant to his very nature, for it condoned the exploitation of labor and failed to take account of whether wealth was acquired by moral or immoral means.[75] He called attention to the fact that political economy was not concerned with a just wage, and he pointed out that the laws of demand and supply did not in practice bring about a just wage:

In practice, according to the laws of demand and supply, when two men are ready to do the work, and only one man wants to have it

[71] Ibid., pp. 29ff.   [72] Ibid., p. 31.   [73] Ibid., p. 32.
[74] Ibid., p. 33.   [75] Ibid., pp. 46–53.

done, the two men underbid each other for it; and the one who gets it to do, is underpaid. But when two men want the work done, and there is only one man ready to do it, the two men who want it done overbid each other, and the workman is overpaid.[76]

He assailed the commercial economists who sought to maintain the existing system by representing the laws of this economy as "natural." [77] And he found the scope of political economy too narrow; it dealt, he said, only with material and marketable goods and neglected the immaterial and nonmarketable, which were equally important and profoundly influenced the amount and the character of the former.[78] It failed to take account of intellectual and moral goods, such as affection in the case of the servant; it thought of man only as a getter and a spender, and forgot that he was also a friend, father, and citizen. And it did not consider how these higher goods might be best created and distributed. Ruskin maintained that political economy could not hope to be scientific unless it dealt with man as the organic unity that he was. The aim of political economy for Ruskin was the maintenance not only of life, but of healthy and happy life.[79]

Ruskin took strong issue with the economist's theory of exchange value. He insisted that the value of a thing did not depend on the money it could bring, nor upon the things it could be exchanged for,[80] nor upon the opinions which people held of it, but on whether it availed toward life. He posited a standard based upon ascertainable principles of health and disease, and of justice and injustice. He would substitute a vital for a money standard of value. His view was summed up in the formula: "There is no wealth but life." He denied that a political economy could be scientific whose laws were merely generalizations drawn from the discreet actions of individual businessmen in their buying and selling operations.

[76] *Ibid.*, p. 64.   [77] *Ibid.*, Appendix, pp. 537–38.
[78] This view appears in many passages in *Unto This Last* (Vol. XVII). See, for example, pp. 81ff.
[79] *Munera Pulveris* (Vol. XVII), p. 149.
[80] *Unto This Last* (Vol. XVII), chap. 4, especially p. 84; *Munera Pulveris* (Vol. XVII), p. 153.

John Ruskin

Ruskin declared that political economy was most perfectly practiced in America, with the result that individualism and vulgarity were triumphant and a republic nonexistent:

. . . it is the freedom to talk of the failure of republican institutions in America, when there has never yet been in America any such thing as an institution, but only defiance of institution . . . every man for himself . . . it is your model science of political economy, brought to its perfect practice. . . . Lust of wealth, and trust in it; vulgar faith in magnitude and multitude, instead of nobleness; . . . perpetual self-contemplation issuing in passionate vanity; total ignorance of the finer and higher arts, . . . and the discontent of energetic minds unoccupied, . . . these are the things that have "failed" in America; and yet not altogether failed — it is not collapse, but collision; the greatest railroad accident on record.[81]

Ruskin, like Carlyle, feared social disruption in the near future, and, like Carlyle, he believed that it would come as a result of the upper classes oppressing the lower, as a result of unjust pauperism in the midst of wealth. The people, he says, have begun to suspect that they have been misgoverned; their masters have set them to do all the work and have themselves taken the wages.[82] What was called governing them meant only wearing fine clothes and living on good fare at their expense. This you will find to be the structure of European society for the thousand years of the feudal system: it was divided into peasants who lived by digging, priests who lived by begging, and knights who lived by pillaging; and, as the luminous public mind becomes fully cognizant of these facts, it will surely not suffer things to be arranged that way any more. Ruskin holds that the unjust oppression by the rich is not the only danger; he sees the aristocracy rapidly losing its power, the imminence of mob violence, the increasing chances of insane war founded on popular passion, whether of pride, fear, or acquisitiveness.[83] And he sees all of these dangers darkened by the monstrous forms of vice and selfishness which the appli-

[81] *Munera Pulveris* (Vol. XVII), p. 246.
[82] *The Crown of Wild Olive* (Vol. XVIII), p. 496.
[83] *Time and Tide* (Vol. XVII), p. 381.

ances of recent wealth and of vulgar mechanical art make possible to the millions.

In order to avoid the disastrous consequences which he believed the exploitation of labor and the abuse of wealth must bring about, he advocated the reorganization of England's industrial system. He advocated the abolition of profit as the chief incentive of production; in its place he would put excellence and cheapness of the product and the maintenance of humane conditions among the workers. Ruskin would make business a profession; he argued for a commerce that was not exclusively selfish. The true function, he says, of the merchant is to provide for the community, just as the true function of the soldier is to defend it, the pastor to teach it, the physician to keep health in it, and the lawyer to enforce justice in it.[84] It is no more the merchant's function to get a profit for himself out of that provision than it is the physician's function to get a profit out of his service. A property reward is a due and necessary adjunct of the function of each, but it is not the object of their lives.[85]

Ruskin insists that in a true commerce there must be capacity for sacrifice as there must be in any honorable calling. In true commerce, he says, it is necessary to admit the idea of occasional voluntary loss — that sixpences have to be lost, as well as lives, under a sense of duty; that the market may have its martyrdoms as well as the pulpit, and trade its heroisms as well as war.[86] It is the duty of the merchant, as it is of the soldier, the pastor, or the physician, on due occasion to give his life to the nation; for, truly, the man who does not know when to die does not know when to live. Because of the nature of his functions the merchant becomes the master and governor of large masses of men; on him falls in great part the responsibility for the kind of life they lead. Therefore it becomes his duty not only to be always considering how to produce what he sells in the purest and cheapest forms, but how to make the

[84] *Unto This Last* (Vol. XVII), p. 39.
[85] *Ibid.*, p. 40.   [86] *Ibid.*, pp. 39–40.

various employments involved in the production most beneficial to the men employed.

In order to appeal to the best side of the worker, to his affections rather than to his selfish side, Ruskin argues for fixed wages irrespective of the demand for labor.[87] It is a curious fact, he says, in the history of human error that though the political economist denies the possibility of thus fixing wages, the wages of all the important and much of the unimportant labor are already fixed. We do not sell our prime-ministership by Dutch auction, nor do we offer the diocese of a bishop at the lowest contract. We do indeed sell commissions, but not openly generalships; sick, we do not inquire for a physician who takes less than a guinea; caught in a shower, we do not canvass the cabmen to find one who values his driving at less than sixpence a mile. It is true that in every case there must be ultimate reference to the present difficulty of the work, or to the number of candidates for the office. In this ultimate sense the price of labor is indeed always regulated by the demand for it; but, so far as the practical and immediate administration of the matter is regarded, the best labor has been, and is, as all labor ought to be, paid by an invariable standard.[88]

In order to make industry a profession, and in order to bring health to a society that was everywhere diseased by industrialism, he advocated thoroughgoing social reconstruction. His many suggestions, which are scattered throughout his writings, may be summed up in the sentence: "Government and cooperation are in all things the Laws of Life; Anarchy and competition the Laws of Death." [89] He would reform at the base; his first requisite of a sound society was that its citizens should be well born. To this end he advocated state permission to marry, with the prohibition of antisocial marriages.[90]

Nothing was more important for Ruskin as a means of reforming English society than education. He held that it was the function of the state to see that its citizens were well edu-

---

[87] *Ibid.*, p. 33.　　[88] *Ibid.*, pp. 33–34.　　[89] *Ibid.*, p. 75.　　[90] *Ibid.*, p. 420.

cated.[91] The aim of education was for him, as for Plato, character rather than knowledge — "the perfect exercise and kingly continence of body and soul." He would have the government establish schools for youth over the whole country.[92] He would train the young people of the state in the laws of health and the exercises enjoined by them; and he would teach them habits of gentleness and of justice,[93] and obedience.[94] Like Plato, Ruskin would develop the aesthetic interests; music and dancing and the study of nature would hold a prominent place in his educational system.[95] The child would be surrounded with beautiful objects and works of art in the schoolroom. And, of course, he would teach alike poor and rich, sailor boy and shepherd, such primary subjects as geography, geometry, astronomy, and the outlines of history.[96]

Not only would the state teach the youth of the nation these things, it would also train the individual in the calling by which he was to live.[97] Ruskin believed strongly in a specialized and technical education as well as in a liberal one. He would have his schools in the fresh country, amidst fresh air.[98] It was the duty of the state, according to Ruskin, not only to see that every child was well educated, but also to see that every child was well housed, clothed, and fed till he attained years of discretion.[99]

In connection with these training schools, government manufactories and workshops would be established for the production of every necessary of life and for the exercise of every useful art.[1] The manufactories, he says, will compete with private enterprise, leaving both to do their best, and setting no

[91] *Sesame and Lilies* (Vol. XVIII), p. 107.
[92] *Unto This Last* (Vol. XVII), Preface, p. 21.   [93] *Ibid.*
[94] *Fors Clavigera* (Vol. XXVIII), pp. 20, 656.
[95] *Ibid.* (Vol. XXVII), p. 96; (Vol. XXVIII), pp. 405–06; (Vol. XXIX), pp. 236ff., 496ff.
[96] *Ibid.*, (Vol. XXIX), p. 495.
[97] *Unto This Last* (Vol. XVII), Preface, p. 21.
[98] *Time and Tide* (Vol. XVII), pp. 397–98.
[99] *Sesame and Lilies* (Vol. XVIII), p. 107; *The Stones of Venice* (Vol. XI), Appendix 8, p. 263.
[1] *Unto This Last* (Vol. XVII), Preface, p. 22.

John Ruskin

restraint or tax on private trade. The government institutions will maintain high standards; they will do exemplary work and their products will be pure. Those who are out of employment will be set to work at government schools; if they are incapable of work through ignorance, they will be taught; if they object to work, they will be set to more painful and degrading forms of toil. Ruskin also held that all enterprise that is constantly and demonstrably profitable should be made a public enterprise; he recommended that roads, mines, and railroads should be owned and administered by the public for public profit.[2]

A society that was attempting to realize a professional view of industry and commerce would subscribe, in Ruskin's view, to the principle that each man should do the job for which he was best fitted. Ruskin would insist that there be no idleness, that aristocrats and men of property must work as well as workers; he held that he who would not work, neither should he eat. Condemning unearned elements of income such as monopoly profits, rent, and interest, on utilitarian as well as on moral grounds, he advocated the establishment of a labor basis of exchange. In making the quantity of labor the basis of exchange for commodities, he adopted the cornerstone of Marxian economic theory.[3] He believed that property reward should consist in the good things a man has honestly got and can skillfully use,[4] and that the amount of property and income of the upper classes should be restricted within fixed limits.[5]

Ruskin did not recommend that private industry should be compelled to accept his professional view; he hoped that his new order might be introduced voluntarily by a system of guilds. He argued that workers in trade-unions could easily transform themselves into guilds.[6] In fact, he said, those who favored honesty in any trade could constitute themselves a guild, elect officers, and regulate methods of production and

[2] *Time and Tide* (Vol. XVII), p. 533.
[3] See *Unto This Last* (Vol. XVII), pp. 95, 133, 183.
[4] *Fors Clavigera* (Vol. XXVIII), p. 713.
[5] *Time and Tide* (Vol. XVII), p. 322.
[6] *Fors Clavigera* (Vol. XXIX), pp. 401ff.

qualities of goods and prices; they would produce only warranted articles.[7] Each firm or guild would regulate its own prices and make its own arrangements with workmen. The guilds would compete with outsiders who made unwarranted products; the formation of guilds would be purely on a voluntary basis. There would be full liberty for employers to remain outside and compete with the public workshops. Though the character of Ruskin's guilds was in many respects socialistic, they were far from being identical with socialism; a master, after meeting a standard wage and providing for sick and superannuated workers, would be allowed to retain for his own use the surplus profits of the business.[8]

Ruskin advocated that all retail traders should become salaried officers in the employ of the trade guilds, thus doing away with the degradation of profit in a large field of commerce.[9] He suggested a well-educated person might hold such an office, no matter how poorly paid, without degradation. Of course, he said, the current objection to such a system would be that no man, for a regularly paid salary, would take pains to please his customers. The answer to that objection is that if you can train a man to so much unselfishness as to offer himself fearlessly to the chance of being shot, you can most assuredly, if you make it a point of honor with him, train him to the amount of self-denial involved in looking you out with care a piece of bacon such as you have asked for.

It followed from his principle of property for use that land should not be monopolized by the few who do not work it;[10] the state, he believed, should encourage peasant proprietorship.[11] It must secure various portions of the land for those who can use it properly, interfering in cases of gross mismanagement or abuse of power. Yet he modified his principle of "land to those who can use it" by advocating the principle of inheritance and of primogeniture;[12] he supported primogeniture

[7] *Ibid.*, p. 401.
[8] *Time and Tide* (Vol. XVII), pp. 319–20. [9] *Ibid.*, p. 427.
[10] *Fors Clavigera* (Vol. XXIX), pp. 404–05. [11] *Ibid.*, pp. 404–07.
[12] *Ibid.*, pp. 404–05.

because he desired to see the agricultural classes bound to the land as the artisans were to the guild.[13] As Ruskin would see that his citizen was well born, properly educated, and provided with the job for which he was best fitted, so would he see that the old and destitute would be taken care of.[14]

Ruskin could no more look to democracy as a government capable of reconstructing society than could Carlyle. For him, as for his master, democracy was destructive; liberty of choice, he says, destroys life and strength.[15] Democracy is destructive in Ruskin's view because the mass of men are fools.[16] He also has a positive reason for rejecting democracy: the people cannot help themselves. "Slavery," that is to say, unqualified and unquestioning submission to a superior will, is an inherent, natural, and eternal inheritance of a large portion of the human race — to whom the more you give of their own free will, the more slaves they will make of themselves.[17]

Although Ruskin believed that universal suffrage was inevitable in the near future, he wished that it were possible to keep the common people from thinking about government. But he realizes that this is not possible, and has not been possible since the invention of printing;[18] the question for Ruskin is how to make the people of exactly the proper weight in the state. In order that the populace might be kept in their place, he suggests that the electors of the nation have votes proportional to their education, age, and wealth.[19] Ruskin looks forward to the time when the populace will have had its day with democracy. When this time arrives he believes that only a despotism will be able to achieve genuine reform, for strong action alone will be capable of extirpating corruption: "A nation once utterly corrupt can only be redeemed by military despotism — never by talking, nor by its free effort. . . . The British Constitution is breaking fast . . . the gipsy hunt is up also . . . and

[13] *Ibid.*, p. 404.
[14] *Unto This Last* (Vol. XVII), Preface, p. 22.
[15] *The Cestus of Aglaia* (Vol. XIX), p. 126.
[16] *Time and Tide* (Vol. XVII), p. 326n.
[17] *Munera Pulveris* (Vol. XVII), p. 256.
[18] *Lectures on Architecture and Painting* (Vol. XII), p. lxxxiii.   [19] *Ibid.*

John Ruskin

the hue and cry loud against your land and you; your tenure of it is in dispute before a multiplying mob, deaf and blind as you." [20]

The government of his ideal is a government of the upper classes, for he believes that the upper classes are the instrument of social progress. He follows Carlyle in accepting the upper classes as he finds them to initiate his ideal; the great old families, he says, always ought to be, and in some measure, however decadent, still truly are, the noblest monumental architecture of the kingdom. [21] The function of the landowners and captains of industry in his ideal society is to keep order among their inferiors, and to raise them always to the nearest level with themselves. [22] Ruskin's artistocracy will be provided for; an amount of land will be granted them in perpetuity such as will enable them to live with all the necessary circumstances of state and outward nobleness. Their income, however, will not be derived from the rent of their land, but will be paid them by the state and will be a fixed amount. [23]

Ruskin's aristocracy is composed not only of landed proprietors and captains of industry but also of professional men. The function of the aristocracy is the disinterested superintendence of public institutions [24] rather than the furthering of their own interests and the accumulation of wealth. A king stands at the head of Ruskin's state authorities; [25] in his early years he was doubtful whether the king should be one or many; in his later years he came to believe in the "one man power." The king is to be the supreme judge in the central court of appeal; other judges in this court are to be nationally elected. The function of ordinary judges, who hold their positions hereditarily, is to administer the national laws under the decisions of juries. There will be state officers charged with the direction of governmental agencies; there will be officers of war and officers of public instruction of various ranks. Last but not least, there will be

[20] *The Crown of Wild Olive* (Vol. XVIII), p. 484; *Fors Clavigera* (Vol. XXVIII), pp. 151–52.
[21] *Time and Tide* (Vol. XVII), p. 439.   [22] *Ibid.*, p. 431.
[23] *Ibid.*, p. 439.   [24] *Ibid.*, p. 322.   [25] *Ibid.*, pp. 440–41.

bishops, and under them pastors, who will act as supervisors of the individual's life.[26] All of these state authorities will be drawn from the aristocracy of the upper classes.

The clergy are to be elected for life.[27] The bishops are to have executive authority over large districts: they will receive reports of the pastors on individuals and on families, which will enable them to discover whom to promote; they will receive reports on the operation of the laws, and will determine measures exceptionally necessary to the public advantage; they will report to Parliament on the operation of public undertakings, such as roads or mines.[28] They will enforce laws against all kinds of thievery, chiefly against the occult and polite methods of it, and of these chiefly the making and selling of bad goods.[29] These laws are to have force only over tradesmen in the guilds. The clergy will enforce a second group of laws, those against dishonest debt. To implement the rule of this theocracy, Ruskin advocates the union of churches into a reconstituted Church.[30] Ruskin's clergy and civil officers will rule together, each supporting and correcting the other, "the clergy hallowing all worldly policy by their influence, and the magistry repressing all religious enthusiasm by their practical wisdom."

Ruskin's society is constructed on the feudal pattern: class distinctions are to be strictly preserved and individuals are to have more or less a fixed status. It is not altogether fixed, for he believes with Plato and Carlyle that everything should be done to develop individual genius. Preaching the gospel of the tools, the land, and the capital to him who can use them, he stands for the principle of opportunity for individual talent.[31] But the mass of men, he holds, are fit only for manual occupations; the children of whom nothing can be made, and who therefore rightly furnish candidates for degradation to common mechanical business, will do the mining, stoking, and forging for society.[32] Ruskin believes that such a class should be continued,

[26] *Ibid.*, p. 441.   [27] *Ibid.*, p. 381.   [28] *Ibid.*, pp. 378–80.   [29] *Ibid.*, pp. 383–85.
[30] *Lectures on Architecture and Painting* (Vol. XII), p. 557.
[31] *Time and Tide* (Vol. XVII), p. 405.   [32] *Ibid.*, pp. 405–06.

for, with very few exceptions, children of unskilled laborers or mere mechanics are by nature and social convenience destined to unskilled and mechanical labor.

In order to achieve the new feudalism Ruskin places his faith in the power of voluntary self-reformation. Making every allowance for the deep corruption in the upper classes, the degrading influences of plutocracy and the degeneration that is born of luxury, he seems to think that these classes can reform themselves and reach a plane of elevation that will justify their social supremacy.[33] Like Carlyle, he looks to the well-born and the captains of industry to change their ways. And he hopes that the supremacy of the upper classes may gradually be brought into force from beneath, without any violence or impatient happenings.[34]

v

If Ruskin thought the society of his time more materialized than was actually the case, his charge that industrialism corrupted the spirit was essentially true. If he carried his attack on machinery too far, he nevertheless showed that "a man who spends his life in opening the valve or in making the eighteenth part of a pin" loses something of his humanity. If he ascribed to capitalism more evil than can fairly be ascribed — if he gave insufficient attention to the fact that men have desires which easily induce them to become materialized, and if he gave insufficient attention to the fact that so long as there is a threat of poverty, money will remain a chief interest with men — he nevertheless showed that a system that makes profit the main incentive encourages selfishness and dishonesty. Nor was this all; he also showed that capitalism, at least in its nineteenth-century form, was an enemy of beauty.

No one expressed more eloquently than he the unjust origin of riches; no one has shown more clearly that the acquisition of wealth is dependent upon an oppressive bargain between those who have and those who have not; nor has anyone shown

[33] *Ibid.*, pp. 430–31, 433.   [34] *Ibid.*, p. 323.

more clearly that wealth consists in power over men. Ruskin was unequaled in his time in succinctly pointing out main elements in the origin, character, and necessary conditions of wealth. By his analysis of wealth he demonstrated that capitalism was profoundly wanting in moral principle; he demonstrated that it was a system of exploitation of the many by the few. By his analysis of the principle of self-interest and competition, he demonstrated that capitalism was a system that could never enlist the loyalty, any more than it could the full cooperation, of workingmen. If he somewhat exaggerated capitalism's appeal to self-interest, and if he underestimated the economic and social utility of the competitive system, he nevertheless showed that capitalism tends to promote discord between man and man. Nowhere did he point this out more ably than in his discussion of war; and it may be observed that his prophecy that "the sun will be redder still" was borne out in 1914. He performed a service to his generation by pointing out the deep antagonism that existed between its profession of Christian morals and the money game it practised in everyday life.

Ruskin did well to point out to a society that accepted capitalism without question that wealth must not only be sound in origin but also in use. He did well to point out to a society that looked upon capitalism as part of the eternal order of things that to make business a profession was to raise it to its proper level. His professional view of industry was a challenge to Victorian minds to bring their actions into line with their conscience, for such a view made excellence rather than reward the aim of effort. He did well to insist that the economic system should serve society and not society the economic system. His functional view of property, which embraced the principle of the tools to him who can use them and restricted the amount of wealth a man could possess within fixed limits, was a fresh approach to a problem that was not recognized to exist. Few have carried the spirit of economic equality so far as he; he believed a man should manage to die poor.

John Ruskin

Ruskin helped to raise the status of the worker, not only by arguing for healthy and pleasant conditions of work and by insisting that the state should educate the worker and provide for his physical welfare, but also by attacking the notion that labor is a commodity. He also helped to promote the interest of the worker by standing for the "right to labor," by holding that the state should furnish work and wages in public workshops to all unemployed persons. So, too, did he support the worker's cause by his demand that degrading work should be reduced to a minimum. Again, he championed the worker's cause by his insistence that men should be able to enjoy their work, and that work should be honest, useful, and cheerful. Again, he promoted the worker's cause by his argument against luxury and by his appeal to society to curb its extravagance until necessities were provided for all.

If in his criticism of political economy he exaggerated the importance placed on self-interest, he showed with striking power the limitations of that assumption as a motive to labor. He made a pertinent criticism of economic thinking by pointing out that economists were prone to neglect the factors they abstracted from their theory when they applied their theory to practice. It was well that he insisted that man could no more be isolated from his affections than he could from society, that man was an organic unity, and that no study could be scientific that failed to take this into account. It was well, too, that he criticized the belief held by economists that inequality is necessary to progress. He did something to humanize economic thought by his insistence on vital value (that a thing must avail toward life) as a measure of economic activity.[35] His application of this doctrine to the processes of production and consumption disclosed immense discrepancies between monetary and human costs. Ruskin was wrong in holding that the lending of capital was unproductive, and that exchange was nugatory. Yet he was right in calling attention to the fact that orthodox

[35] John A. Hobson, *John Ruskin*, pp. 89, 106–07, 309. Cf. his *Work and Wealth* (rev. ed., London, 1933), p. 9.

88

political economy, which derived its theories from the working of capitalism and which was unable to imagine an economic order based on different assumptions, lent support to that system.

In all these ways — in his attack on the spirit of acquisitive gain, in showing that labor did not receive a just reward, in revealing the degradation of unhealthy conditions of work, in his argument for a social service state, and in his attack on political economy — he helped to soften the harshness of competitive capitalism. Yet clear-sighted as he was in revealing the shortcomings of the society of his day, the chief method by which he proposed to change society could not by itself effect the change. Like Carlyle, he held that the sins of society were fundamentally the sins of individuals; even more than Carlyle, he looked to the self-reformation of the individual to bring about a new order. He did not appreciate, any more than did Plato and Carlyle, that basic social evils come not only from the individuals who compose a system of society, but also from the principles of its organization. History since the Industrial Revolution shows that there is a great deal of truth in the thesis of Marx, that the character of the principles by which men make their living determines in general their values of life. No one can deny, for example, the profound effect of machine production upon the mass of men, of herding them into cities and of rendering them propertyless.

History would seem to show that there is little likelihood that the owners of economic power will voluntarily reform themselves and surrender their control. Captains of industry are convinced that there is nothing dishonest about their conduct.[36] They think that they are entirely within their rights in taking as much rent, profit, interest, and other emoluments as they can and in spending them for their own private purposes; or they think that such action simply reflects the unalterable character of human nature. Perhaps most of the captains of industry are incapable of following an analysis such as Ruskin's, which

[36] See John A. Hobson, *John Ruskin*, pp. 197–99.

shows that their activity has been built upon wrong principles. Moreover, of the few who could rise above long-established habits and modes of thought, not many would be likely to change their ways. Yet, even if we assume that employers are open to the "conviction of sin" and desire a new order, Ruskin's remedy of voluntary action cannot be successful. For a number of individuals acting independently cannot effect a social remedy; social evils require a social remedy.

Though Ruskin looked for an aristocracy of the wisest and best to lead men out of the evil ways of materialism, he never told us, any more than did Carlyle, by what method other than freedom such an aristocracy was to be found. Though history taught him that priest, king, and aristocrat had grossly abused their power, he was prepared, in spite of this, to turn the government over to the aristocracy. Even assuming that his aristocracy would not betray its trust, the authority he would give it over the lives of common men was such as must needs destroy their self-reliance. The far-reaching control he would give the clergy over private life would turn the workingman into a mere child — which was, of course, to no small extent just what he wanted.

In his failure to find any value in freedom he denied a condition essential to the attainment of the ends that he desired. If industry and commerce are to be true professions, if for the mass of men work is to be creative in the fine sense that he desired, and if the individual is to be in harmony with himself and with his fellows, there must be scope for free activity such as would be impossible under his despotism. The suspicion and fear that despotism creates would alone prevent any satisfactory approximation to his ideals. Enforced cooperation under a despotism of the upper classes would be more destructive of his ideals than the competition which he decried under competitive capitalism. Carlyle and Ruskin might create Sparta, but never Athens. All the arguments that were brought against Carlyle's autocracy hold against Ruskin's.[37]

[37] See above, pp. 48–50.

John Ruskin

Though no one was ever more aware than Ruskin of the abuse of political power when exercised by part of the community over the whole, he was unable to see that democracy was a means of coping with the abuse of power by the few. He never considered that rulers are more inclined to act for the common good when they are held accountable to the community, and less inclined when they are held accountable to a class. Hoping that his rulers might one day become an aristocracy of intellect, he confused the need for experts, whose proper function is to advise government, not to direct it, with the need for a whole community taking part directly or indirectly in the governmental process. He failed to see that a complicated economic system and a complex society cannot hope to work effectively unless the mass of men take a real part in working them. Efficient administration in the modern state is out of the question unless the citizen body can criticize and report on the working of the administrative services without fear of penalty. A free, universal electorate is indispensable to the detection of error and to its effective communication to the sources of power.

Ruskin, however, was unable to accept democracy, for he held with Carlyle and Plato that the common man is not competent to exercise political power. This view of the common man also vitiated his conception of society as organic. To hold that the common man is inferior and on this view construct a hierarchical society, as did Plato and Carlyle as well as Ruskin, is to construct a society that is not organic enough. Under a hierarchical system the mass of men are reduced to a subservient position; they are in no sense ends in themselves, living for the things they wish to live for, but a means to the ends of others. They do not participate in a common purpose. In a truly organic view, every part is, in a very real sense, something of an end in itself, yet participates in a common purpose. A truly organic conception cannot admit a hierarchical "caste" system.

Ruskin could never have a very high regard for the common man, for he was strongly impressed with the virtues of the few. Ruskin had learned of kings from Homer and Sir Walter Scott, and had been taught the superiority of the few by Plato and Carlyle. He stood for authority not only because extensive power was necessary to manage men who could not manage themselves, but also because he was, like Carlyle, an egoist who had a temperamental affinity for absolutism.

Both Carlyle and Ruskin had little capacity for considering ideas in an impartial spirit and of appreciating opposing views. This, in part, explains why their thought was frequently inconsistent, muddled, and sometimes absurd. Though Ruskin held that the ordinary man was not fit to be entrusted with power, he could testify against himself by saying that "the feelings of the mob are on the whole generous and right, but they have no foundation for them." Though he execrated war in modern times, he found that it was often noble in ancient times; on one occasion he said that true war is a means of deciding which is the best man, "which has the strongest arm and steadiest heart."

Such defects, however, do not prevent Ruskin from being a stirring critic of life, rich in ideas. In his power to move the moral feelings and to quicken the minds of his countrymen, he ranks second only to Carlyle. Carlyle pointed to the source of this power when he wrote to Emerson that "There is nothing going on among us as notable to me as those fierce lightning-bolts Ruskin is copiously and desperately pouring into the black world of Anarchy all around him. No other man in England that I meet has in him the divine rage against iniquity, falsity, and baseness that Ruskin has." [38]

[38] *The Correspondence of Thomas Carlyle and Ralph Waldo Emerson, 1834–1872* (Charles E. Norton, editor, 3d ed., 2 vols., Boston, 1883), II, 352.

MATTHEW ARNOLD

I

IF CARLYLE and Ruskin refreshed the moral insights of men but did little to shape their minds, Arnold neither shaped their minds nor refreshed their moral insights. He exerted little influence as a political and social writer; his age refused to take him seriously. If it did not ridicule him as inept, it brushed him lightly aside as inconsequential, or it thought of him simply as a wholesome irritant to prejudice. Frederick Harrison spoke for those who had only contempt when he referred to the man of culture in politics as "a well-preserved Ariel tripping from flower to flower."[1] The description of Arnold as "a Hebrew prophet in white-kid gloves"[2] expressed the view of those who were merely amused by him. Leslie Stephen spoke for those who looked upon Arnold as a propagandist for light when he described him as an effective agent in breaking up old crusts of thought, and as one who aroused many to a new perception of their needs.[3] And if Arnold gained little recognition as a political writer in his own time, his reputation has hardly increased since he wrote; he is generally thought of in terms of Ernest Barker's estimate, as an artist-critic whose chief claim to remembrance lies in a witty satire of laissez faire and in the championship of authority.[4]

[1] Saintsbury could say that Arnold had "no 'ideas,' no first principles in politics at all." *Matthew Arnold* (New York, 1899), p. 152.

[2] George W. E. Russell, *Matthew Arnold* (New York, 1904), p. 135.

[3] Leslie Stephen, *Studies of a Biographer* (4 vols., London, 1898–1907), II, 121.

[4] Ernest Barker, *Political Thought in England, 1848 to 1914* (rev. ed., London, 1928), pp. 183, 198ff.

Matthew Arnold

Many were unable to understand Arnold because of his style; his banter, his delicate sarcasm, his raillery, his ability to dissolve pompous gentlemen with ridicule, all these accomplishments were considered bad taste by not a few serious minds. He did not declaim, as did Carlyle; he persuaded. He employed ideas and the aesthetic charm of the insinuating phrase; in his writing he was French rather than English. Many did not grasp what he had to say because he wrote in the classical tradition, because he was too refined and too urbane. Arnold directed his thoughts not to a wide reading public, but to those in high places in society, to the graduates of Oxford and Cambridge. Many, too, were denied the opportunity of grasping what he had to say because a great part of his most penetrating social analysis was buried in educational reports; though these reports were reprinted for a wider audience, his analysis nevertheless remained buried. Again, many were put off by Arnold's views in the field of practical politics; for if a number of his ideas here had about them the wisdom of Burke, one or two had about them the prejudices of an elderly lady of the Victorian period, and some the brutality of a reactionary. Many were unable fully to appreciate Arnold — and this would seem to be true of Leslie Stephen — because their mental horizon was limited to the liberal middle-class tradition of the nineteenth century.

Pre-eminently a critic of civilization, Arnold held that English society fell far short of a humane ideal. He charged, as did Carlyle and Ruskin, that it was degraded by materialism, that it was in danger of anarchy through laissez faire; and he charged that its culture had been debased by puritanism. In his eyes it was a hard, raw, unlovely, and dangerous civilization. Though he criticized the middle class most severely of all, the aristocracy was in his eyes the great enemy of English society. It stood for materialism and inequality; it stood for a class society, which was fatal to the development of the lower, no less than to that of the middle, class; it rendered impossible the creation of a true social spirit, without which there could be no humane civilization. Though Arnold held that the middle class was totally without culture, he looked to it to promote his ideal of a true civilization.

Like Carlyle and Ruskin, Arnold attacked middle-class liberalism, centering his attack on laissez faire; and he urged, as they did, the need for an acting rather than a do-nothing state. He championed public authority, above all in the field of education. He set, as they did, an "organic" view of society over against the individualistic conception of the liberals. But, unlike Carlyle and Ruskin, he did not turn to reaction for a solution of the anarchy of individualism. Rather than advocate an aristocracy governing in the military fashion, he looked for a remedy within the framework of democracy, though he, too, feared the ignorance of the multitude and had confidence in the few. Arnold would see the élite working in democracy, analyzing ideas, standing for culture, and making intelligence prevail. He would see the élite drawn largely from an educated middle class, and he would see it playing its part in the higher posts of the state, in the universities, in the civil service, and in the professions.

Arnold was not a critic essentially of industrialism; he did not point out, as did Carlyle, the great social cost and the profound injustice of an industrial system whose chief impulse was gain. Nor did he demonstrate, as did Ruskin, that the employers, in virtue of their ownership of the means of production and their control of capital, had the workers at their disposal as if they were so many slaves. He was not as acutely aware as Ruskin, nor was he even as cognizant as Carlyle, that capitalism, in making profit the goal of effort, degraded the workers and materialized the whole of society. Yet he penetrated more deeply into the social structure of Victorian society than did either of these men, or even Marx. With the intellectual outlook of a rationalistic puritan, of one who had accepted science, who had been humanized by the classics and mellowed by the study of letters, he saw the great importance of education; he saw education as a means not only of civilizing men but also of governing them. His demonstration of the aristocracy's control of the administration of the state through their control of the public schools showed an insight into the instruments of power unequaled in his day except by Bagehot's.

Arnold saw more clearly than Carlyle and Ruskin that great inequalities of wealth are disastrous to a civilized society. He analyzed the psychological and cultural effects of inequality more keenly than anyone else in the nineteenth century. It is not a little astonishing that a poet, a literary critic, an inspector of schools, saw that democracy without equality could never mean freedom; Arnold anticipated the Fabians by two decades.

II

Born in 1822 to parents of the professional class, Arnold never ceased to show his heritage. He was deeply influenced by his father, the noted headmaster of Rugby, the conspicuous liberal and Broad Churchman. Not that he was his father's image, for his temperament was very different: never was he vehement or pious, seldom was he intolerant; he was distinguished for good spirits and a gracious manner; he was, in the French sense of the term, social. Swinburne aptly caught the difference between him and his father when he referred to Arnold as "David the son of Goliath."

Arnold inherited from his father a strong puritan strain; he was indebted to him for his belief, fundamental to all that he had to say, that conduct was "three-fourths of life." He inherited from him a deep interest in the welfare of society, and an untiring zeal to reform it. He was indebted to his father's influence for a sense of authority and of order, though it seems that a sense of both was inborn in his temperament. The father undoubtedly gave to the son a belief that all the world is in eternal progress, that nothing is so unnatural and convulsive to society as the strain to keep things fixed, that the deadly error is to preserve and not to improve.[5] Arnold testified to his in-

[5] Arthur P. Stanley, *The Life and Correspondence of Dr. Arnold* (new ed., New York, 1898), p. 155.

heritance when, in a letter to his mother, he said that in his notions of the state he was quite his father's son.[6] If the term liberal Whig most accurately describes Arnold's father, it is too narrow a term to apply to the son; Arnold may be called a speculative liberal, whose imagination carried him on fundamental ideas considerably beyond the Liberals.

Arnold's father taught him the classics, and the classics were one of the most important influences in his development; Arnold himself said that he inherited from his parent a deep sense of what was sound and rational in the Greek and Roman world. The classics gave Arnold ideals and principles that formed the very basis of his criticism. From the Greeks Arnold learned that the aim of criticism is the perfection of all sides of our humanity. Sophocles represented to him the most harmonious development of human nature; of Sophocles he said that he saw life steadily and saw it whole; he saw the object as in itself it really is. Arnold learned from the Greeks what is meant by a finely tempered spirit.

Few things in the classics impressed him more than the emphasis on order, harmony, unity, and the conception of society as an organic whole. For his view of these things he seems to owe a special debt to Plato, as he does also for his emphasis on reason and authority. Here Arnold seems to have found ideas that were congenial to his own nature and a reinforcement of it. Arnold's training in the classics seems to have had not a little to do with his aversion to disorder, his hostility to laissez faire, and his desire to see the noble prevail in human affairs. The classics undoubtedly impressed upon him the great need of education and of high standards; and they undoubtedly bred in him a kind of contempt for uncultivated minds, just as they bred a confidence in the wisdom of the few.

Oxford, where Arnold went into residence in 1841, played, as it inevitably must with a sensitive nature, a notable part in his development. Contact with contemporary currents of thought

---

[6] *Letters* (De Luxe Edition of works, 15 vols., London, 1903, Vol. XIII), p. 299. All future references to the works of Arnold will be to this edition. Each volume will be identified in the edition by a number in parentheses after the title.

enriched his intellectual background, as further contact with the classics increased his knowledge of a civilization that for him was ever a source of inspiration and guidance. In the Oxford of Arnold's day Newman was at his zenith and the Tractarian Movement was in full swing. Newman never gained a strong hold over Arnold's intellect, but attracted him morally and aesthetically.[7] Newman revealed to him that Catholicism provided a spiritual discipline for which the world has found no substitute; but the effect on Arnold's rationalistic mind was to strengthen a belief, which his father had implanted in him, in the Church of England.[8]

But the voice of Newman was not the only one heard by young Oxonians. "There was," says Arnold, "the puissant voice of Carlyle; so sorely strained, over-used, and misused since, but then fresh, comparatively sound, and reaching our hearts with true pathetic eloquence." Arnold later paid tribute to Carlyle and to puritanism when he said that he valued the prophet's perception of the sole importance of truth and justice, and his appreciation of the dignity of labor, and of the necessity of righteousness.[9] Through Carlyle, says Arnold, came a greater voice still — the greatest voice of the century — the voice of Goethe, with *Wilhelm Meister* and its large, liberal view of human life.[10] And there was still another voice, from the other side of the Atlantic — Emerson's — a clear and pure voice, which brought a strain both new and refreshing; it said "judge a man's wisdom by his hope." [11] Though Arnold could criticize Oxford in those unforgettable words, as "the home of lost causes, and forsaken beliefs, and unpopular names, and impossible loyalties," he nevertheless thought of it as an outpost in the darkness that stood for sweetness and light.[12] For

[7] See Arnold's essay on Emerson in *Discourses in America*, in *Essays in Criticism*, second series (Vol. IV), pages 350ff. See also such essays as "The Literary Influence of Academies" and "Pagan and Mediaeval Religious Sentiment," in *Essays in Criticism*, first series (Vol. III).

[8] George W. E. Russell, *Matthew Arnold*, p. 61.

[9] "Emerson," *Discourses in America*, in *Essays in Criticism* (Vol. IV), p. 351.

[10] *Ibid.*   [11] *Ibid.*, pp. 352, 375.

[12] *Culture and Anarchy* (Vol. VI), pp. 30–33.

him, Oxford exemplified high standards and was an impressive argument for established institutions.

In 1847 Arnold became private secretary to the Marquess of Lansdowne, who was a member of the Russell ministry; this connection enabled him to become intimately acquainted with the aristocracy. By temperament Arnold had much in common with the aristocratic way of life and could therefore appreciate the virtues of the aristocracy, but he could never be one of them. The man who had in him a strong element of "Hebraism," who believed that conduct was three-fourths of life, could never identify himself with the "barbarians." Rather of necessity must he become their critic; at the time of the revolutions of 1848 he says that "the hour of the hereditary peerage and eldest sonship and immense properties has struck."[13] He admires in France what he calls the *"intelligence* of their *idea-moved masses,"* yet he is critical of the revolution there and resents the "hot, dizzy trash" people are talking in regard to it.[14] He thinks England as it is "not liveable-in," but is convinced that a government of Chartists would not mend matters.[15]

Though Arnold believes that aristocracy must go, he does not rejoice in its going when he considers "what a middle class and people we have in England: of whom Saint-Simon says truly: 'Sur tous les chantiers de l'Angleterre il n'existe pas une seule grande idée.'"[16] Arnold valued the aristocracy for the same reason, it seems, as his father; he thought it provided an element both necessary and precious to the national life — a sense of the greatness of public affairs and a power of social life and manners. For want of an aristocracy, he was convinced that America with the "intolerable *laideur*" of her masses was a threat to civilization.[17] It seems, he says, as if few stocks could be trusted to grow up properly without having a priesthood and an aristocracy to act as their schoolmaster at some time or other of their national existence.[18] Yet he says he agrees

[13] *Letters* (Vol. XIII), p. 5.   [14] *Ibid.*, p. 4.   [15] *Ibid.*, pp. 5, 9.   [16] *Ibid.*, p. 66.
[17] *Ibid.*, p. 7.   [18] *Ibid.*, p. 152.

with all the men of soul from Pythagoras to Byron in thinking that an aristocratic society is the most drying, wasting, depressing, and fatal thing possible.

In 1849 Arnold appeared as a poet and was not long in winning a place in the English tradition. He is, says J. M. Robertson, our greatest master of elegy; what Gray was for his age, Arnold is for the larger world of ours.[19] Arnold's poetry showed that he could not accept orthodox religion but must follow the "main movement of the mind" and hold with rationalism. He described his position in *The Grand Chartreuse:*

> For rigorous teachers seized my youth,
> And purged its faith, and trimmed its fire,
> Showed me the high, white star of Truth,
> There bade me gaze, and there aspire.

The rejection of religion in the old fundamental sense made Arnold aware of a profound uncertainty, as lines from the same poem show:

> Wandering between two worlds, one dead,
> The other powerless to be born,

The rejection of religion also meant that he could look upon the future as dark with confusion and struggle; he said in *Dover Beach:*

> And we are here as on a darkling plain
> Swept with confused alarms of struggle and flight,
> Where ignorant armies clash by night.

Though Arnold passed out of these moods, which pervaded much of his poetry, they nevertheless reflect a stoical strain that influenced his criticism. That he was, like Job, resigned not to expect too much from life made for a conservative temper. This temper was already noticeable in a poem *To a Republican Friend,* written as early as 1848; he says, "God knows it, I am with you," and proclaims with heart and soul that he is with the victims of a false civilization — "the armies of the homeless and unfed." Yet he does not believe that man can be

[19] John M. Robertson, *Modern Humanists Reconsidered* (London, 1927), p. 128.

liberated overnight; and is distrustful of changes that do not take full account of the limitations of human nature:

> ... when I muse on what life is, I seem
> Rather to patience prompted, than that proud
> Prospect of hope which France proclaims so loud.

Arnold, as we have said, conquered the occasional moods of depression and gloom that his poetry reflects. To make, he remarked in his thirty-fourth year, habitual war on depression and low spirits, which in early youth one is apt to indulge and be somewhat interested in, is among the things one learns as one gets older; they are noxious alike to body and mind, and already partake of the nature of death.[20] The writer of that passage, Stuart Sherman says, had very deliberately taken his own nature under criticism and cultivation.[21] As he presents himself, Sherman continues, through his prose to our later time, he is the most rigorously disciplined of men, the most coherently purposeful of writers. From his perception that what is has been and will be again, Arnold had acquired a wholesome tranquillity about the universe, a certain humility about his own function in it, and just that touch of superiority to transitory things — to the passing show — which enables a man of his rigorous social sense and fundamental seriousness to do his duty lightly and even gaily. Arnold's *Notebooks* show well the measures he took to discipline himself; he turned to writers like Joubert, whose singular felicity of nature, he says, sought happiness as a flower seeks the sunshine, and he looked for counsel in the aphorisms of men of action.

In 1851 Lord Lansdowne procured for Arnold the post of inspector of schools; apart from his father and his temperament, his work in education is the key to understanding him. He made a number of trips to the Continent to report on foreign schools. His comparison of Continental schools with English, and of Continental societies, above all the French, with

[20] *Letters* (Vol. XIII), p. 69.
[21] Stuart Sherman, *Matthew Arnold, How to Know Him* (New York, 1932), p. 4.

English, led him to the chief recommendations that he made for the improvement of English civilization. He wrote:

For twenty years, ever since I had to go about the Continent to learn what the schools were like there, and observed at the same time the people for whom the schools existed and conditions of their life, and compared it with what was to be found at home — ever since that time I have felt convinced that for the progress of our civilization, here in England, three things were above all necessary: a reduction of those immense inequalities of condition and property amongst us, of which our land system is the base; a genuine municipal system; and public schools for the middle classes.[22]

Greatly impressed by government supervision of foreign education, especially in France, he became imbued with the idea of state action. In his travels on the Continent Arnold's official position, as well as his own reputation, brought him into contact with many eminent men of letters. In France he came to know such leaders in literature as Saint-Beuve, Prosper Mérimée, and Ernest Renan; through these friends he came to admire the French Academy, which, as his essay on "The Literary Influence of Academies" shows, became another argument for established, authoritative institutions.

Arnold was elected to the professorship of poetry at Oxford in 1837, though by this time his inspiration had passed. When he announced in 1859 that his special line of endeavor was to "inculcate intelligence" [23] upon the nation, it was clear that the educator and the critic had got the upper hand of the poet. Profoundly discontented with English culture, he set himself to rouse his countrymen by raillery and satire to the shortcomings of English civilization. Finding a need for criticism on all sides, he wrote on education, politics, social affairs, literature, and religion. Not only did the classics furnish him with materials for criticism, but also the English, French, and German traditions of literature, the Bible, and moralists like Marcus Aurelius. Burke was the chief source of his inspiration in political affairs: Burke gave him a sense of the importance of

[22] "Ecce, Convertimur ad Gentes," *Irish Essays* (Vol. XI), pp. 113–14.
[23] *Letters* (Vol. XIII), p. 147.

government and strengthened his belief in the state; Burke lent him support in his attack on laissez faire; to Burke he was indebted for his liberal treatment of Irish affairs; and Burke reinforced his conservative temper. John Stuart Mill appealed to his liberal side, and he was indebted to Mill for his practical remedy for inequality of property. He found De Tocqueville, who made a profound impression on him,[24] congenial in the same way that he did Mill; De Tocqueville supported his case for equality, and was an authority against the "barbarians."

Arnold's first political writing, *England and the Italian Question* (1859), showed a liberal point of view; he thought that the ideas of the French Revolution were in the main true, and he could see the common people moved by ideas and the aristocracy inaccessible to them. By 1861 he had developed his main political ideas, which he set forth in that year in the introduction to his first publication on education, *Popular Education in France,* later reprinted in *Mixed Essays* under the title of "Democracy." Arnold argued that democracy was inevitable and argued for its inevitability, but he insisted that the masses were not ready to rule; neither was he willing to see the aristocracy or the middle class impose its culture on the community. He looked to the state to set an ideal for the governance of Englishmen. In 1864 *A French Eton* appeared; this essay, which was an unofficial product of the tour he made to the Continent in 1859, is a brilliant plea for state action in education; it is a plea to the middle class to support the establishment of public secondary schools.

The publication of Arnold's *Essays in Criticism* (first series) in 1865 was something of an event in the literary world. His essay, "The Function of Criticism at the Present Time," which sparkles with ideas, showed why he was concerned with the social question as an artist. He argued that there could be no great artistic productions like those of Sophocles and Shakespeare unless materials were at hand, that is, fresh ideas, and unless there was an atmosphere of vitality, a national glow of

[24] Joshua Fitch, *Thomas and Matthew Arnold* (New York, 1898), p. 202.

Matthew Arnold

life. As a critic, he conceived it his function to stimulate the flow of fresh ideas (this made rather for a progressive outlook) and he held that the problem of great art was not only an aesthetic problem but also a social one. As an artist, no less than as a puritan, Arnold was driven into social criticism.

In "The Function of Criticism at the Present Time" he set forth his aim as a critic—the disinterested endeavor to learn and to propagate the best that is known and thought in the world. And he made a strong plea for detachment as a necessary condition for the pursuit of his aim. He held that the critic performs his function best by dealing with ideas themselves, not with their practical consequences and applications; the latter aspects, he said, will never fail to have due prominence given them. The true teacher must not encumber himself by any alliance with tendencies; he must be one thing to all men, the voice of reason and of truth. "The Function of Criticism at the Present Time" is an attack on the practical mind as well as a plea for detachment. At the same time, this essay reflects his conservative strain; he can say that the great error of the French Revolution was the failure to observe the principle of "force, or the existing order till right is ready."

Schools and Universities on the Continent appeared in 1868; here Arnold contended that the establishment of a sound municipal system in England was essential to the development of a public system of education. In his preface to the second edition of part of the report, entitled "Higher Schools and Universities in Germany," Arnold asked for the establishment of a Catholic university for the Catholics in Ireland and presented an acute analysis of the Nonconformist opposition.

Arnold's strongest attack on the middle class was made in *Culture and Anarchy,* which was published in 1869, and dealt with the middle-class spirit. For all its defects, it remains his richest work in social, as distinct from political, criticism; it is a devastating attack on the man of action. And it shows that Arnold is convinced more strongly than ever that the aristocracy must go. If *Culture and Anarchy* reveals more clearly than any other of his social writings the weakness of his puritanism, it also reveals more clearly than any other his debt to Greece.

In *Culture and Anarchy* Arnold's conservative side is more apparent than in his previous writings; though this side was exhibited in his letters, in his poetry, and in his essay "The Function of Criticism at the Present Time," it stands out here. In the first edition (though not in subsequent ones) he can say of the Hyde Park demonstrators that the old Roman method is the right one for dealing with rioting — "flog the rank and file, and fling the leaders from the Tarpeian Rock." This is a method for dealing with disorder which his father had recommended. The demonstrations that accompanied the passing of the Reform Act of 1867 and the action of the Fenians no doubt influenced Arnold to state his conservative side in clearer terms than before, and probably strengthened this side in him. Perhaps the most significant evidence for Arnold's conservative temper is the frequency with which he identifies the working class with brutality and violence.

Between 1866 and 1871 Arnold published a series of letters, in which he spoke through an imaginary German visitor, satirizing with delicate but telling irony the foibles of his countrymen. These letters, which were collected under the title of *Friendship's Garland* (1871), continue the attack on laissez faire, and contain Arnold's finest satire on English education. Perhaps no work of his showed so clearly that the age had produced a new controversialist to act as a foil to the seriousness of Carlyle and Ruskin.

From 1870 till 1877 Arnold was mainly concerned with religious criticism. In these years he directed his barbs against the religion of the middle class, Nonconformity. His criticism combined, as has been said, the spirit of Voltaire with that of a bishop. Standing for what he himself would call a scientific conception of Christianity, he asked the Nonconformists to give up their "hole-and-corner" religion, to cast out their belief in miracles and a supernatural God. He asked them to look upon the Bible as furnishing the best guide to the achievement of righteousness: to value the Old Testament for its emphasis on conduct and the New because Christ showed the way by which conduct might best be achieved — through renunciation, through finding life by losing it. His message to Nonconformity appeared in *St. Paul and Protestantism* (1870), *Literature and Dogma* (1873), *God and the Bible* (1875), and *Last Essays in Church and Religion* (1877). In his preface to *St. Paul and Protestantism* Arnold argued for the comprehension and union of all Protestant churches within the Church of England. For him the Church was a society for the promotion of goodness; its establishment by the state was important, for he believed that an interest so deep and abiding as religion should be publicly and splendidly recognized. Arnold's most important religious writing from the standpoint of his politics was "Bishop Butler and the Zeit-Geist," which was published in *Last Essays on Church and Religion* (1876); here he developed his view of human nature.

Arnold returned to political and social criticism in *Mixed Essays* (1879), in which he published two outstanding papers, "Democracy" and "Equality"; these two essays set forth his fundamental political and social ideas. In "Equality," which he had delivered as an address before a distinguished audience at the Royal Institution in 1878, he made his most searching attack on the aristocracy, virtually advocating its abolition by his criticism of the inequality of property. "Irish Catholicism and British Liberalism" showed the influence of Burke. In this essay he again presented his case for the establishment of a Catholic university for Ireland; he also showed that one of his main reasons for an established church was an aesthetic one. In "Irish Catholicism and British Liberalism" he could say that the middle class was the best stuff of which the nation was made. It is of interest, too, that he said the middle class should be thankful they do not have to be abolished. "Porro Unum Est Necessarium" was another plea for the establishment of a sound secondary system of education for the middle class.

Matthew Arnold

From 1880 onward Arnold was mainly concerned with Irish affairs. *Irish Essays,* which appeared in 1882, showed a generous spirit and his debt to Burke. In "The Incompatibles" he accused the landlords of confiscation, misgovernment, and tyranny, and recommended that England should break with the past by a striking and solemn act — the expropriation of landlords. "Ecce Convertimur ad Gentes" argued for the three things which, as we saw above, he held were necessary to the progress of English civilization — reduction of the inequality of landed property, a genuine municipal system, public schools for the middle class. "The Future of Liberalism" contained a searching criticism of the Liberal and Conservative parties. Arnold found the Conservatives unpromising; they had an excessive regard for existing fact, they had not the secret of life. He thought that the Liberals had at least a sound sense of direction. Their instinct, he says, is right, for their appeal to the love of liberty is an appeal to an instinct healthy and commendable in itself, and the instinct of the country is profoundly liberal. But in practical affairs they fall short; for rational action they substitute a mechanical procedure and a blind worship of conventional ideas. They appreciate no instinct save that of an unrestrained play of individuality. Trade and industry are the chief expressions of their instinct for expansion. When this instinct is emphasized to the exclusion of all others, it is, like the lean kine of Pharaoh's dream, apt to destroy all its fellows. Arnold sounded a new note in "The Future of Liberalism"; he went beyond mere condemnation of industrialism and ascribed the social distress to the action of unscrupulous capitalists.

Discourses in America was published in 1885; in "Numbers" he stated more flatly than before his doubt of the multitude, though he still held on to a belief in democracy. He thought that the unsound majority could be saved only by a remnant of the wise. And he was certain that the German stock, from which Americans and Englishmen derive, was the soundest the world had ever seen. Arnold's second book dealing with

Matthew Arnold

America, *Civilization in the United States,* appeared in 1888; he pointed out that America was the same as England "with the aristocracy left out and the populace nearly," and with the Philistines more lively than in England. He found American democracy to work naturally, in contrast to the English, which worked under tension and strain; American democracy, unlike the English, enjoyed social equality. Yet American civilization was wanting in the human element; it was not interesting, there was no beauty, and there was no distinction. Lincoln, he said, was a man without distinction. He was deeply impressed with federalism and advocated it for England. And he insisted that a House of Lords had no place in a modern government and that a nominated second chamber was fantastic; he proposed that England should construct an upper house like the American Senate, which he thought was the most successful of American institutions.

As we said above, Arnold disagreed with the practical program of the Liberals; in *Culture and Anarchy* he had criticized such leading measures as the Irish Church Disestablishment Bill and free trade. The "Nadir of Liberalism" (1886) showed that though he still looked upon himself as a liberal of the future, he was convinced of the utter failure of the Liberal party and was beginning to see hope in the Conservatives. He criticized the Home Rule Bill on the ground that it would loosen the ties between England and Ireland and proposed, as an alternative to Home Rule, to give Ireland three local legislatures, each with power to establish by majority vote the church of its preference. He thought that England would never be successful in conciliating Ireland until Catholics were able to establish their own church. In the following year Arnold told the Conservatives, in the "Zenith of Conservatism" (1887), that they were at the height of their power and he counseled them to deal with the pressing problems in Ireland, above all to suppress anarchy and the inflammatory speeches of Irish leaders and to give Ireland control of local affairs. "Up to Easter"

(1887) was a vigorous defense of the Coercion Act; somewhat impatient with the Conservative policy of law enforcement in Ireland, he asked for bold action against the mischief-makers; for, he said, a large part of Ireland was revolutionary. Arnold's *Reports on Elementary Schools (1852–1882),* published in 1889, a year after his death, show once again the mark of a creative mind in a field distinguished by their scarcity.

III

Arnold maintained, as did Carlyle, that man was destined to progress; he believed that the good was ultimately bound to triumph in the world.[25] It was bound to triumph not because, as for Carlyle, a puritan God had ordained it, but because it was in the nature of things. All things, according to Arnold, have a law of their being and tend to fulfill it.[26] The law of man's being, which he tends to fulfill, is righteousness: "There is a real power which makes for righteousness; and it is the greatest of realities for us."[27]

Man, according to Arnold, is able to achieve righteousness or to act for the good through conscience or reason; by reflection he is able to discover what he ought to do irrespective of his arbitrary wish or fancy. This view lies at the bottom of his doctrine of the two selves. Arnold believes that all experience shows that there are two selves in man, an inferior and a higher self, or, as he puts it in *Culture and Anarchy,* an ordinary and a best self:

. . . all experience brings us at last to the fact of two selves . . . contending for the mastery in man: one, a movement of first impulse and more involuntary, leading us to gratify any inclination that may solicit us, and called generally a movement of man's ordinary or passing self, of sense, appetite, desire; the other, a movement

[25] "Bishop Butler and the Zeit-Geist," *Last Essays on Church and Religion* (Vol. IX), p. 339.

[26] *Literature and Dogma* (Vol. VII), p. 43. Arnold says it is a matter of taste what we call this fact that all things have a law of their being and tend to fulfill it, but it may be called God; "for science God is simply a stream of tendency by which all things fulfill the law of their being." *Ibid.,* pp. 42–43.

[27] *Ibid.,* p. 43.

of reflection and more voluntary, leading us to submit inclination to some rule, and generally called a movement of man's higher or enduring self, of reason, spirit, will.[28]

It is no less an established fact for Arnold that to obey the best self, to submit inclination to some rule, brings happiness, while to obey the ordinary self can bring only misery and death.[29] The end of man is for Arnold the attainment of happiness,[30] not righteousness, as it is for Carlyle. Happiness, it may be observed, is rather a democratic ideal, all can participate in it; while righteousness is a theocratic ideal, only the few are elected. Thus where is was easy for Arnold to look with favor on democracy, it was easy for Carlyle to look upon it with contempt.

Arnold was aware that it was difficult to follow reason; he realized that it required struggle and discipline to renounce the immediate impulse in order to achieve excellence. He held, especially toward the end of his life, that only the few could really follow reason; in his essay on "Numbers" the majority was unsound and the remnant was wise. Convinced that the majority of men in English society were subject to their ordinary, their class selves, he looked to the state to act as the representative of the best self, to furnish a means of criticism.[31] The state would promote the ideal of a humane life through authoritative institutions — a national system of education, a national Protestant church, and, if it were but possible, a literary academy.

The nineteenth century was for Arnold an age of progress, and democracy, like science, was one of its inevitable and salutary revolutions. Democracy represented an expansion of man's spirit, an expansion manifested by the mass of men. Arnold could say that the need of expansion is as genuine an instinct

[28] Preface to *Last Essays on Church and Religion* (Vol. IX), p. 183. Cf. *Culture and Anarchy* (Vol. VI), pp. 74ff.

[29] Preface to *Last Essays on Church and Religion* (Vol. IX), p. 184.

[30] "Bishop Butler and the Zeit-Geist," *Last Essays on Church and Religion* (Vol. IX), pp. 304, 308.

[31] *Culture and Anarchy* (Vol. VI), pp. 74ff.

in man as the need in plants for the light. Arnold, unlike Carlyle, saw real potentialities for development in the common man; where Carlyle emphasized the great superiority of the few, Arnold emphasized rather the humanity of mankind. His emphasis on the common element in man was a factor that made him sympathetic to equality and hostile to laissez faire. And this emphasis on the common element probably saved him from giving way to hero worship and to aristocracy.

Not only was democracy, according to Arnold, a manifestation of the spirit of expansion; so also were liberty and equality. Like democracy, these were essential to human development.[32] If the aristocracy had been instrumental in the winning of liberty, and the middle class even more so, equality was the quest of democracy; the mass of men now desired to explore their faculties just as the few had desired to explore theirs.[33] Hence it was clear to Arnold that democracy could not fulfill itself in a society where there was great inequality in the conditions of life; it was natural that he should advocate the abolition of the great inequalities of property.

He believed that man could not reach the best that was in him unless he aspired to be a complete human being, to develop all sides of his nature. Of the powers he thought necessary for man's humanization none was so important as character, the power of conduct. To be strict, he says, and sincere with oneself, to be earnest, is the discipline by which alone a man is enabled to rescue his life from thraldom to the passing moment and to his bodily senses, to ennoble it, and to make it eternal.[34] Just as the power of conduct was so felt and fixed by Israel in the ancient world, so is it felt and fixed by England in the modern; our feeling for religion is one part of this power, our industry is another, our public spirit, our love, amidst all our liberty, for public order and for stability are parts of it too.[35]

[32] *Mixed Essays* (Vol. X): Preface; "Democracy," pp. 8–18; "Equality."
[33] "Equality," *Mixed Essays* (Vol. X), p. 71.
[34] *Culture and Anarchy* (Vol. VI), p. xlvi.
[35] "Equality," *Mixed Essays* (Vol. X), p. 63.

Arnold asserted that the culture of a nation must be frivolous, vain, and weak if the power of conduct is wanting.[36]

Yet he was equally certain that the culture of a nation must be raw, blind, and dangerous if the power of conduct is not aided by other powers.[37] The power, he holds, of intellect and knowledge, the power of beauty, and the power of social life and manners are also necessary to perfection; these are what Greece so felt, and fixed, and may stand for.[38] At the present time the Italians are pre-eminent in feeling the power of beauty; the power of knowledge is pre-eminently a feeling with the Germans; and perhaps even the Athenians have hardly felt the power of social life and manners so much as the French.[39] Arnold places not a little emphasis on the power of social life and manners. It is, he says, by no means identical with the moral impulse to help our neighbor and to do him good,[40] yet in many ways it works to a like end. It brings men together, makes them feel the need of one another, be considerate of one another, understand one another. But, above all things, it is a promoter of equality. It is by the humanity of their manners that men are made equal.

It may be said that Arnold looked forward to a society like that of the Athens of Pericles, with the slaves left out; this society in his view was the most civilized the world has ever known.[41] His ideal of a humane life was both aristocratic and democratic. It was aristocratic in that only a few could hope to pursue it adequately; it was democratic in that all could participate in it to some extent. Where Carlyle laid stress on the discovery of talent — an aristocratic ideal, for only the few are gifted — Arnold laid stress on the discovery of the individual's humanity. Where Carlyle saw the need of heroes acting for society, Arnold saw the need of a common life with men acting for themselves.

[36] "Democracy," *Mixed Essays* (Vol. X), p. 36.
[37] *Ibid.*, p. 37; cf. "Equality," *Mixed Essays* (Vol. X), pp. 75–81.
[38] "Equality," *Mixed Essays* (Vol. X), pp. 62–63.
[39] *Ibid.*, pp. 64–65.   [40] *Ibid.*, p. 66.
[41] "Democracy," *Mixed Essays* (Vol. X), p. 37.

Matthew Arnold

IV

Arnold found that England suffered from social and cultural anarchy; there was, he thought, no true society. Though there was some splendor and some beauty, these were not of the spirit, but external in character, and were confined to the aristocracy. There was some social life, life in the *grand* style, but it was the exclusive possession of the aristocracy, and therefore not generous, but limited. There was, indeed, a sense of conduct, and this represented the most considerable effort England had made toward perfection, but it was hard, narrow, and unlovely; it was characteristic of the puritan middle class. There was a sense of curiosity, a desire for ideas, but it was scarcely articulate; it was discernible in the lower classes, where it was all but swamped by ignorance and coarseness.

Society was not civilized, not humane. With too much splendor at the top, with too much seriousness in the middle, and with too little humanity at the bottom, it was divided, each class separated from another. And with the aristocracy and the lower class sharing the middle-class philosophy of individualism, of everyone doing as he likes, men were the servants of prejudice, not the followers of reason. There was in England no sense of a common purpose, of a life lived in common, lived at its best, on a plane truly civilized.

Arnold saw, as Carlyle and Ruskin had seen before him, that English life was dominated by materialism; and though he believed that it characterized all classes, he thought that the aristocracy was its special representative. With, he insisted, no longer any social function to fulfill, yet with great reserves for the means of life, the aristocracy had given itself over to material pleasures. Tempted, flattered, and spoiled from childhood to old age, standing for the splendor of wealth and the weight of property, the aristocratic class was inevitably materialized — and the more so as the development of industry and ingenuity augmented the means of luxury.[42] Arnold saw the ideal of

[42] *A French Eton* (Vol. XII), p. 78; "Equality," *Mixed Essays* (Vol. X), p. 85.

113

materialism affecting the whole of society, above all, the middle class. The possession, he says, of wealth, power, and consideration becomes a kind of ideal for the rest of the community.[43] It operates on the middle class; to be as rich as they can that they may reach the splendor of wealth and weight of property and, in time, the importance of the actual heads of society, is their ambition.[44]

The middle class, Arnold holds, has developed a materialistic spirit in its own right, though he believes that it is not as strong as that of the aristocracy. The middle class, he says, with its bent for industry and commerce, has great faith in machinery, in mechanical and external things — not in an inward condition of the mind and spirit, but in having something.[45] The middle class believes that the greatness of England depends on the coal supply, that its welfare is proved by its being rich; this belief about its wealth is held by nine out of ten Englishmen at the present time.[46] Arnold does not deny that industrialism is necessary; what he criticizes is its excess. It brings men to worship mechanically the production of wealth and the increase of population as ends in themselves. He makes the charge that the free-trading Liberals are above all guilty of mechanically worshipping these ends. He insists that Liberalism so emphasizes wealth and population for their own sakes that it is prepared to tolerate a sunken multitude, as if it were part of the necessary order of things.[47]

Capitalism, Arnold observes, builds industrial towns like St. Helens, Bolton, and Wigan — what Cobbett called hell-holes and what Lord Derby and Mr. Bright called centers of manufacturing — towns which afford their inhabitants no satisfaction of man's instinct for beauty, but develop in them uneasiness and stoppage.[48] Capitalists produce as much as they can without asking how long the demand will last, provided it lasts

[43] *Culture and Anarchy* (Vol. VI), p. 185.
[44] *A French Eton* (Vol. XII), p. 78.
[45] *Culture and Anarchy* (Vol. VI), p. 13.
[46] *Ibid.*, p. 17.   [47] *Ibid.*, pp. 204–07.
[48] "The Future of Liberalism," *Irish Essays* (Vol. XI), p. 149.

long enough to make their own fortunes. Capitalism leads to overproduction, depression, and distress.[49] It does not make the fortunes of the clusters of men and women whom it has called into being; these it leaves to the chances of fortune and the further development, as Lord Derby says, of great manufacturing industries. People begin to discover that "free political institutions do not guarantee the well-being of the toiling class."

English civilization, according to Arnold, was not only impaired by its belief in materialism, but also by its belief in an extreme form of freedom. The philosophy of individualism, the philosophy of the middle class, was, he maintained, leading the nation toward anarchy. The worship of free trade in industry meant, as did the belief in materialism, the mechanical increase of manufactures and the creation of poverty-stricken multitudes.[50] And individualism ascribed this result to the working of natural law! The *Times* said: "The East End [of London] is the most commercial, the most industrial, the most fluctuating region of the metropolis . . . a wilderness of small houses, all full of life and happiness in brisk times, but in dull times withered and lifeless, like the deserts we read of in the East. . . . There is no one to blame for this; it is the result of Nature's simplest laws!" [51]

Arnold was hardly less concerned with the freedom permitted the working class. This and that body of men all over the country, he said, are beginning to assert and put into practice an Englishman's right to do what he likes: his right to march where he likes, meet where he likes, enter where he likes, hoot as he likes, threaten as he likes, and smash as he likes.[52]

Arnold attacked individualism not only in the economic and political sphere, but also in the intellectual. He held that it was good to have freedom of speech, but argued that what was said was equally important, that liberty and publicity were not substitutes for right thinking. Denouncing the claptrap of politi-

[49] *Ibid.*, pp. 150–51.
[50] *Culture and Anarchy* (Vol. VI), pp. 200–02.
[51] *Ibid.*, p. 201.   [52] *Ibid.*, p. 50.

cians and their flattery of class prejudices, he insisted that freedom in England had come to mean freedom to affirm the irrational, ordinary self.[53] Perhaps Arnold's most devastating criticism of freedom of thought was his charge that Englishmen had placed so much emphasis on freedom that there had been a grave deterioration in the quality of thinking. He contended that in literature, religion, education, and journalism there was a marked decline in rational thought — above all, there was a throwing overboard of standards.[54] Extreme individualism in thought, Arnold held, was characterized by a tendency to anarchy, for it implied the equality of all values and was against the triumph of right reason.[55]

Puritanism, in Arnold's view, was another great obstacle to a genuine civilization. Not that puritanism was without virtue; in seizing upon the importance of character, it had placed its hand on the greatest element necessary to man's humanization. Nor was this all. It had fought ecclesiastical domination and made an invaluable contribution to the achievement of freedom of thought. And with its great store of energy it had helped to build modern industry. On the other hand, it stood for superstition in religion; it believed in miracles. It made a mechanical and misleading use of the Scriptures; it believed that children were *sent,* and that the divine nature took a delight in swarming the East End of London with paupers.[56] And though it sent missionaries to the masses, it accepted more or less their degradation.[57] It was almost as powerless as the free-trading Liberals to deal efficaciously with the ever-growing pauperism. It was hostile to speculation. It had created a type of life and manners that was fatally condemned by its hideousness, by its immense ennui; and its spirit was immune to a sense of beauty.[58] To judge puritanism by its works, what could be said

[53] *Friendship's Garland,* in *Culture and Anarchy* (Vol. VI), p. 237; *Culture and Anarchy* (Vol. VI), pp. 100–06.
[54] *Culture and Anarchy* (Vol. VI), pp. 95, 96–97, 107–08, 109–10.
[55] *Ibid.,* pp. 109–11.
[56] *Ibid.,* pp. 206–07.   [57] *Ibid.*
[58] "Equality," *Mixed Essays* (Vol. X), p. 76.

of that grand center of life, London! — "London, with its unutterable external hideousness, and with its internal canker of *publice egestas privatim opulentia,*—to use the words Sallust put into Cato's mouth about Rome, — unequalled in the world." [59] With all of these imperfections, a religion not true, the claims of intellect not satisfied, the claims of manners and of beauty not satisfied, puritanism could not even employ its sense of conduct aright. [60]

Against the materialism that was so prevalent, against an individualism that bordered on anarchy, and against a religion that made for a harsh culture, Arnold appealed to what he called right reason, that is, to his ideal of a humane civilization. The problem was to decide what class should be entrusted with setting this ideal, with determining how men should be governed. Arnold was convinced that of the three main classes in English society, the aristocracy was least fitted to set his ideal of a humane life. The aristocracy, he thought, was unfitted not only because it stood for materialism — the false ideal of wealth and station, pleasure and ease [61] — but also because it had lost its hold on the people. It is, he says, almost inevitable with aristocracies that they fail to appreciate justly, or even to consider, the instinct pushing the masses toward expansion and a fuller life. It is the old story of the incapacity of aristocracies for ideas, the secret of their want of success in modern epochs. Though they can, and often do, impart a high spirit, a fine ideal of grandeur, and thus lay the foundations of a great nation, they leave the people still the multitude, the crowd; they have small belief in the power of ideas which are the people's life. [62] "Themselves a power reposing on all which is most solid, material and visible, they are slow to attach any importance to influences impalpable, spiritual, and viewless . . . in one most important part of general human culture — openness to ideas

[59] *Culture and Anarchy* (Vol. VI), p. 27.
[60] "Equality," *Mixed Essays* (Vol. X), pp. 80–81.
[61] *Culture and Anarchy* (Vol. VI), p. 185.
[62] "Democracy," *Mixed Essays* (Vol. X), p. 14.

and ardour for them, — aristocracy is less advanced than democracy." [63]

Nor could Arnold look to the middle class to set his ideal. It stood, he maintained, for industrialism, for a freedom of industrial enterprise that put a premium on wealth and impaired the humanity of workingmen. And it represented a defective type of religion, a narrow range of intellect and knowledge, a stunted sense of beauty, and a low standard of manners.[64] Again, the middle class could not set the ideal because its political creed, Liberalism, was a power of yesterday; Liberalism had lost the future to the new force, democracy. Democracy, which was different from Liberalism in its cardinal point of belief, had little confidence in Liberalism: "It loves and admires neither the legislation of middle-class Parliaments, nor the local self-government of middle-class vestries, nor the unrestricted competition of middle-class industrialists, nor the dissidence of middle-class Dissent and the Protestantism of middle-class Protestant religion." [65]

Unlike Carlyle and Ruskin, Arnold had faith in democracy; he believed, as we have seen, that it responded to a primary element in human nature — the instinct of expansion. He looked upon democracy as a movement in which the mass of men were beginning to discover themselves:

Ever since Europe emerged from barbarism, ever since the condition of the common people began a little to improve, ever since their minds began to stir, this effort of democracy has been gaining strength; and the more their condition improves, the more strength this effort gains. So potent is the charm of life and expansion upon the living; the moment men are aware of them, they begin to desire them, and the more they have of them the more they crave.[66]

And he argues for democracy on the ground that common men are more likely to attain their wants if they have political

[63] *Ibid.*, pp. 15–16.
[64] *Ibid.*, pp. 34–38; "Equality," *Mixed Essays* (Vol. X), p. 88.
[65] *Culture and Anarchy* (Vol. VI), p. 32.
[66] "Democracy," *Mixed Essays* (Vol. X), p. 8.

power.[67] It is well, he says, for any great class of men to be able to say for itself what it wants, and not to have other classes, the so-called educated and intelligent classes, acting for it as its proctors. They do not really understand its wants, they do not really provide for them. A class of men may often itself not either fully understand its own wants, or adequately express them, but it has a nearer interest and a surer diligence in the matter than any of its proctors, and therefore a better chance of success. Moreover, the exercise of power by the people tends to educate the people.[68]

Arnold believes that democracy eventually means the triumph of reason and intelligence, but that it is not yet ready to come into its own. He does not idealize the masses; in his view they are still crude and raw, with a tendency to brutality and violence, even though they are distinguished by a flair for ideas. Though he favors democracy, he does not favor the mass of men setting the ideal by which English society shall be governed, for he firmly believes that the majority of the populace need to follow an ideal.

Finding each class unfitted to act as a center of authority, Arnold looked to the state to set the proper ideal through a system of public education. He argued that his ideal might be best promoted through an educated middle class, in spite of the fact that this class had failed in civilization. It furnished, he thought, the best basis on which to build a true culture, not only because of all classes it had made the greatest stride toward perfection, but also because it provided a broad basis on which to build a true culture. A broad basis of culture was for him the secret of rich and beautiful epochs of national life, the epoch of Pericles in Greece, of Michael Angelo in Italy, and of Shakespeare in England.[69]

Arnold also thought that the middle class was promising because he observed a ferment of ideas there [70] and, not least,

[67] "The Future of Liberalism," *Irish Essays* (Vol. XI), pp. 140–41.
[68] "Numbers," *Discourses in America*, in *Essays in Criticism* (Vol. IV), p. 286.
[69] *A French Eton* (Vol. XII), p. 72.   [70] *Ibid.*, pp. 69, 80.

because this class was in power.[71] As the dominant class in the state, it could make education something of its own, and more easily transform itself. Still another reason prompted Arnold to concentrate his efforts on improving middle-class education. The lower classes naturally looked up to the middle class, which was the educator of the lower class; unless the middle class could give direction to the lower, whose sympathies were already wider and more liberal than their model, society was in danger of falling into anarchy:

They arrive, these masses, eager to enter into the possession of the world, to gain a more vivid sense of their own life and activity. In this their irrepressible development, their natural educators and initiators are those immediately above them, the middle class. If these classes cannot win their sympathy or give them their direction, society is in danger of falling into anarchy.[72]

Arnold believed that this was especially true in view of the decline of the aristocratic element, which, he said, in some sort supplied an ideal to ennoble the spirit of the nation and to keep it together.[73]

Arnold wanted the state to provide public secondary education, yet he found state action discredited in his day, above all, in the eyes of the middle class; laissez faire was the dominant political philosophy.[74] His task was to persuade the middle class to accept state action. He said he understood the antagonism of the middle class to the state; for in the youth and early manhood of this class, the action of the state was at the service of an ecclesiastical party which used state power against its religion.[75] In its struggle to repel the conformity enforced upon it by the High Church, the middle class underwent great suffering and injustice. The state tried to do it violence, so it does not love the state; the state failed to subdue it, so it does not respect the state. The middle class naturally regards the state with something of aversion and contempt.

[71] "Democracy," *Mixed Essays* (Vol. X), p. 39.
[72] *Ibid.*, pp. 38–39.   [73] *Ibid.*, p. 38.
[74] *Culture and Anarchy* (Vol. VI), p. 47.
[75] *A French Eton* (Vol. XII), pp. 58–59.

Matthew Arnold

Arnold suggested that another cause indisposed the middle class to state action: the men of this class were of the Gaulish rather than of the Germanic races, and therefore characterized by the preponderant action of individuals instead of by the preponderant action of bodies of men.[76] Still another cause, he believed, indisposed the middle class to state action; it was not very open to new ideas, not easily ravished by them; it was not a great enthusiast for universal progress. He suggested that the bent of this class for keeping things as they were was a product of its national well-being and a cramped mental life:

Poverty and hope make men the friend of ideals, therefore the multitude has a turn for ideals; culture and genius make men the friend of ideals, therefore the gifted or highly trained few have a turn for ideals. The middle class has the whet neither of poverty nor of culture; it is not ill-off in the things of the body, and it is not highly trained in the things of the mind; therefore it has little turn for ideals; it is self-satisfied.[77]

Arnold admitted that there was justice in the contention of the middle class that things managed by the government are often managed ill. He says that a class with a strong practical sense and habit of affairs must see the government sometimes act remissly, sometimes vexatiously, now with a paralyzing want of fruitful energy, now with an overbusy fussiness, with rigidity, with formality, without due consideration of special circumstances.[78] Yet, he adds, it is no wonder state action often bungles and does its work badly. It is exercised by a class to whose cherished instincts it is opposed — the aristocratic class; and it is watched by a class to whose cherished prejudices it is opposed — the middle class.[79] Since it is hesitatingly exercised and jealously watched, it works without courage, cordiality, or belief in itself. Arnold argues that because state power has been used against the middle class as an engine of oppression is no reason for believing that state power must of necessity be an evil. State action, he says, is not in itself unfavorable to individual perfection; indeed, on the contrary, we see the individual

[76] *Ibid.*, p. 59.   [77] *Ibid.*, p. 60.   [78] *Ibid.*, p. 61.   [79] *Ibid.*, p. 65.

in ancient Greece, where state action was omnipresent, at his very highest pitch of free and fair activity.[80]

For want of adequate secondary education England suffers from both a social and an intellectual inconvenience, which falls most heavily on the middle class. The middle class is brought up on the second plane; on the Continent, where the state has organized secondary schools, the upper and middle classes are brought up on the same plane.[81] Though the middle class in England dominates Parliament, the aristocracy very largely governs. In France the Government is composed of professional and middle-class men; in England it is composed of a string of aristocratic personages and one or two men from the professions.[82] Still more important, the aristocracy dominates the administration; and, with Mirabeau, he who administers governs. Half a dozen famous schools, Oxford or Cambridge, the army or navy, and those posts in the public service supposed to be for gentlemen — these are the schools all or any of which give a training, a stamp, a cast of ideas that make a sort of association of all who share them. This cast of ideas is naturally that of the most powerful part of the association, the aristocracy.[83] Though the professions recruit the governing force of the aristocracy and assist it to rule, though they are the more numerous part of the association, they form the less prominent part; in no country do the professions so generally share the cast of ideas of the aristocracy as in England.

Arnold is the first to admit that there is a good side to this cast of mind imposed by the aristocracy: a high spirit, dignity, and a sense of the greatness of great affairs are characteristics necessary to the governing of men.[84] The bad side, he points out, is an indisposition and incapacity for science, for systematic knowledge, which is communicated to the professions.[85] The

---

[80] *Ibid.*, p. 69.
[81] "Higher Schools and Universities in Germany," *A French Eton* (Vol. XII), p. 408.
[82] "Porro Unum Est Necessarium," *Mixed Essays* (Vol. X), p. 158.
[83] "Higher Schools and Universities in Germany," *A French Eton* (Vol. XII), p. 408.
[84] *Ibid.*   [85] *Ibid.*, pp. 408–09.

want of adequate secondary schools for the middle class means that England presents a spectacle, unexampled anywhere else, of a middle class cut in two, the professions separated from the commercial and industrial class, with which in social standing they are naturally on a level [86] — the profession, with governing qualities, but without science; the commercial and industrial class cut off both from the aristocracy and the professions, without science or governing qualities. "He that wandereth out of the way of understanding shall remain in the congregation of the dead."

Arnold, in fine, appealed to the middle class to support a system of secondary schools on the ground that it could never reach a position of leadership in the state, to which is was entitled, so long as it failed in education. In his eyes the secondary schools of Nonconformity were narrowly religious; they gave no real training in the humanities and practically none in science. Yet, he said, a knowledge of the former was a means of power over men, a means of governance, as a knowledge of the latter was a means of power over things. The middle class was training men neither to govern nor to compete successfully with other nations in the trade, the industry, and the technical professions of the world.

Arnold called upon the middle class to take the initiative in creating a system of secondary education. He told them that they could never expect the aristocracy to take the lead, for the aristocracy must of necessity be against state action.[87] The aristocracy was a relatively large class and only a small part of its members could directly administer the state; therefore it was not to the interest of the remainder to give this small part an excessive preponderance. Where the aristocracy, he remarked, was a small oligarchy, able to find employment for all its members in the administration of the state, it was not the enemy, but the friend, of state action; for state action was then but its own action under another name. Again, he says, the aristocracy

[86] *Ibid.*, p. 409.
[87] *A French Eton* (Vol. XII), pp. 55–56.

must oppose state action because of its dominance in local government. The true aristocratic theory of civil government was to leave as much as possible to the individual, to local government. Why? Because aristocrats were preponderating individuals; the local government was in their hands. Though the middle class, he says, talks of self-government, the aristocracy *is* the self-government. Its hostility to state action affects even those members of the Government who are not of the aristocratic class; in the beginning they are overpowered by it, in the end they share it: "When the shepherd Daphnis first arrives in heaven, he naturally bows to the august traditions of his new sphere . . . by the time the novelty has worn off, he has come to think just as the immortals do." [88]

Again, how can the middle class expect the aristocracy to establish secondary schools for it in view of the fact that the aristocracy has no need for them? Still more important, the establishment of secondary schools like Eton and Harrow for the middle class would create competitors for the children of the aristocracy. Why should the aristocracy labor to endow another class with schools which develop those great instruments of power — a public spirit, a free spirit, a high spirit, a governing spirit, characteristics which make up what the aristocracy call "tone," which are the first things the aristocracy requires of the public schools, and which explain why it continues to govern.[89]

Arnold's appeal to the middle class to establish schools went beyond an appeal to its interests. He held that education was the proper function of the state because of its great importance; organization by the state would impart to education a certain gravity and grandeur that private institutions could never hope to impart to it. The state was properly just what Burke called it: the nation in its collective and corporate character. The state acted for the English nation; and the genius of the English nation was greater than the genius of any individual, greater even than Shakespeare's genius, for it included the genius of Newton also. Arnold wanted to see the state establish schools in order

[88] *Ibid.,* p. 55.   [89] *Ibid.,* p. 66.

to avoid the bias that must come from any purely voluntary group, and in order to avoid the sectarian bias of puritanism. He favored the state, too, because collective action was more efficient than isolated individual efforts.[90] Arnold realized that the state might not set a high ideal inasmuch as the nation might choose inferior representatives to govern. If it should do this, he said, it is the nation's responsibility.[91] However, even if the members of the executive are no wiser than the rest of the world, they have two great advantages from their position: access to almost boundless means of information, and the enlargement of mind which the habit of dealing with great affairs tends to produce.[92] The agents of the state are more apt to act with a sense of responsibility than any private group, because they are responsible to the nation.[93]

Arnold did not make a special plea for elementary state education, for he believed that nearly everyone in his day had reached the notion that popular education was the state's duty. It was his opinion that not many saw the need of a sound civil organization, yet he was convinced that there could be no satisfactory educational system without a true municipal system universally diffused.[94] The countries, he says, on the Continent which had established satisfactory elementary and secondary schools, France, Italy, Switzerland, Germany, and Holland, had transformed their civil organizations in order to meet the needs of a modern society.[95] In England the civil organization still remains what time and chance have made it; the country districts have only the feudal and ecclesiastical organizations of the Middle Ages or of France before the Revolution.[96] In England there is confusion, there is no idea of *co-ordering* things, as the French say — that is, of making them work fitly to a fit end.[97] Therefore there is waste of power, extravagance, and poverty of result. Modern states, he declares, "cannot either do

[90] "Democracy," *Mixed Essays* (Vol. X), p. 43.
[91] *Ibid.*, p. 42.   [92] *Ibid.*, p. 40.   [93] *Ibid.*, pp. 40–41.
[94] "Higher Schools and Universities in Germany," *A French Eton* (Vol. XII), pp. 403–07.
[95] *Ibid.*, p. 403.   [96] *Ibid.*, pp. 403, 406.   [97] *Ibid.*, p. 403.

without free institutions, or do without a rationally planned and effective civil organization." [98] We can form ourselves into the best and most efficient voluntary societies for dealing with education, that is, we can make state action upon it a genuine local government of it.[99] We can make the central government that mere court of disinterested review and correction which every sensible man would always be glad to have for his activity.

Not only did Arnold believe that a public educational system — above all, secondary education for the middle class, and a sound municipal organization — was necessary to the progress of English civilization, but he also believed that the signal reduction, if not the abolition, of great inequalities of property and conditions of life, of which the land system was the base, was no less necessary. In his view equality was essential if the middle class was to be brought up on the first plane, just as it was if society was to become civilized. Immense inequality of conditions and property, he says, is a defeat to the instinct of expansion — that impulse which no longer drives individuals and limited classes only but society as a whole to develop itself with the utmost possible fullness and freedom.[1] On the one side inequality pampers, on the other it vulgarizes and depresses. To live in a society of equals tends to make a man's spirit expand and his faculties work easily and actively; while to live in a society of superiors tends generally to tame the spirits and to make the play of the faculties less secure and active. To be heavily overshadowed, to be profoundly insignificant, has on the whole a depressing and benumbing effect on the character. De Tocqueville, who had no love for democracy, but rather a terror of it, has remarked that the common people are more uncivilized in aristocratic countries than in any others because they are overwhelmed with the weight of their own inferiority. While equality has not improved the upper classes of French

[98] *Ibid.*, p. 404.
[99] *A French Eton* (Vol. XII), p. 63.
[1] Preface, pp. vii–viii, "Democracy," pp. 10–12, *Mixed Essays* (Vol. X).

society, it has undoubtedly given to the lower classes, to the body of the common people, a self-respect, an enlargement of spirit, a consciousness of counting for something in their country's action, which has raised them in the scale of humanity.

Inequality, he contends, obstructs the development of a true culture. It splits society into classes, weakens them, and throws them back upon their own limited culture. Inequality has an unfortunate effect on the large class of gentlemen not of the landed class, but cultivated and refined, of the class which embraces the men of the professions. Not having all the dissipations and distractions of the aristocracy, more alive to the power of intellect and knowledge and to the power of beauty, they are nevertheless somewhat materialized.[2] Their contiguousness to the aristocracy has the effect of blocking their mental horizon and limiting the possibilities of things to them; they are deficient in openness and flexibility of mind, in faith, and ardor.[3] Civilized they are, but they are not much of a civilizing force; they are somehow bounded and ineffective. So in the middle class they produce singularly little effect.

What the middle class see, he says, is that splendid piece of materialism, the aristocratic class, with a wealth and luxury utterly out of their reach, with a standard of social life and manners, the offspring of that wealth and luxury, seemingly out of their reach also. And thus they are thrown back upon themselves — upon a defective type of religion, a narrow range of intellect and knowledge, a stunted sense of beauty, a low standard of manners. And the lower class see before them the aristocratic class, and its civilization, such as it is, infinitely more out of their reach than out of that of the middle class; while the life of the middle class, with its unlovely types of religion, thought, beauty, and manners, has naturally, in general, no great attractions for them either. And so they are thrown back upon themselves; upon their beer, their gin, and their fun. Inequality materializes our upper class, vulgarizes our middle

[2] "Equality," *Mixed Essays* (Vol. X), p. 88.   [3] *Ibid.*

class, brutalizes our lower.[4] As a remedy for inequality Arnold recommends Mill's proposal of a law fixing the maximum, whether of land or money, that any individual may take by bequest or inheritance.[5]

As we saw above, Arnold held that a public system of secondary education for the middle class was what was most needed to remedy the greatest of wants in English civilization, the want of mind. He also thought that if a real attempt was to be made to remove this deficiency, a system of higher education would be necessary. He recommended that the state should plant faculties in eight or ten principal seats of population, providing each faculty with a dean.[6] The prime minister, he thought, was not the person to appoint the faculties, for he was above all a political functionary, who felt political influences overwhelmingly. Nor was a school board fit to appoint, for men would connive at a job as members of a committee who singlehanded would never consider it. Arnold would entrust the power of appointment and dismissal of professors to a minister of education.[7]

A minister of education, he says, supplies you with the discharge of certain critical functions; he is the agent who will perform them in the greatest blaze of daylight and with the keenest sense of responsibility. Directly representing all the interests of learning and intelligence in the country, he is a full mark for their criticism and is conscious of his responsibility to them; he alone supplies a center upon which to fix that responsibility. The minister should be aided by a High Council of Education, comprising without regard to politics personages most proper to be heard on questions of public education. Its function should be consultative only, but the minister should be obliged to take its opinion on all important measures not purely administrative. Some eight or ten provincial school boards, like those in Germany, should be established to repre-

[4] *Ibid.*, p. 88.   [5] *Ibid.*, p. 92.
[6] "Higher Schools and Universities in Germany," *A French Eton* (Vol. XII), p. 425.
[7] *Ibid.*, pp. 415, 429–30.

Matthew Arnold

sent the state in the country for the purposes of administration.[8] Arnold looked to Oxford and Cambridge to provide professors for the provincial universities. At the old universities, which he called *haut lycées,* and considered inferior to Continental universities, he wished to see more science introduced and higher standards prevail.

Through his system of superior instruction Arnold would provide training for all the professions and services of the state that required it; thus he would train ministers of religion, doctors, lawyers, and civil servants of the higher ranks.[9] His system of university training, in which science would be given its full weight, would help to remedy the intellectual inconvenience in English civilization due to the Englishman's disbelief in ideas.[10] His system of university training would bring to English life a true sense of the power of intellect and knowledge, and circulate through it a current of ideas.

A state system of education — elementary, secondary, and superior — a democratic municipal system, and equality, were for Arnold not the only means of promoting the welfare of English civilization. He advocated, in addition, a national Protestant church, comprehending all sects; though it would be a state church, he believed that the Dissenters should be permitted to keep their democratic system of the election of ministers by the congregation.[11] Such a church, he held, would establish unity where there was separatism; instead of emphasizing differences, it would give itself over to worship and a cultivation of the spirit; it would put the puritan religion of the middle class in touch with a national tradition and impart to it a historical spirit; it would replace an unattractive ritual with one of beauty. For Arnold a national church would help to supply Nonconformity with a remedy for its chief defects, its want of beauty and intelligence; it would help to correct Hebraism by Hellenism.

[8] *Ibid.,* pp. 416–17.　　[9] *Ibid.,* p. 431.　　[10] *Ibid.,* p. 414.
[11] "Puritanism and the Church of England," *St. Paul and Protestantism* (Vol. IX); "The Church of England," *Last Essays on Church and Religion* (Vol. IX).

Matthew Arnold

Another institution that Arnold would have liked to see established by the state was a literary academy like that of the French.[12] Though he did not advocate it directly, on the ground that the Englishman's inordinate desire to do as he likes would for a long time be an obstacle to its establishment, he strongly favored such an institution. For in his eyes it represented Hellenism; it would help to make the best that has been known and thought in the world prevail. Like a national system of education and a national church, it too was a source of "sweetness and light," of beauty and intelligence.

V

Unlike Carlyle and Ruskin, Arnold understood the democratic movement, the main political movement of his time; he saw as clearly as Mill that its genius was equality, and he grasped its relation to the middle class and to the aristocracy even more clearly. Carlyle pointed out that the impulse of the democratic movement was in conflict with the inequality of property and conditions of life, and he analyzed the psychological and cultural effects of its frustration just as he did of its fulfillment. No one in his generation saw more acutely that a concentration of wealth in the hands of the few must impede the free, creative development of a society. No one saw more acutely that social position, born of great wealth, is an instrument of political power. In his analysis of the influence of the aristocracy on the leading secondary schools of the nation, he demonstrated how a class could govern that was no longer able to rule. His discussion of how the aristocracy imposed its cast of mind on the professional classes, above all on the administrators of the state, showed him to be a gifted political psychologist; few have given a more convincing demonstration of the subtle and far-reaching influence of attitudes. No one has brought out more clearly the power of the aristocracy and the method of its exercise in the middle-class state of the nineteenth century.

[12] "The Literary Influence of Academies," *Essays in Criticism* (Vol. III).

Matthew Arnold

In contrast to Carlyle and Ruskin, Arnold strove to discover the virtues as well as the defects of English civilization; if a want of mind, a stunted sense of beauty, a want of social spirit, and a narrow religion were its chief defects, its power of conduct was its chief virtue. With an understanding of institutions gained through his experience as an inspector of schools, Arnold, unlike Carlyle and Ruskin, presented in detail a practical program for the promotion of his ideal of a better life. The system of education he recommended, his suggestions for its administration — his discussion, for example, of the function of the minister of education — show a sense of statesmanship. That English education has developed to no small extent along the lines that he advocated is testimony to his grasp of what was possible. His turn for the practical was also expressed in his method of attacking inequality of property — a law of bequest limiting gifts and inheritance. Again, his practical sense was expressed in his demand for a democratic municipal system. In short, his main recommendations for the improvement of English civilization show a knowledge of the working of institutions.

If he did a little something to discredit laissez faire but could not match the work done here by Carlyle and Ruskin, his attack was more intellectual than Carlyle's and more felicitous than Ruskin's. In his criticism of the middle-class doctrine of a minimized state, which was at its best in *A French Eton,* he did not shock his reader loose from stock notions, as did Carlyle and Ruskin, but he persuaded him to give them up freely. He disarmed his opponent before he criticized him, he found value in his argument and won his friendship before disposing of his views. And he frequently dissolved the prejudice of his opponent by tracing its history; and by an appeal to reason, he could disabuse him of the fear of shadows. If Arnold did not appreciate as deeply as did John Stuart Mill the value of liberty and the moral argument for self-government, he saw more clearly than Mill the need of restraints if true freedom was to be attained.

Though Arnold was aware of the superficial nature of Liberal reform — that it was "machinery" and not fundamental reform — his own horizon was limited by the middle-class point of view. He underestimated the materialism engendered by the profit-system, and he did not probe the problem of inequality in relation to industrial property, though from the economic angle the major problem was here. His suggested law abolishing freedom of bequest as a means of reducing the great inequalities of property would undoubtedly destroy the landed aristocracy, but it would not necessarily destroy the aristocracy of industry and finance. In fixing the limits of inheritance, Arnold aimed at establishing equality of bequest; for, whether by the Code Napoléon as in France, or by custom as in America, equality of bequest in his view had brought about social equality. Yet both France and America show that equality of bequest does not prevent the accumulation of great wealth in the hands of the few, and does not prevent the development of practically all of the social, cultural, and psychological disadvantages of inequality. His view of the workers was frequently a typical middle-class view, the Roman view; the working class was the populace, and was characterized by brutality and a tendency to violence. Such an assumption along with a strong belief in order made it easy for Arnold to discover in *Culture and Anarchy* that street meetings were meetings for the purpose of disorder, and should be suppressed; and it was easy for him to recommend the method of the Tarpeian Rock. It should be observed that brutality and violence are more characteristic of the middle and upper classes than of the lower throughout history.[13] It should be further observed that even if the explanation of this fact is that the former have been in power while the latter have not, this explanation does not alter the fact.

Arnold's insistence, with Burke, on order before reform led him to speak of Bradlaugh, who defended the right of public meeting for workingmen in Hyde Park, as an irresponsible

[13] For further discussion of this point see the chapter on Maine, page 198.

tribune. It led him to speak of Frederick Harrison, who showed vigor in supporting the working class, as an exponent of fierceness. It led him to advocate putting down disorder in Ireland with a sternness that was excessive. To say that Arnold's judgment of practical politics was unreliable because he was a man of letters who was detached from the world, is to offer but part of the explanation; the greater part lies in his view of the common man, and in his belief in order. Arnold's concern with order and with authority prevented him from seeing the arguments against an established church; he never considered Lord Morley's charge that historically the English Church has been the "ally of tyranny, the organ of social oppression, the champion of intellectual bondage."

Yet, in spite of his shortcomings, Arnold made a stronger appeal to reason than Carlyle or Ruskin, stronger even though he had the Englishman's distrust of abstract thought, which is itself a distrust of reason. We may say of him, as he said of Burke, that he mixed politics with ideas. In the ideal he urged upon his generation, he called attention to the elements of a humane life, and, in the criticism he made of English society, he pointed to some of the conditions necessary to its attainment. Though he was little understood in his own time, and is less well known today, he remains a civilizing force; to read the best that he wrote is to have a heightened sense of our humanity. He is, as he himself said, a liberal of the future.

JAMES FITZJAMES STEPHEN

I

UNLIKE Carlyle, Ruskin, and Arnold, Fitzjames Stephen was not of the blood of the prophet; he was capable neither of moving the minds of men nor of giving new significance to old ideas. His talent lay rather in a smashing criticism. He was the severest critic of the advanced democratic thought of the 1860's and 70's. Stephen found in his day a growing enthusiasm for what he called the "Religion of Humanity," a creed of liberty, equality, fraternity — the belief, as he put it, that the human race has splendid destinies before it, and that the road to them is to be found in the removal of all restraints on human conduct, in substantial equality, and in general love.

Though Positivism, Stephen thought, was the most definite form in which the "Religion of Humanity" had expressed itself, its most accredited representative was John Stuart Mill, not the early but the later John Stuart Mill, the one who wrote *Liberty, Subjection of Women,* and *Utilitarianism.* Stephen focused his attention on Mill, dissecting his philosophy as if the process of criticism were something like the operations of an anatomist. He dissected Mill's ideas minutely in order more surely to wither them with logic. Stephen, however, was more than a technical critic. He submitted Mill's ideas to a sledgehammer rhetoric, of which at times even Dr. Johnson might have been proud. Nor were logic and rhetoric his only weapons. He brought to bear against his opponent the moral zeal of an indignant puritan, who was out to save the world from the devil. And he brought to bear a philosophy that could hardly have been better constructed for opposing Mill's democratic views.

Stephen set over against Mill a view of human nature like that of Hobbes and of Calvin, and opposed Mill with ideas of authority and of obedience which these older writers would have admired. He emphasized the virtue of the few and held that the few ought to rule, though he accepted democracy on the ground that it was inevitable. An adherent of the pleasure-pain philosophy of Bentham, he appealed to the Utilitarianism of the master against that of the disciple; this served to sharpen his attack on Mill. Stephen set forth his criticism of Mill and the Positivists in *Liberty, Equality, Fraternity,* which was the most trenchant and elaborate criticism of the democratic tendencies of the Utilitarian school of thought of the day.[1]

There can be no doubt that Stephen destroyed Mill's principle of liberty — that neither the government nor public opinion is entitled to interfere with the actions of the individual except for the purpose of self-protection. Nor can there be any doubt that he showed some weakness in the argument Mill made from history in support of equality, and that he discredited the extravagant claims made by Mill and the Positivists on behalf of fraternity. Stephen, however, was not able to impugn the spirit of freedom for which Mill stood; nor was he able to refute Mill on the essentials of his argument for equality.

If Stephen, as Ernest Barker said, gave the finest expression of conservative thought in the latter half of the nineteenth century,[2] yet he was a conservative with a difference. He did not fear change, which is the fundamental characteristic of the conservative, so much as he denied that the mass of people were capable of improvement. He feared anarchy, but the kind of anarchy that the puritan rather than the conservative fears.

[1] Cf. Leslie Stephen, *The English Utilitarians* (3 vols., London, 1900), III, 244n.
[2] Ernest Barker, *Political Thought in England, 1848 to 1914* (rev. ed., London, 1928), p. 172.

Like Carlyle, he feared the anarchy of disobedience; and he feared the anarchy of the appetites, of experiments in free living, of that kind of liberty which might destroy all social bonds. If his politics were not based directly on religion, as were Burke's, they were very much affected by it. If he went very far with the rationalists on religious matters, he accepted the probability of religious truth, in order, it seems, to have a sanction for inducing men to be good. If Calvin provided him with weapons to attack liberalism, so also did Hobbes; on almost every front he held that the rule of force was the rule of life.

His authoritarianism, however, was restrained within the utilitarian mold; he did not stand, as did Carlyle, for a strong social service state, let alone a military one. Though he believed in safe reforms like education and codification of the criminal law, he did not support extensive state action. He stood broadly for a laissez-faire state and for economic individualism. Though he believed that the state could not and should not be neutral in regard to fundamental religious and moral problems, he did not believe that the state should go so far as to determine what creed the churches should teach.

Matthew Arnold spoke of Burke as the author of an epoch of concentration; Stephen was not the author of an epoch, any more than of a school or a movement. He did not count as an influence, though Lord Morley thought it necessary to make a vigorous reply to *Liberty, Equality, Fraternity*.[3] Stephen was the leader of the conservative intellectual reaction against democracy in the second half of the nineteenth century; neither Maine nor Lecky, who followed him, stated the case against democracy as strongly as he. His case was stronger than Carlyle's and is perhaps the strongest after Plato's. He was not content merely to assert that the mass of men cannot be improved by liberty and free discussion; he supported this assertion by arguments from history. No one has surpassed him in

[3] Francis W. Hirst, *Early Life and Letters of John Morley* (2 vols., London, 1927), I, 239, 243.

showing the importance of coercion in human affairs. In a minor way, he stands to the democratic movement in the nineteenth century as Hobbes stood to the religious struggles in the seventeenth; both represent the peak of opposition to forces of expansion.

II

Nothing was so important for Stephen's political ideas as his early family training. Born in London in 1829 to parents who were zealous adherents of the Clapham sect, Stephen's mind was fashioned in the Calvinist mold.[4] Stephen was indebted to Calvinism for his conviction that politics cannot be divorced ultimately from religion any more than can morals. Calvinism gave him an appreciation of the depravity of human nature, and led him to admire vigor and strength; and Calvinism taught him that most men must be compelled to be good. The reading course given Stephen in his very early years undoubtedly left an impression upon him. He was brought up on a diet of the Bible and *The Pilgrim's Progress,* which was occasionally thinned by the lighter fare of *Robinson Crusoe* and heroic poetry. Such literature strengthened the traits for which he was remarkable as a child, strong-mindedness and independence, traits which never ceased to be characteristic of him.

Though Eton is always important for anyone who enters its doors, it is seldom of outstanding importance, as it was for Stephen. An intense individualist, his life at Eton was not a happy one. Eton exasperated him; he saw in it an institution that could boast of no better ideals than proficiency in athletics and pliability in social life. Failing to find any virtue in the accepted type, he refused to conform to it. Thus in a real sense his life resolved itself into one of conflict; fighting with his classmates became part of his daily routine. Eton, Stephen says, taught him forever that to be weak is to be wretched, that the state of nature is the state of war, and *vae victis* the great

[4] Leslie Stephen, *Life of Sir James Fitzjames Stephen* (London, 1895), pp. 69ff., 78, 116.

law of nature.[5] This view of life, which had so much in common with Hobbes', was fundamental to Stephen's political philosophy. Along with his Calvinism, it accounts for his view of human nature in the mass.

In 1847 Stephen went into residence at Trinity College, Cambridge. But his lack of accurate scholarship and of proficiency in mathematics made his academic career more or less unsuccessful. Except for his acquaintance with Maine, which paved the way for his Indian appointment, Cambridge counted little in his career. Stephen's conservative sympathies were at this time unmistakably clear. The record of the Union debates shows that he favored Establishment and opposed Sir William Harcourt on his motion to extend the suffrage without regard to education or property.[6] At a meeting of the "Apostles," the most distinguished literary and philosophical club at Cambridge, he denied that society needed reconstructing, though some of his friends, including Maine, not only favored reconstruction but insisted that some elements of socialism were desirable.[7]

The French Revolution of 1848 brought boiling to the surface his deepest convictions. Writing in 1867 of his feelings toward the revolution, he says, "they were then, as always, feelings of fierce, unqualified hatred for the revolution and revolutionists; feelings of the most bitter contempt and indignation against those who feared them, truckled to them, or failed to fight them whensoever they could and as long as they could; feelings of zeal against all popular aspirations and in favour of all established institutions whatever their various defects or harshnesses (which, however, I wish to alter slowly and moderately); in a word, the feelings of a scandalized policeman towards a mob breaking windows in the cause of humanity." [8] No remark better illustrates the underlying tendency of Stephen's political thought and its debt to a temperament.

On leaving Cambridge, Stephen, despite his father's wish that he should take up a clerical career, decided to take up law.

[5] *Ibid.,* p. 80.   [6] *Ibid.,* p. 99.   [7] *Ibid.,* p. 104.   [8] *Ibid.,* p. 107.

James Fitzjames Stephen

While preparing at the University of London, he came into full contact with Benthamism and, with certain modifications, was soon a thoroughgoing disciple. To a man whose predominant faculty was strong common sense and who held nothing but hatred for sentimentalism, there was an obvious fascination in the Benthamite mode of thought. But Stephen found a rich response in Benthamism mainly because of its empirical quality.[9] Knowledge was to be sought not by what he would call metaphysical or logical jugglery, but by scrupulous observation and systematic appeals to experience. From this time on, says Leslie Stephen, his philosophical position was substantially that of Bentham and John Stuart Mill and the empiricists, while the superstructure of his belief was a modified evangelicism.[10] When Stephen, however, came to write his political work *Liberty, Equality, Fraternity* (1873), his Calvinism dominated the liberal view he drew from the Utilitarians.

Called to the bar in 1854, Stephen divided the next fifteen years of his life between the practice of law and a vigorous career in journalism. He wrote successively for the *Saturday Review, Fraser's Magazine,* the *Cornhill Magazine,* and the *Pall Mall Gazette.* His articles were usually heavy dissertations on morals, theology, and politics. A master of intellectual quarterstaff play, Stephen became, according to one authority, the most vigorous controversialist of the age.[11] Hobbes was his favorite philosopher; he read the *Leviathan* during hours of recreation. He believed with Hobbes that life is a battle and that the strongest will always rule, and that the state must be supreme if conflict is to be avoided.[12] While practising law and writing for the reviews, Stephen's ideas underwent little change. Yet it is interesting to note that he manifested two different attitudes toward politics. In keeping with his discipleship to Bentham, he displayed a genuine liberal strain; in an essay on Burke he maintained that the development of democracy justi-

---

[9] *Ibid.*, p. 123.   [10] *Ibid.*, p. 124.
[11] A. W. Benn, *The History of English Rationalism in the Nineteenth Century* (2 vols., London, 1906), II, 302.
[12] Leslie Stephen, *Life of Sir James Fitzjames Stephen*, p. 330.

fied the revolutions in both France and England.[13] And it is an interesting commentary on his later Indian experience that in a paper on Hobbes he showed little sympathy with the principle of autocracy.[14]

Stephen's conservatism got the better of his liberal side when he acted as counsel for the Jamaica Committee in 1867. The object of the Jamaica Committee, which was headed by such outstanding liberals as John Stuart Mill, Spencer, and Huxley, was the prosecution of Governor Eyre and his officers for having hanged Gordon, whom the Governor believed to have brought about insurrection by advocating the rights of negroes. Stephen held that the defendants were guilty of legal murder, but extended considerable sympathy to them and intimated that they were probably morally justified.[15] From then on Mill was cool to him. In the same year the behavior of the Conservative Government in the case of the Hyde Park riots excited his contempt, as did the party maneuvers which attended the passing of the Reform Bill.[16]

It is not strange that Carlyle was an influence that helped to give final shape to Stephen's ideas. True enough, Stephen was not drawn to Carlyle by affinity of intellect; Stephen's mind was of the logical and practical order, Carlyle's of the intuitive. But this difference was not great enough to keep the two men apart; they were obviously drawn to each other on the ground of temperament. Stephen was first and foremost a product of the Evangelical circle; both he and Carlyle were spiritual descendants of the old Covenanters. As Stephen advanced in years, he found Carlyle's denunciation of the parliamentary system more and more congenial, especially was this so after his return from India.[17] He admitted that his association with Carlyle may have made him increasingly gloomy.[18] Stephen began to

[13] *Horae Sabbaticae* (reprint of articles contributed to the *Saturday Review*, 3 vols., London, 1902), III, 149.

[14] *Ibid.*, II, 67ff.

[15] Leslie Stephen, *Life of Sir James Fitzjames Stephen*, pp. 227–30.

[16] *Ibid.*, p. 224.

[17] *Ibid.*, pp. 225, 315.   [18] *Ibid.*, p. 305.

hold Carlyle's view of the parliamentary system; he began to see it as the petty game of wire-pulling and of pandering to shallow prejudices. His conversations with Carlyle on Sunday afternoon walks strengthened his conviction that strong government was sorely needed.

India, however, was a more important influence than Carlyle in the development of Stephen's ideas. In 1868 Stephen went to India, as the result of Maine's recommendation, to take his place as legal member of the Viceroy's commission. As Stephen himself said, his work in India was that of a Benthamee Lycurgus. Stephen saw and took part in the actual application of many of his principles under what were for him perfect conditions. In India he thought he had found his ideal realized.[19] There, regardless of shortcomings, the rulers ruled. Governors acted upon their convictions, and government was powerful and capable of despatching business. The law of force was indisputably the law of life. Hobbes had greater vitality than ever: his philosophy written for the England of 1660 was vindicated by the India of 1870; and the England of Queen Victoria still had much to learn from the gospel of authority. Stephen reached the conviction that absolutism was as legitimate a form of government as any other.[20] Just as surely was he convinced that a bureaucracy had its merits. A government, he thought, unhampered by a legislature and an electorate was capable of an efficiency utterly unknown to a democracy.

India left Stephen an ardent imperialist. No one, it seems, has more vigorously defended empire.[21] There is no disgrace, he declares, attaching to the conquest of India by England. It is only the transfer of political power from one hand to an-

[19] *Ibid.,* p. 315.

[20] See his article "Foundations of the Government in India," in the *Nineteenth Century,* 14:551ff. (October, 1883). Frederick Harrison interestingly suggests that India had something to do with Stephen's insistence in *Liberty, Equality, Fraternity* that the state should take cognizance of religion. He points to the possible influence of the Brahmanical and Mohammedan theocracies. *Fortnightly Review,* old series, 19:693 (January–June, 1873).

[21] See "Foundations of the Government in India," *Nineteenth Century,* 14:551ff. (October, 1883).

other.[22] The object of British rule in India is for India's own greatest good, "the natural and legitimate advantages which flow from the honourable enterprise of substituting civilization for barbarism." [23] Though he grudgingly admits that representative government may some day have to be introduced into India, he does not believe that it is the moral duty of Englishmen to educate natives so that they may institute democracy, especially when the present arrangement suits all parties concerned, with the exception of a few malcontents in India and a few radicals in England.[24] To introduce parliamentary government into India at the present time, he affirms, would produce unqualified anarchy.[25]

On the voyage home from India in 1872 Stephen began *Liberty, Equality, Fraternity,* which he well described when he spoke of it as "virtually a consideration of the commonplace of British politics in the light of his Indian experience." [26] He was appointed Professor of Common Law at the Inns of Court in 1875; his lectures upon the law of evidence led to a "digest" of that law, published in 1876. He had previously written, in 1863, *A General View of the Criminal Law of England,* which met with much success; this study led him to a digest of the criminal law, which he published in 1877. His suggestion that this might be converted into a code was favorably received by the government of the day. In codifying he was carrying out the theories of his teachers, Bentham and Austin. That the bill he prepared never came before Parliament strengthened his predilection for strong government.[27] His most distinguished service was his *History of the Criminal Law of England,* published in 1883.

Stephen still considered himself a Liberal. In 1873 he decided to stand for Dundee as a supporter of Gladstone. When he made this decision he apparently did not realize how deeply India had undermined his liberalism. In the election he was de-

[22] *Ibid.,* p. 546.   [23] *Ibid.,* p. 567.   [24] *Ibid.,* pp. 561–66.   [25] *Ibid.,* p. 557.
[26] Leslie Stephen, *Life of Sir James Fitzjames Stephen,* p. 316.
[27] See Leslie Stephen's biography of his brother in the *Dictionary of National Biography,* LIV, 166–67.

feated by a large majority; his want of sympathy for the popular sentiment, said Leslie Stephen, led him to see that he was less averse to the Conservatives.[28]

III

Stephen's political ideas are founded essentially on his view of human nature. The mass of men, he thinks, are ignorant or indifferent, and a great many are selfish and venal. He holds with Hobbes that life is inevitably a conflict.[29] "Struggles," he says, "there must and always will be, unless men stick like limpets or spin like weathercocks." This view led him to exalt coercion; because men are base and because they struggle, they must be restrained and compelled in nearly every action of their lives.[30]

His view of human nature led him, not unlike Hobbes, to posit force as the keystone of the social arch. In fact, with Stephen force tends to identify itself with morality. "Force," he says, "is always in the background, and the invisible bond which corresponds to the moral framework of society."[31] If the majority of men are ignorant, it follows that the few are wise; Stephen believes that the wise minority are the rightful masters of the foolish majority. Stephen's view of human nature, needless to say, made him hostile to democracy; mankind was ignorant and petty, and consequently could not be improved by freedom.

His utilitarian view of society, that the individuals making up society are like an aggregate of independent atoms, led him to place a disproportionate emphasis on force, for atoms in the last analysis can only be held together by force. He believed with Bentham that government was a necessary evil, but, unlike the individualists of the Manchester school, who emphasized the "evil," he emphasized the "necessary." As a puritan, he found that utilitarian ethics were not altogether satisfactory;

[28] *Ibid.*, p. 166.
[29] *Liberty, Equality, Fraternity* (2d ed., London, 1874), pp. 96, 108, 155, 180.
[30] *Ibid.*, pp. 34–35.   [31] *Ibid.*, p. 31.

the ethics of self-interest and happiness did not put morality on a plane of law. Thus Stephen, though broadly a Benthamite individualist, justified in theory, and in special circumstances in practice, state interference for moral and religious ends.[32] For Stephen the state was a great teacher of the moral law so far as its arm could reach.[33] Since morality depended on religion, the state, he held, should not shrink from exercising authority in this sphere.[34] Though he would disclaim that he advocated a state church, his doctrines seem to imply it.

IV

Liberty, Equality, Fraternity was, as we have said, essentially an attack on the social philosophy of John Stuart Mill. Stephen agreed with Mill that the mass in all countries constituted collective mediocrity, but he denied that Mill's philosophy would improve the mass; he insisted that so far from developing individuality, it threatened to undermine the foundations of society. He summarized Mill's philosophy as follows: "Mill appears to believe that if men are all freed from restraint and put, as far as possible, on an equal footing, they will naturally treat each other as brothers, and work together harmoniously for the common good."[35] "The great instrument for bringing about this result is a social sentiment which promises to be sublimated into a new religion; a general love of the human race."[36]

Stephen insisted that Mill's doctrine of liberty, which held that there was no warrant for interfering with the action of an individual except for the end of self-protection, was not only unsound but mischievous. He agrees with Mill's view that the strongest of all arguments against the interference of the public with purely personal conduct is that when it does interfere the odds are that it interferes wrongly.[37] But he dissents with vehemence from Mill's attempt to develop such a view into a sweeping principle. Stephen begins his attack by distinguishing, from

---

[32] *Ibid.*, pp. 53ff.
[33] Leslie Stephen, *Life of Sir James Fitzjames Stephen*, p. 324.   [34] *Ibid.*, p. 325.
[35] *Liberty, Equality, Fraternity*, p. 280.   [36] *Ibid.*, p. 291.   [37] *Ibid.*, p. 8.

the utilitarian point of view, between voluntary acts and acts done under compulsion: acts, he says, are free when hope is their motive, and acts are done under compulsion when fear is their motive.[38] If Mill's doctrine of liberty is true, he continues, no one is ever justified in trying to affect anyone's conduct by exciting his fears except for the sake of self-protection. Mill's doctrine of liberty is contradicted by all systems of religion, and morality, and methods of changing government or social institutions, for all these, in so far as they aim at affecting human conduct, appeal far more to fear than to hope; and they are coercive for ends other than self-protection.[39]

For one person who is restrained by the fear of the law of the land, many are restrained by the fear of the disapprobation of their neighbors, or by the fear of punishment in a future state, or by the fear of their own disapprobation.[40] Now, in the great majority of cases disapprobation, which is a moral sanction, has nothing whatever to do with self-protection, and the fear of punishment in a future state is by its nature altogether independent of it. Coercion is habitually employed for the purpose of making alterations in existing forms of government and social institutions; all the great political and social changes since the sixteenth century, which Mill and his disciples would be the last persons to say were not beneficial to mankind, have been brought about by force.[41] It would surely be as absurd to say that the French Revolution or the Reformation was brought about freely and not by coercion as to say that Charles I walked freely to the block. Stephen holds that morals, religion, and law are not only forms of coercion for purposes extending beyond self-protection, but also that they are on the whole good.[42]

Mill's principle, he says, would condemn all taxation to which the party taxed did not consent, unless the money produced by it was laid out either upon military or upon police purposes or in the administration of justice, for these purposes only can be described as self-protection.[43] To force an unwilling

[38] *Ibid.*, p. 9. [39] *Ibid.*, pp. 10, 16ff. [40] *Ibid.*, p. 10.
[41] *Ibid.*, p. 21. [42] *Ibid.*, pp. 15n, 17. [43] *Ibid.*, p. 16.

person to contribute to the support of the British Museum is as distinct a violation of Mill's principle of liberty as religious persecution. Mill's error is that he falsely assumes that some acts concern the agent only and some other people. The fact is that by far the most important part of our conduct concerns both ourselves and others, and revolutions are the clearest proof of this.[44]

In his consideration of Mill's views on liberty of thought and discussion, Stephen says that he agrees with Mill that there should be greater freedom of discussion on moral and theological subjects, and that he thinks that Mill's illustrations are valuable.[45] But he finds that Mill has developed a theory to support a general view which is far from the truth. Mill, he says, advances the theory of unlimited freedom of opinion on all subjects. Mill argues that no one can have a rational assurance of the truth of any opinion unless there is absolute freedom to contradict it. This is not true. A man may be a thief, though no one is at liberty to say so from fear of the law of libel; but this does not mean that there is no rational assurance that the man is a thief.[46] Mill argues that to deny freedom of opinion is to assume infallibility. This is not true, says Stephen. An opinion may be silenced without any assertion on the part of the person who silences it that it is false. It may be suppressed because it is true, or because it is doubtful whether it is true or false, or because it is not considered desirable that it should be discussed; in these cases there is obviously no assumption of infallibility in suppressing the opinion.[47] When Henry VIII and Queen Elizabeth silenced to a certain extent both Catholics and Puritans, and sought to confine religious controversy within limits fixed by law, they did not assume themselves to be infallible.[48] What they thought — and it is by no means clear that they were wrong — was that unless religious controversy was kept within bounds there would be a civil war, and they muzzled the disputants accordingly.

[44] *Liberty, Equality, Fraternity,* p. 24. [45] *Ibid.,* pp. 37–38.
[46] *Ibid.,* pp. 40–41. [47] *Ibid.,* p. 41. [48] *Ibid.,* p. 42.

James Fitzjames Stephen

Mill argues that freedom of discussion is necessary in order to develop a true appreciation of the truth of an opinion. Is this true? asks Stephen. The notorious result of freedom of thought and discussion is to produce general skepticism on many subjects in the vast majority of minds.[49] If you want zealous belief, set people to fight. Few things give men such a keen perception of their own opinions and the vileness of others as the fact that they have inflicted and suffered persecution for them.[50] Doctrines come home to people in general, not if and so far as they are free to discuss all their applications, but if and in so far as the doctrines happen to interest them and appear to illustrate and interpret their own experience.[51] Mill says that after doctrines take their place as received opinions their living power declines. This is not true. A doctrine that really goes to the hearts of men never loses its power; millions of men hold with a living perception the doctrine that honesty is the best policy. If, however, it is true, as Mill says, that a doctrine is full of meaning when it is struggling for ascendency and its living power declines when it has become a received opinion, surely that proves that coercion and not liberty is favorable to its appreciation.[52]

Mill, says Stephen, assumes that the people of Europe and America have reached a stage in which discussion takes the place of compulsion. But no such period has been reached anywhere, and there is no prospect of its being reached anywhere within any assignable time.[53] Where, in the most advanced and civilized communities, will you find any class of persons whose views or whose conduct on subjects in which they are interested are regulated even in the main by the results of free discussion?

If we look at the conduct of bodies of men as expressed through their laws and institutions, we shall find that, though compulsion and persuasion go hand in hand, from the most immature and the roughest ages up to the most civilized, the lion's share of the results obtained is due to compulsion.[54]

[49] Ibid., p. 44.   [50] Ibid.   [51] Ibid., p. 89.
[52] Ibid., pp. 89–90.   [53] Ibid., p. 29.   [54] Ibid., p. 30.

Can a single case of a great change be mentioned, in which the passions of men were interested, where the change was not carried by force — that is to say, ultimately by the fear of revolution?[55] Look at small matters which involve more or less of a principle, but do not affect many men's passions, and see how much reasoning has to do with their settlement. Such questions as the admission of Jews to Parliament and the legislation dealing with marriage between brothers- and sisters-in-law drag on and on after the argument has been exhausted, till in the course of time those who take one view or the other grow into a decided majority and settle the matter their own way.

Parliamentary government, Stephen observes, is simply a mild and disguised form of compulsion. We agree to try strength by counting heads instead of breaking heads, but the principle is exactly the same.

It is not the wisest side that wins, but the one which for the time being shows its superior strength (of which no doubt wisdom is one element) by enlisting the largest amount of active sympathy in its support. The minority gives way not because it is convinced that it is wrong but because it is convinced that it is a minority.[56]

Stephen declares that the mass of men cannot be improved by free discussion, for in favorable cases mankind is just beginning to be conscious of its ignorance.[57] Estimate, he says, the proportion of men and women who are selfish, sensual, frivolous, idle, absolutely commonplace, and wrapped up in the smallest of petty routines, and consider how far the freest of free discussion is likely to improve them.[58] The only way by which it is possible to act upon them is by compulsion; the utmost conceivable liberty would not in the least tend to improve them.

In support of his theory of liberty Mill advances the view that freedom is essential to originality and individuality of character. Stephen denies that this is true; he holds that the growth of liberty in the sense of democracy tends to diminish, not to increase, originality and individuality:

[55] *Liberty, Equality, Fraternity,* p. 30.　　[56] *Ibid.,* p. 31.
[57] *Ibid.,* p. 32.　　[58] *Ibid.,* p. 34.

James Fitzjames Stephen

Make all men equal so far as laws can make them equal, and each unit is rendered helplessly feeble in the presence of an overwhelming majority. The existence of such a state of society reduces individuals to impotence, and to tell them to be powerful, original, and independent is to mock them. It is like plucking a bird's feathers in order to put it on a level with beasts, and then telling it to fly.[59]

He insists that habitual exertion is the greatest of all invigorators of character, and restraint and coercion in one form or another is the great stimulus to exertion.[60] A life, he remarks, made up of danger, vicissitude, and exposure is the sort of life which produces originality and resource.

The great defect of Mill's later writings is that he has formed too favorable an estimate of human nature.[61] Mill, says Stephen, is so desirous of encouraging individuality that he makes out a case for eccentricity. Surely eccentricity is far more often a mark of weakness than a mark of strength; originality consists in thinking for yourself, not in thinking differently from others.[62]

In advancing his own view of liberty, Stephen says that liberty is a negative term. Whether liberty is a good or bad thing is as irrational a question as whether fire is a good or a bad thing. It is both good and bad according to time, place, and circumstances; no general rules can be ascertained about it.[63] Liberty is good not as opposed to coercion in general, as Mill believes, but as opposed to coercion in certain cases. These, Stephen believes, are to be ascertained by a Benthamite principle of "expediency"; force is good when the end is good, when the means employed are efficient, and when the cost of application is not excessive.[64] Stephen, unlike Mill, is willing on his principle to apply compulsion to thought. He holds that the legal establishment and disestablishment of various forms of opinion — religious, political, and moral — are perfectly justifiable.[65] He is convinced that there is some truth in religion, and that there is great good in many moral and political opinions, and that all these can be promoted successfully without bringing about more harm than good. He holds that the state is

[59] *Ibid.*, p. 46.   [60] *Ibid.*, p. 47.   [61] *Ibid.*   [62] *Ibid.*, p. 52.
[63] *Ibid.*, p. 53.   [64] *Ibid.*, p. 54.   [65] *Ibid.*, p. 57.

entitled to interfere and promote the belief of the fundamental doctrines of religion not only on the ground of their truth, but also on the ground that virtue is good and that virtue depends on religion: "If, then, virtue is good, it seems to me clear that to promote the belief of the fundamental doctrines of religion is good also, for I am convinced that in Europe at least the two must stand or fall together." [66]

He argues that the difference between paying a single shilling of public money to a single school in which any opinion is taught of which any single taxpayer disapproves and the maintenance of the Spanish Inquisition is a difference of degree.[67] Stephen, however, condemns persecution on the ground that it involves far more evil than good.[68]

He sees some danger in the American arrangement of considering all religions as equally true; the fatal defect, he says, of this arrangement is that it tends to emasculate both church and state.[69] It cuts human life in two; it cuts off religion from active life, and it reduces the state to a matter of police. Moreover, this arrangement is not an act of neutrality but of covert unbelief. He is afraid that if the state is reduced to mere police functions, associations like Mormonism might take its place and push it to one side.[70] Experiments in living, he says, have nothing whatever to do with liberty.

Stephen has little patience with Mill's plea for tolerance, that many promising intellects have been discouraged from thinking boldly and independently for fear of being considered irreligious or immoral. Speculation, says Stephen, on government, morals, and religion is a matter of vital importance, and not mere food for curiosity.[71] To attack opinions on which the framework of society rests is and ought to be dangerous. It should be done sword in hand, and a man who does it has no more right to be surprised at being fiercely resisted than a soldier who attacks a breach.[72] The true ground of moral

[66] *Liberty, Equality, Fraternity*, p. 76.
[67] *Ibid.*, p. 58. [68] *Ibid.*, pp. 81–82, 105, 111.
[69] *Ibid.*, p. 71. [70] *Ibid.*, p. 72.
[71] *Ibid.*, p. 85. [72] *Ibid.*, p. 84.

tolerance lies in this—that most people have no right to any opinions whatever upon these questions, except in so far as they are necessary for the regulation of their own affairs.[73] Stephen believes that men who really study these questions should feel themselves at liberty not merely to dissent from, but to disapprove of, opinions which they think wrong. Toleration, Stephen thinks, is in its proper sphere so long as its object is to mitigate inevitable struggles.[74] The complete suppression of struggle, which would produce indifference and isolation, would be the greatest of all evils. Though Stephen holds that nothing can be said about liberty apart from specific cases, he asserts that if human experience proves anything at all, it proves that if restraints are minimized, if the largest possible measure of liberty is accorded to all human beings, the result will not be equality but inequality.[75]

Stephen criticized Positivism, which was the most definite expression of the "Religion of Humanity," on the ground that it divided life into two spheres, when in fact life was a unity.[76] Positivism, he says, distinguishes between a spiritual and a temporal sphere, the former corresponding to Mill's province of liberty, and the latter corresponding to the province of law. Such a distinction is impossible; life is one and indivisible, at the same time spiritual and temporal.[77] Laws concerning marriage and education, for example, obviously belong to each. The Positivists would have well-instructed persons speak with authority in the spiritual sphere in regard to morals and politics, as scientists now speak with authority in scientific fields.[78] Government would be carried on by an inferior class of persons in obedience to principles laid down by the spiritual experts. Positivism would have a priesthood and a spiritual rule, but rejects the condition that makes this possible: it denies hell. Positivism has nothing whatever to say to the selfish, the worldly, the indifferent; yet without an appeal to such natures a religion is powerless. You can never persuade the mass of men till you can

[73] *Ibid.*, p. 92.   [74] *Ibid.*, p. 180.   [75] *Ibid.*, p. 198.
[76] *Ibid.*, pp. 144ff.   [77] *Ibid.*, pp. 166ff.   [78] *Ibid.*, pp. 122–23.

threaten them; "Here and there a horse may be disposed to go by himself, but you cannot drive a coach without reins and whip." Considered as an organized religion, Positivism is superfluous to those who like it, and impotent against those who like it not; Positivism will never be anything more than a "Ritualistic Social Science Association." [79]

Stephen was as strongly opposed to Mill's theory of equality as to his theory of liberty; he took issue above all with Mill's theory of equality as it was set forth in *Subjection of Women*. Stephen condemned Mill's plea for the equality of women, which was perhaps his most cherished doctrine, as the "most ignoble and mischievous of all the popular feelings of the age." [80] The general argument that Mill brought to bear in support of his case for equality of women, that justice requires that all people should live in society as equals, was rejected by Stephen. He says that from the utilitarian point of view equality has no connection with justice except in the narrow sense of judicial impartiality; waiving this point of view, he denies that equality is expedient in the most important relations of social life.[81] As applied to the sexes, he declares, it is unsound, for it is based on a notorious error; woman is not man's equal, in every test of strength she is inferior. Men have greater muscular and nervous force, greater intellectual force, and greater vigor of character.[82] If in marriage the two parties are treated as equals, marriage, like other partnerships, will be dissolved at pleasure; if women are treated as equals, they will become slaves of their husbands.[83] Women are not able to remarry as easily as men, for they lose the qualities that make them attractive earlier than men. Again, marriage itself creates inequality; a woman, as a result of marriage, generally renounces any means of earning her living, while the man's occupation is little affected by marriage. The law ought to recognize such inequalities if women are to be treated justly. Stephen believes that if marriage is to be a permanent institution, one party must be

[79] *Liberty, Equality, Fraternity*, p. 133.   [80] *Ibid.*, p. 220.
[81] *Ibid.*, pp. 224ff., 254.   [82] *Ibid.*, p. 228.   [83] *Ibid.*, p. 231.

stronger; husbands, he says, must govern, for no one proposes that the wife should.[84]

In support of his plea for the equality of women, Mill argues that history shows human progress to have been a progress from a "law of force" to a condition wherein obedience and command become exceptional. Stephen insists that this implies a theory of progress for which there is no validity. Progress, he says, has been mixed, partly good and partly bad; in many ways we have progressed from strength to weakness:

I do not myself see that our mechanical inventions have increased the general vigour of men's characters, though they have, no doubt, increased enormously our control over nature. The greater part of our humanity appears to me to be a mere increase of nervous sensibility in which I feel no satisfaction at all.[85]

Mill's statement that the "law of force" is being abandoned more and more implies that today force is less important in human affairs. This is untrue. Lincoln and Moltke commanded a force which would have crushed Charlemagne and his paladins like so many eggshells.[86] All that is proved by the fact that status, to use Sir Henry Maine's expression, tends to be replaced by contract is that force changes in form.[87] The power of a French minister of the interior over an immense multitude of subordinates is as real and quite as formidable as the power of a feudal lord over his vassals ever was. Society rests ultimately upon force in these days, just as much as it did in the wildest and most stormy periods of history. The difference is that it reigns in a more quiet manner: "The force which goes to govern the Scotland of these days is to the force employed for the same purpose in the fourteenth century what the force of a line-of-battle ship is to the force of an individual prize fighter."[88] To say that the law of force is abandoned because force is regular, unopposed, and beneficially exercised is to say that day and night are now such well-established institutions that the sun and moon are mere superfluities.[89]

[84] *Ibid.*, pp. 232ff.   [85] *Ibid.*, p. 237.   [86] *Ibid.*, pp. 32, 112.
[87] *Ibid.*, p. 243.   [88] *Ibid.*, p. 244.   [89] *Ibid.*, p. 248.

Another theory, Stephen affirms, involved in Mill's position is that the abandonment of the "law of force" is equivalent to the growth of equality. Surely the opposite is true. Never have inequalities of wealth, of talent, of education, of sentiment, and of religious belief been so great as at this present moment. Today we have inequality in its harshest form; never has it been so great.[90] It is doubtful if in any other age the power of particular persons over their neighbors has been so well defined and so easily and safely exerted as at present. If in old times a slave was inattentive and his master abused him, he damaged his own property. If a modern servant misconducts himself, he can be turned out of the house at once and another hired as easily as you would call a cab. Such punishments are inflicted without appeal, without reflection, without the smallest disturbance of the smooth waters of ordinary life.

In setting out his more positive view on equality, Stephen maintains that it has nothing to do with democracy. Establish universal suffrage, he says, and you are still as far as ever from equality.[91] The result of cutting up political power into little bits is simply that the man who can sweep the greatest number of them into one heap will govern the rest. The strongest man in some form or other will always rule; in a pure democracy the ruling men will be the wire-pullers and their friends. Stephen concludes that equality, like liberty, is a big name for a small thing; if equality is not, like liberty, a word of negation, it is at best a word of relation.[92] What little can be said for equality, he remarks, is that as a fact human beings are not equal, but fundamentally unequal.[93] To try to make them equal by altering social arrangements is like trying to make the cards of equal value by shuffling the pack. In their dealings with each other men ought to recognize real inequalities where they exist as much as substantial equality where it exists.[94] He admits that equality has been successful in America, which, he thinks, is due to the fact that a large number of people who were sub-

[90] *Liberty, Equality, Fraternity*, pp. 249ff.   [91] *Ibid.*, p. 256.
[92] *Ibid.*, p. 272.   [93] *Ibid.*, p. 271.   [94] *Ibid.*

stantially equal recognized that fact and did not set up unfounded distinctions.

Stephen was not without an ideal solution for the problem of equality, one which, he said, was the only way of obtaining the greatest amount of equality. His method was to establish a system of distinctions, a social hierarchy corresponding as nearly as possible to the real distinctions between men, and make the members of each class equal among themselves.[95] Something not unlike this, he says, has been done by the caste system in India; this society in some ways is elastic and possessed of a considerable power of assimilating new ideas, and is stable and conservative to a degree utterly unknown and hardly imaginable in Europe. Though this is an ideal that cannot be attained, he adds, the maintenance of broad and well-marked distinctions is a step toward it. The alternative to recognizing distinctions among men is inequality in its harshest form.

Stephen held that the doctrine of fraternity was entitled to no more respect than the doctrines of liberty and equality. He insisted that Mill's attempt to sublimate self-love and affection for one's friends into a general love of the human race was impossible. He declared he could not love human creatures indiscriminately, the bad as well as the good.[96] Moreover, the human race, he says, is so big, so various, so little known, that no one can love it; it is impossible to love a shadowy abstraction.[97] Stephen believes that fraternity, mere love for the human race, is not fitted to be a religion for still other reasons. Fraternity, he says, does not demand self-sacrifice and does not make it a duty to be virtuous.[98]

Though Stephen thinks that the utilitarian morality, outlined by Mill in *Utilitarianism*, is satisfactory as far as it goes, it does not go far enough. Stephen is convinced that it must be supplemented by religion if morality is not to be left to individual taste. Stephen argues for a belief in Providence and in a future state in order that morality should be a law:[99]

[95] *Ibid.*, pp. 251–53.   [96] *Ibid.*, p. 304.   [97] *Ibid.*, p. 306.
[98] *Ibid.*, pp. 293ff., 322.   [99] *Ibid.*, pp. 320ff.

Utilitarianism appears to me to rest on its own foundations. It is a consequence from the ultimate fact that men have powers and wishes. Add a future state, and you give happiness a special meaning, and establish a scale among different kinds of happiness. Add a belief in God, and virtue ceases to be a mere fact, and becomes the law of a society.[1]

In Stephen's view it is necessary to make morality a law in order to affect the conduct of selfish men and to control the brutes.[2]

If Stephen believed that the democratic ideals of liberty, equality, fraternity did not warrant the blind admiration which was lavished on them, neither did he think that democratic government was deserving of the enthusiasm with which it was received. He realized, he said, that the whole stream of human affairs was settling irresistibly in the direction of democracy, but he did not see "why as we go with the stream we need sing Hallelujah to the river god."

He admits that he has no substitute for universal suffrage; and he believes that taxation must be subject to popular consent. Yet he is convinced that democracy does not secure the rule of the good and the wise over the bad and the foolish.[3] He thinks, moreover, that democracy makes for inefficient administration. The very essentials of good government, he argues, are some degree of permanence, some amount of discretionary authority, and continuity; under the present system of universal suffrage these are almost entirely wanting.[4] The real difficulty that causes so much public business that ought to be done, such as law reform, to be neglected, lies in the constitution of Parliament; it lies in the system of party government, which makes every man who is out of office pick holes in the work of every man who is in office.[5] And every man who is in office considers not what is the best thing to be done, but what is most likely to carry in spite of opposition. This condition of things is aggravated by endless discussion, by continual explanation, and by

---

[1] *Liberty, Equality, Fraternity*, pp. 321–22.   [2] *Ibid.*, pp. 132, 320.
[3] *Ibid.*, p. 259.   [4] *Ibid.*, pp. 262–63.   [5] *Ibid.*, p. 265.

James Fitzjames Stephen

constant restatement of every matter on which government is to act, all of which hamper to the last degree the process of governing.[6] Again, party government prevents men from being chosen members of Parliament on the score of ability. It involves great waste of talent; half the ablest men in the country spend the greater part of their lives fighting the other half.[7] Parliament, moreover, is ill fitted to elaborate details of legislation, and worse fitted to keep close and stringent control over problems of administration.[8] It does not possess special knowledge; and its rules of parliamentary procedure, together with the uncertainty of office, make systematic legislation practically impossible.[9]

The present constitution of the Cabinet and the public offices, he continues, is about as ill conceived an arrangement for the real dispatch of public business as could be contrived.[10] Each department is a little state with its own king for the time being, and the control of the whole over the parts is loose and vague to the highest possible degree. The Colonial Office, the War Office, the Admiralty, and the India Office, have very little to gain and everything to lose by uncertainty of tenure and continual accountability to every voter in England through his representative. The Home Office is burdened by a heterogeneous, complex structure which lacks unity and central control. If anyone was to attempt to say what the internal government of England is, he would be smothered under a chaos of acts, charters, commissioners, boards, benches, courts, and vestries of all sorts and conditions. All the defects that reside in such a jungle of institutions are supposed to be atoned for by "le self-government," which not infrequently means the right to misgovern your neighbors without being accountable for it to anyone wiser than yourself.

If we examine the Cabinet, we find that there is no unity,[11]

[6] *Ibid.*, p. 263.
[7] "Parliamentary Government," *Contemporary Review*, 23:6 (December, 1873).
[8] *Ibid.*, p. 5.   [9] *Ibid.*, pp. 7ff.
[10] *Liberty, Equality, Fraternity*, p. 266.
[11] "Parliamentary Government," *Contemporary Review*, 23:16 (December, 1873).

no common center, no clear, well-defined connection between the departments. A greater evil still is that a Parliamentary head may treat any member of his department as a mere clerk.[12] And it is no small defect that Parliamentary heads are appointed upon party considerations rather than upon grounds of special fitness. Finally, the great evil of the administrative system in regard to the management of particular affairs is the way in which special knowledge is divorced from experience, and authority from responsibility.[13] Stephen objects to the extent and nature of the principle of Cabinet responsibility.[14] It makes, he says, for a weak executive; every act and thought of the Cabinet is dependent on the shifting currents of public and Parliamentary opinion. "As matters now stand, a disaster on the west coast of Africa would very probably alter the complexion of popular education in this country, by changing the Ministry, which appears to me about as rational as changing your lawyer because you discharge your cook." [15] A king, he deplores, has been reduced to a cipher.[16]

As a remedy for these shortcomings, he would like to restore a considerable degree of power to the king, but regrets that this is impossible.[17] He would, therefore, mitigate conditions: [18] first, by arranging that nonparty questions should be handled by an independent department, subject only to the general control of Parliament; second, by reforming the Civil Service. The latter would be accomplished by appointing the ablest men in the country as permanent heads of departments, by conferring honor and dignity upon the positions, and raising salaries. Permanent heads, says Stephen, ought not to be clerks to Cabinet ministers, but councilors. Their opinion might be overruled if necessary, but should be recorded so that Parliament and the public might know how decisions were taken. Lastly, he would introduce more change in the upper ranks of the Civil Service; this would increase competence through enlarged experience and make the officials more receptive to new ideas.

[12] *Ibid.*   [13] *Ibid.*, p. 19.   [14] *Ibid.*, p. 14.   [15] *Ibid.*, p. 179.
[16] *Ibid.*, pp. 14–16.   [17] *Ibid.*, p. 179.   [18] *Ibid.*, pp. 179ff.

James Fitzjames Stephen

It cannot be denied that Stephen's criticism of Mill was as powerful as it was searching. In spite of his ponderous style, he was never at a loss for a telling epigram; and if his argument at times developed into an exercise in logic, it seldom failed to reach the heart of the matter. His criticism of Mill's principle of liberty, that there should be no interference with the actions of an individual except for the sole end of self-protection, was a demonstration that a state which limited its activity to the duties of a policeman was inadequate. Indeed, he showed that the "let alone" state for which Mill stood in his *Essay on Liberty* must be unjust, for it permitted some persons, in virtue of their favorable economic positions, to exercise a tyrannical power over others. Though Stephen greatly overemphasized the part played by coercion in human affairs, he showed that Mill's theory of liberty did not take sufficient account of the value of restraints. There is a refreshing realism in Stephen's argument that the state cannot, and should not, avoid taking a position on important moral and religious issues. His criticism of Mill's theory of liberty from beginning to end brought out that the individual is a member of society and that he is interested in the acts, ideas, and character of his fellows, and that his actions affect others directly or indirectly; in short, he showed that Mill's fallacy lay in the distinction he drew between self-regarding acts and acts which regard others.

Stephen not only showed that Mill's principle of liberty could not be maintained; he also showed that Mill's theory of absolute freedom of thought and discussion was untenable. He proved that Mill was wrong in holding that a denial of freedom of thought necessarily assumed infallibility, and he convinced us that freedom of discussion was not necessarily essential to a live appreciation of opinions. Few have more successfully argued the view that discussion plays a small part in bringing about a change of mind among men. Stephen did well to insist that discussion in the modern world, in Europe and America, has not supplanted coercion to the extent that Mill seemed to think. By emphasizing the many areas in which coercion operates, he promoted the interests of freedom; he indicated the great distance that freedom still has to travel before it can come into its own. Yet he did not show that Mill was essentially mistaken in holding that physical force is less important in human affairs in Europe and America than formerly, that it operates less arbitrarily and less frequently in man's everyday life than in earlier times; and he did not show that Mill was wrong in holding that there had been a growth of equality. His criticism of Mill's argument for absolute freedom of thought and discussion showed not least that Mill assumed men to be more rational than they actually are.

If Stephen misunderstood Mill's plea for equality, he nevertheless showed that inequalities as well as equalities between the sexes must be recognized in marriage. And if he did not dissuade us from believing that men moved by a social feeling can and do act unselfishly, in fact, even sacrifice their lives, as such examples as the American Civil War and the Russian Revolution of 1917 obviously show, he nevertheless exploded the attempt of Mill and the Positivists to exalt a feeling for humanity into a religion.

The weakness of Stephen's criticism of Mill was that he did not see any great value in freedom. Liberty for him was merely a word of negation; he was incapable of appreciating freedom either as a value in itself or as an essential condition of development. He thought of liberty solely in terms of the classical definition — absence of restraint. The nominalism of his utilitarian philosophy, which asserted that only the particular, concrete thing is real, prevented him from reaching an appreciation of freedom as a thing of worth in itself and of seeing its significance in general. His insistence that nothing can be said of liberty apart from an application of the Benthamite formula — of applying the questions, is the end good? are the means efficient? is the cost of the means greater than the end? — is certainly useful up to a point. But it underestimates the significance of the part played by values in the judgment of the three questions in the Benthamite formula.

To say as Stephen does that the purpose of toleration is to mitigate an inevitable conflict contains no little truth, but it misses the main point of Mill's plea for freedom of thought and discussion. Stephen was not really convinced that freedom of thought was indispensable to the process of discovering truth. Part of the explanation of Stephen's want of appreciation of freedom of thought lies in his utilitarianism; as Leslie Stephen has said, utilitarianism lowers the ground of toleration because it regards exclusively the coercive elements of law. Utilitarianism emphasizes the coercive elements because, as we have seen, its view of law is based on an atomistic conception of society. From another angle the atomistic conception of society lowers the ground of toleration: holding that men are so many units in an aggregate, it tends to maximize their identity and to minimize their difference; it lowers respect for personality. If Mill escaped from his Benthamite inheritance and advocated the manifold development of human personality to such a point that he stood for eccentricity, Stephen committed the opposite error; he had little regard for individuality except in the puritan sense of a strong and vigorous character. He saw little potentiality for development in the mass of men.

Stephen's view of equality was confined to a legal, utilitarian interpretation of it; equality had no meaning for him apart from judicial impartiality. He rejected Mill's claim that justice requires all men to live in society as equals, for he believed that men were fundamentally unequal. Though he held that equalities should be recognized where they existed, he was satisfied that for all practical purposes the state of his day recognized most of the necessary equalities. That he stood for economic individualism, though he was aware that it gave the strong great power over the weak, showed how far he was from believing in the democratic doctrine of equality.

He did not understand this doctrine as it is understood by a democrat, that men are equal in respect of the characteristics they have in common, that men are equal as regards their essential humanity. Whether a man is saint or criminal, he is part of an ultimate oneness, from whence it may be said the real meaning of equality derives.[19] It follows from this that it is the duty of the state to secure equality of opportunity for men on the basis of their common needs. Stephen did not see that the state must abolish not only the privilege of birth, and religious and civil privilege, but also economic privilege. It did not occur to him that unless accidental and artificial differences were broken down between men, there could be no real civilization, let alone genuine equality before the law.

Stephen's suggestion that a caste system would attain the greatest amount of equality is, from the point of view of a democrat, one that would for the most part attain the very reverse of equality. Such a system would secure the full institutional recognition of individual distinctions, of individual differences, not of the things men have in common. Such a system would arrange men according to a hierarchy of classes, placing them on different levels; it would embody equality in the sense of recognizing differences equally, while it would destroy equality in the far more basic sense of recognizing what men have in common. Such a system would be the very opposite of that aimed at by a democrat. In criticizing the doctrine of equality Stephen made the mistake, which is so often made by the conservative, of thinking that the doctrine aims at making individuals equal in all respects. The doctrine really aims at maximizing the possibilities of individual development by providing equal opportunity for all. It stands for the maintenance of those conditions — such as adequate housing, adequate education, and opportunity for work — that are essential to a decent existence; it insists that these be provided for the whole community. The doctrine aims not at an identical, but at a common environment, in the sense of conditions equally good in quality, so that individuality will have a chance of flowering among the mass of men.

[19] Leonard T. Hobhouse, *Liberalism* (London, 1911), p. 121.

James Fitzjames Stephen

It is clear that Stephen's chief criticism of the philosophy of liberty, equality, fraternity, that it threatened to loosen the social bonds, can hardly be maintained. Though he pointed out the shortcomings of Mill's theory of liberty, he did not show that it threatened dissolution. If he showed that Mill had somewhat overstated his argument for equality of women, he did not discredit Mill's plea for giving women greater equality, let alone show that it would impair the social fabric. And he did not convince us that Mill's utilitarian ethics would render society powerless against evildoers.

The chief argument that Stephen urged against the philosophy of liberty, equality, fraternity was that force is the essence of life. That Stephen was able to claim so much for force was due to a confusion in the use of terms; he did not distinguish between force in the sense of physical power and force in senses other than this. If his argument is to merit consideration it must be construed in the sense of physical power; otherwise it is so vague and general that it means next to nothing. Clearly physical force plays a minor not a major part in man's life. What is vastly more important, for example, is toil.[20] What is vastly more important than force in the development and the expansion of states is intelligence, enterprise, character, cooperation, and a common purpose. Imperialism in modern times has developed, not so much because Western states have had great military force at their disposal, as because they have had vast industrial systems that needed to sell their surplus products — in a word, because of the economic activity of their citizens. The defeat of the Spanish Armada did not prevent the gradual permeation of Mexico and South America by Spanish civilization. Modern wars, like the Hundred Years' War or the World War of this century, destroy but do nothing to create.

Most men obey the law not because of the threat of physical penalty, as Stephen seemed to think, but because of habit and because they recognize the necessity of obeying rules if men are

[20] I am indebted to Robert M. MacIver's *Modern State* (Oxford, 1926), pp. 221ff. in the argument that follows.

to reap the benefits of organized life. Force by itself holds nothing together; it is only an instrument for helping to hold things together. Since it is a delicate as well as a crude instrument, it must be used with great caution if it is not to defeat its own purpose. Men praise the sword only because it gives them victory over the sword. Force breaks habit and the order of life; if suffered to prevail it would destroy civilization. Stephen tended to identify force with other aspects of human nature and of human activity not only because he stretched that term to mean power in the broadest sense, but also because he failed to distinguish clearly in his use of the term between cause and effect. It may be noted that there is no reason for accepting Stephen's proposition that force changes in form only, not in amount; as his own example of Lincoln and Charlemagne shows, modern man, through science, has far greater physical force at his disposal than man in earlier times.

Stephen's thesis of force, however, rests at bottom on a distorted view of human nature; this view of mankind, which he drew from Hobbes, Bentham, puritanism, and his experience in India, underestimates man's gregarious nature, his social sympathies, and countless instincts which bind him to his fellows. Stephen, as a result of his utilitarianism, with its assumption of self-interest and its assumption of society as atomistic, overemphasized the selfish side of man and the motive of fear. As a result of his puritanism, which Frederick Harrison called "Calvinism minus Christianity," he conceived of mankind in harsher terms than the facts will bear out. Given Stephen's view of human nature, it was more important for him to control men than to promote the expression of their individuality. Command and obedience, in his view, must be the laws of life for the mass of men, not self-direction and individual responsibility.

Stephen's criticism of democracy, that it does not secure the rule of the good and the wise over the bad and the foolish, may be answered by saying that the bad and foolish would never have come to power if the good and the wise had been discovered.[21] His criticism of democracy as a method of government involves a mistaken view of the primary purpose of the franchise and the party system. The main purpose of the franchise is not to enable us to communicate expert judgment, as most administrators would have us believe. Rather is it to enable us to communicate needs and wants, which, if the franchise did not exist, would not be so easily communicated and, eventually, so well satisfied. Stephen sees the party system as an obstruction to government rather than as an indispensable factor making for responsibility, for criticism, for the clarification of issues, for the education of the citizen body, and as a means of representation.

Stephen hardly appreciates the principle of Cabinet responsibility. He maintains that Parliament should decide issues of policy; but his plea for a stronger Cabinet and his desire to restore power to the king imply autocratic control. In a word, Stephen pre-eminently embodies the traits that usually typify the Indian administrator of the nineteenth century. No better proof of this can be found than his letters to the *Times* on the Home Rule dispute of 1886. He recommended for Ireland the methods of rule employed in India. As is so often the case with those who have wielded power where there has been no electorate to hold them accountable, Stephen mistook a movement of freedom for a movement of disruption. The Irish demands for Home Rule and land legislation, he says, are simply corollaries from the general principles of Jacobinism and socialism, whose acceptance threatens destruction of the empire.[22] It is not strange, as Frederick Harrison remarked, that the only character in the Bible whom Indian administrators seem to be acquainted with is Pontius Pilate.[23] It may be noted that Stephen's Indian experience gave him insight into the needs of the English Civil Service; some of his suggestions have been carried out since he wrote, and some have still to be realized.

[21] For a fuller treatment of ability and power, see pages 51 and 90–91 above.

[22] Leslie Stephen, *Life of Sir James Fitzjames Stephen*, pp. 461ff.

[23] See Stephen's defense of Pontius Pilate in *Liberty, Equality, Fraternity*, pp. 96–104.

James Fitzjames Stephen

Few books have been more the product of a temperament than *Liberty, Equality, Fraternity*. Stephen's deep interest in force is the manifestation of a powerful character that found enjoyment in struggle; his combativeness, it would seem, found an outlet in theories of power. With a natural admiration for strength, the liberal philosophy of Mill appeared to him as an expression of weakness. Stephen's feeling for stability and order were violated by views of "liberal emancipation." That a new age was developing which he could not understand led him to appeal to an untheological Calvinism; he would prevent undesirable change by making virtue a law. It is not unsignificant that he spoke of his *History of Criminal Law* as an expression of the second table of the Ten Commandments.[24]

[24] Leslie Stephen, *Life of Sir James Fitzjames Stephen*, p. 427.

HENRY MAINE

I

MAINE was probably the most searching critic of democratic optimism in the Victorian era. Stephen, it will be remembered, was the critic of the advanced school of liberal thought of the nineteenth century, the school of John Stuart Mill. It was given to Maine to criticize not a philosophy of democracy, but democratic beliefs; where Stephen attacked the philosophy of "liberal emancipation," Maine took issue with the claim that democracy was the harbinger of progress. With the liberal movement gaining power in the third quarter of the nineteenth century, with the bright outlook created by the passing of the Reform Bill of 1867 and the success of Gladstone's first ministry, and with all the hopes that were bred of Victorian prosperity, there developed strong enthusiasm for democracy. Some of the more ardent exponents, like Carpenter, were coming to believe that democracy promised all kinds of blessings to mankind. Maine conceived it his task to show that such enthusiasm was a delusion. As Stephen had attacked a philosophy that saw in the ideals of liberty, equality, fraternity the promise of a new society, Maine attacked an attitude that saw in democracy the coming of a new world.

Maine was even more of a technical critic than Stephen. Unlike Stephen, there was very little of the moral fire of the puritan in him; not that he never spoke out with righteous indignation, only that he seldom did so, and when he did, he spoke not from the judgment seat but from the study. Unlike

Henry Maine

Stephen, he hardly ever touched upon the ethical aspect of his problem. If Maine was less concerned than Stephen with exposing the logical shortcomings of his opponents, he was more concerned with making a frontal attack upon them with the ammunition of the specialist. He measured the claims of the optimistic democrats in a perspective of history. He criticized them by means of a detailed analysis of the institutional arrangements of democracy. He judged them in terms of a view of man based upon anthropological and historical findings. He pitted against them a conservative philosophy that marshaled weapons from the sciences of political economy and biology.

There can be no doubt that Maine discredited the excessive optimism of his opponents; he showed that Benthamite democracy had placed its hopes too high; he demonstrated that eighteenth-century rationalism had assumed too much. But he did not destroy the philosophy of which the extravagant democratic beliefs were the expression, any more than Stephen destroyed the democratic essentials for which Mill stood. Maine's criticism, which was set forth in his *Popular Government* in 1885, was eagerly welcomed by the *Quarterly Review,* and solid opinion at Oxford considered it the last word on democracy. But Maine, like Stephen, addressed only a small audience and, like Stephen, exercised little influence.

Maine, however, was the intellectual leader of the conservatives, who had become alarmed, especially after the passing of the franchise act of 1884, at the advancing flood of Liberal Gladstonian democracy.[1] Realizing, as Stephen had done, that the political tide had turned in favor of democracy, Maine was on the defensive. As one who had studied the past, and had observed that change was rare and that most men were creatures of custom and habit, he had nothing but distrust for democratic change. Maine was an expert who saw in the advance of the common man a threat to all science and progress. Like

[1] Cf. Ernest Barker, *Political Thought in England, 1848 to 1914* (rev. ed., London, 1928), pp. 127, 167–70.

Henry Maine

Stephen, he held the aristocratic view that democracy is opposed to the rightful rule of ability and intelligence, which is the exclusive possession of the few. Maine reflected the new alignment that had for many years been forming between the landed aristocracy and the middle class. He did not advocate an alliance between the aristocrats and the captains of industry, as Carlyle had done. Nor did he advise the aristocracy and the plutocracy to unite against the rule of a lower intelligence, as Bagehot did; nor did he really combine the theory of aristocracy with that of middle-class rule. In his thought are to be found the claims of an aristocracy that had lost its economic power but still retained great social power, and the claims of a middle class that had come of age. No longer able to justify the aristocracy on the grounds of a fundamental social function, Maine sought in history a theory of progress and in biology a theory of heredity to support the rule of the few. But he was less anxious to persuade men to believe in aristocracy, which he seemed to realize had little hope of returning in anything like its original form, than to defend private property as organized under the system of economic competition.

Perhaps in the final analysis Maine represents the best attempt in the nineteenth century to justify conservatism to a new age. Following the rationalist movement of his era, he broke with the conservative tradition of Burke, Coleridge, and Stephen, and rejected religion either as a basis upon which to construct a conservative philosophy, or as a factor essential to its building. Believing in the two dominant intellectual movements of his age, the historical and the scientific, he turned to both for the building of his politics; history provided him with fundamental ideas, and science with sanctions, for a conservative creed. That up to the present Maine is not only the first but also the last "scientific conservative" in English political thought is perhaps significant. However that may be, Maine stands in England, like Taine in France, as something of an innovator who strove to wed science to a conservative philosophy.

Henry Maine

II

Few thinkers have come under more unusual and diverse influences in the molding of their political ideas than Maine. Unlike Stephen, he was indebted neither to his parents nor to his public school. What was important for Maine's political thought during his early life was that he went to Cambridge and studied law, not so much because he had an exceptionally brilliant career there and was appointed Regius Professor of Civil Law at the age of twenty-five, but because he approached the study of law under the guidance of the German school of historical jurisprudence which had formed itself around Eichhorn and Savigny. Before discussing his debt to the German writers, it might be well to note one or two other things about his life during this period.

In politics, Maine, so far from being with the Conservatives, was distinctly with the Liberals. He denounced Disraeli, who had placed himself at the head of the great Conservative majority of 1847, as one who believed in protection "with the same intensity of faith which animated General Bonaparte to profess Islam."[2] In 1849 he warned French conservatives that they would not gain as much as they would lose if the young democracy was destroyed.[3] Though called to the bar in 1850, Maine on account of ill-health never attempted the practice of law. While keeping up his legal studies he turned to journalism, writing many of the leaders for the *Saturday Review*.

To return to the German historical school, we may say that it seems to have been the leading influence in shaping Maine's political ideas. It was the source of inspiration for his philosophy of history, and thus for his conservatism.[4] The distinctive characteristic of the German school was its so-called historical method: the application of history or, as Sir Frederick Pollock has put it, the application of the doctrine of evo-

[2] M. E. Grant Duff, *Sir Henry Maine: A Brief Memoir of His Life* (New York, 1892), p. 11.
[3] *Ibid.*, p. 12.
[4] Paul Vinogradoff, *The Teaching of Sir Henry Maine* (London, 1904), pp. 9–10.

lution to human institutions. Needless to say, it was important that Maine should have learned from the German school to apply the doctrine of evolution to human institutions; but it was equally if not more important for his politics that he accepted the philosophy that lay behind it.

The German historical school, like the French and English historical schools of the same period, represented a reaction against the French Revolution. It was, as Ernest Barker says, opposed to revolutionary rationalism as embodied in the French Republic and in Napoleon's empire.[5] It had nothing but derision for the revolutionary assertion of natural rights and the revolutionary belief in an ideal system of society that was everywhere and always valid. It placed its faith, on the other hand, in history; and history revealed to Eichhorn and Savigny that law and institutions are the product of all the factors that influence a nation, that they show a continuous growth, and are formed by the slow working of custom, not by the arbitrary will of the legislator.[6] This is also one of the fundamental positions of Maine's *Ancient Law*. It may be said, then, that the German historical school showed Maine above all that law and institutions grow and are not made, and that human nature is subject to little change. This was, indeed, to direct him along the conservative path, for such a view enjoins the acceptance of things as they are and insists that change by human action, by legislation, is all but futile.

Ancient Law, which appeared in 1861, created a prodigious stir, exercising in its own field an influence comparable to that of Darwin's *Origin of Species* in the realm of science. It was followed by *Village Communities* (1871), *Early History of Institutions* (1875), and *Dissertations on Early Law and Custom* (1883).[7] In *Village Communities* he shows his deep attach-

[5] Ernest Barker, *Political Thought in England, 1848 to 1914*, p. 162.

[6] George P. Gooch, *History and Historians in the Nineteenth Century* (3d ed., London, 1920), pp. 45, 50, 51.

[7] For an excellent brief summary and criticism of the leading ideas in Maine's legal works, see K. B. Smellie, "Sir Henry Maine," *Economica*, 8:64–94 (March, 1928).

ment to private property; he says that the substitution of several property for collective ownership was the most powerful influence making for civilization, and that no one who values civilization is at liberty to attack several property.[8] These later works, however, made no fundamental addition to the political and legal philosophy set forth in *Ancient Law*.

In order to see a little more clearly the conservative direction in which Maine's mind was moving in *Ancient Law*, it would be well to consider his remarks on Rousseau. The law of nature, he says, which in the hands of the Romans had been the instrument of a most creative development in civilization, had with Rousseau helped most powerfully to bring about the grosser disappointments of which the first French Revolution was fertile.[9] It gave birth, he continues, or intense stimulus, to the vices of mental habit that were all but universal at that time — disdain of positive law, impatience of experience, and the preference of *a priori* to all other reasoning. With minds of smaller observation, he says, its tendency was to become distinctly anarchical. Whether or not this outburst against Rousseau was inspired by the German historical school, it nevertheless was an outburst that could hardly have been written by a democrat.

Maine, says Vinogradoff, not only stood under the influence of the German school of the preceding generation, but also under the sign of his own time with its craving for a scientific treatment of the problems of social life. Science, that is to say, exact knowledge based on the strict observation of fact and aiming at the formulation of general laws, had become a passion with Maine. So convinced was he of its possibilities that he claimed for history scientific characteristics such as even a physicist would hesitate to put forward today for his science. In an impressive address delivered at the University of Calcutta, he said that if there be truth in history, it must be scientific truth. He continued:

[8] *Village Communities in the East and the West* (3d ed., New York, 1876), p. 230.
[9] *Ancient Law* (1st American ed., New York, 1870), pp. 73–79, 91.

Henry Maine

There can be no essential difference between the truths of the Astronomer, of the Physiologist, and of the Historian. The great principle which underlies all our knowledge of the Physical world, that Nature is ever consistent with herself, must also be true of human nature and human society which is made up of human nature . . . if indeed history be true, it must teach that which every other science teaches, continuous sequence, inflexible order, and eternal law.[10]

What was the effect of science on Maine's political ideas? His conception of science partly explains his antipathy to Rousseau; he held that many of Rousseau's ideas could not be supported by historical fact and were purely *a priori*. Vinogradoff said that Maine conceived his whole literary career as a constant struggle against pure abstractions and *a priori* assumptions. His antipathy to Rousseau partly explains his antipathy to democracy, for he believed that Rousseau was the chief source of democratic thought. Maine's belief in scientific method partly explains why he gave so much attention to political institutions and machinery, and why he failed adequately to consider their motivating ideas. The science of political economy, standing as it did for laissez faire, lent support to Maine's individualism. And Darwin's idea of "the survival of the fittest" provided him with a kind of crowning scientific sanction for his belief in acquisitive economics. Whether the source was Darwin or Lamarck, science also gave him, in the idea of inherited characteristics, an argument for aristocracy.

If the influence of historical research upon Maine is not of the same importance as that of the German historical school or of science, nonetheless it must be taken into consideration. Dicey in his discussion of Maine has indicated the effect that historical research seems to have had upon Maine. Historical research, Dicey says, just because it proves that forms of government are the necessary outcome of complicated social conditions, leads to the conclusion that the wisest legislation can do far less than both philanthropic philosophers and the ordinary public suppose, and that it seems to be a waste of energy to trouble

[10] *Village Communities*, pp. 265–66.

oneself greatly about the amendment of law.[11] Historical research, continues Dicey, brings into prominence, and exaggerates the dissimilarities between, different classes and different races of mankind, and thus tends to quench the confident enthusiasm necessary for carrying out even the most well-approved and most beneficial among democratic innovations.

An influence no less potent upon Maine than historical research was what Ernest Barker has called the professional instinct of the lawyer, though we cannot go as far as Barker and claim that it was a leading influence.[12] If the political theorist, as Barker says, deals with the ideas that lie behind rules and the ideals that lie behind order, the lawyer deals with their external manifestation, with the instruments of their practical embodiment, with the rules that direct actions in an ordered community.[13] Thus the lawyer is engaged in what might be called the search for objective mind; he is preoccupied with concrete detail, with form, with methods of regulation and execution, with all those objective factors that enter into the making and applying of the rules that order society. Perhaps the main effect of his intellectual activity is to engender an outlook that overvalues form and mechanism to the detriment of spirit. It is not therefore astonishing that much of Maine's criticism of democracy dealt with its form and machinery.

That no force was more powerful in molding Maine's political beliefs than the German historical school is undeniable, but it does not explain why Maine's legal writings were superior to his political work, *Popular Government*. If we are to know why he did such violence in *Popular Government* to a method of history and a high standard of criticism that had been productive of valuable results throughout his previous work, we must search elsewhere. So must we search elsewhere if we are to explain why by 1869 Maine had changed from a liberal to a conservative in politics.

[11] Albert V. Dicey, *Lectures on the Relation between Law and Public Opinion in England in the Nineteenth Century* (1st ed., London, 1905), pp. 457–59.
[12] Ernest Barker, *Political Thought in England, 1848 to 1914,* p. 168.
[13] *Ibid.,* pp. 15–16.

Henry Maine

In 1861 Maine went to India to fill the post of legal member of the Council. As an Indian legislator and administrator, Maine showed none of the characteristics of an autocrat nor of one who favors government by an aristocracy. Moreover, beyond the shadow of a doubt, Maine's speeches and minutes are notable for their lack of partisanship with any political party or any particular form of government. During his stay in India there does not appear to be any perceptible sign that his political views underwent change. But it seems that new habits and modes of thinking, which were to constitute a different outlook, were nevertheless woven into the fabric of his experience. The different point of view which he seems to have unconsciously acquired in India was not manifest until he again encountered the English environment.

In India Maine had become accustomed, in fulfilling his own duties, to the exercise of power. He had seen the results of bureaucratic government manipulated by a small group, responsible not to the people over whom it governed, but to an external sovereign. To him it had seemed effective and efficient. The majority of the inhabitants over whom it ruled were ultraconservative; they were steeped in the rigid ancestral traditions and customs of the ages, and were rabidly opposed to change. It would seem that India bore out his conviction that any innovation in government or extension of its sphere of control had to be carried out with the utmost caution; that there must be respect for the maxim that law and institutions grow and are not made.

England, on the other hand, presented to Maine a situation very nearly the direct opposite. The political and social order was passing through a period of transformation. Between the time when Maine returned from India and the writing of *Popular Government* (between 1869 and 1885) political democracy had become a certainty which remained only to be more fully established. From the franchise acts it seemed clear that there would be a great increase in the activities of the state. The very thing Maine most distrusted, legislative change, carried on not by the qualified few, but by the unqualified many, marked the English political scene.

Maine himself testified to the effect India had upon him. Writing after his return, he says, "If there were an ideal Tory-ism I should probably be a Tory . . . The truth is, India and the Indian Office make one judge public men by standards which have little to do with public opinion." [14] Lord Morley aptly referred to the influence of India upon Maine when he said: "The truth is that scientific lawyers have seldom been very favorable to popular government, and when the scientific lawyer is doubled with the Indian bureaucrat, we are pretty sure beforehand that in such a tribunal it will go hard with democracy." [15] Lord Acton ascribed to Maine characteristics that his Indian experience might easily have brought out. "Maine's nature," he says, "is to exercise power, and to find good reason for adopted policy. Augustus or Napoleon would have made him Prime Minister." [16]

One more influence must be reckoned with. Maine's unsan-guine temperament, which seems traceable to the trying and tedious illnesses which afflicted him through most of his life and caused his premature death, undoubtedly accentuated his conservatism. Sir Frederick Pollock aptly expressed the effect Maine's temperament seems to have had upon his outlook when he said: "I have long thought that the general colour of a man's estimate of the greatest objects of human interest — the characters of his fellow-citizens, the affairs of his country, the nature of man and his relation to the universe — depends much more on temperament than on intellect. No very wide margin of debatable ground is required to enable two thinkers to draw from the same data, without manifest violence either to evidence or to logic, the one optimist and the other pessi-mist conclusions. Sir Henry Maine's temper was not a sanguine

[14] K. B. Smellie, "Sir Henry Maine," *Economica*, 8:91 (March, 1928).
[15] John Morley, "Maine on Popular Government," *Oracles on Man and Govern-ment* (rev. ed., London, 1923), p. 79.
[16] *Letters of Lord Acton to Mary Gladstone* (Herbert Paul, editor, London, 1904), p. 26.

one." [17] When *Popular Government* appeared, in 1885, it attracted attention and was not long in taking a leading place in conservative thought. Sir Louis Mallet said of it that nothing would profit Toryism so much as Maine's essays.

III

As we have seen, Maine was too much of a modernist to be able to build his political ideas on religion. We have also seen that it was only natural for one so attached to the historical method to arrive at his fundamental views by the study of history. So, too, have we observed that of all the principles that Maine drew from history none was so important as that institutions grow and are not made. Behind this principle was a view of human nature that was the most basic conception in Maine's thought: man is subject to little change, and most men dislike change.[18] It followed for Maine that it was both futile and dangerous for men to make much of an attempt to alter the course of their lives. Thus to him democracy, legislation, and governmental activity were to be discouraged, for they placed an emphasis on change. Where change had been rendered difficult Maine had only admiration; the fathers of the American constitution, he thought, had shown great wisdom in devising a complicated system of amendment.[19] For simplicity, he maintained, led straight to absolutism.[20]

Maine was distrustful of democracy not only because he thought it went contrary to man's inherent conservatism, but also because he believed that the mass of men were ignorant and unintelligent with a tendency to disorder.[21] The natural counterpart of a contempt for the masses is a faith in the competence of the few. History demonstrated to Maine that aristocracy was the form of government from which all improvement

---

[17] Sir Frederick Pollock, *Oxford Lectures and Other Discourses* (London, 1890), p. 160.

[18] See his *Ancient Law*, pages 22–24 and 117; also the chapter on "The Age of Progress" in *Popular Government: Four Essays* (New York, 1897), especially pages 132–44, 170, and 171.

[19] *Popular Government*, pp. 124–25, 240–46.   [20] *Ibid.*, p. 169.

[21] *Ibid.*, pp. 35, 38, 45, 68, 86.

had hitherto sprung.[22] He seemed to think it was the mother of talent.[23] But he rejected rule by an intellectual aristocracy, by scientists, such as Renan suggested, apparently on the ground that scientists might become too absolute.[24] Rather was he in favor, as an ideal so it would seem, of an hereditary aristocracy. Biology, he believed, supported the case for an aristocracy of birth. If the proper qualities, he argued, for the conduct of government can be secured in a limited class, there is a strong probability that they will be transmitted to the corresponding class in the next generation, although no assertion is possible as to individuals.[25]

The above analysis suggests that apart from religion Maine was closer to Burke on basic assumptions than was Stephen; he was more deeply opposed to change than Stephen and, unlike Stephen, he identified the rule of the few with an hereditary aristocracy. In the stand he took for private property, Maine found arguments for both the old landed type and the new industrial type. He could say of the former that there might come a time when it would be recognized that the possession of a great estate implies more administrative power and kindlier relations with other classes having subordinate interests than almost any kind of superiority founded on wealth.[26] Maine, however, made an even stronger plea for private property of the new type; he went out of his way to defend the economic system of competition, which he thought democracy might impair, if not destroy.[27] From another angle he gave support to the new kind of property. He called the attention of Englishmen to how well the constitution of the United States safeguarded freedom of contract,[28] which was the legal instrument that afforded protection especially to industrial and commercial property. It was, he said, the bulwark of American individualism against democratic impatience and socialistic fantasy.[29] It must be pointed out that America was for Maine

---

[22] *Popular Government*, p. 42.   [23] *Ibid.*, pp. 42, 188.
[24] *Ibid.*, p. 189.   [25] *Ibid.*, p. 188.   [26] *Ibid.*
[27] *Ibid.*, pp. 47–52.   [28] *Ibid.*, pp. 247–48.   [29] *Ibid.*, p. 248.

the best illustration of the triumph of the principles of competition.[30] So important was freedom of contract to Maine that he could say that all modern progress seemed to be intimately connected with the completest freedom of contract and in some way almost mysteriously dependent upon it.[31]

IV

Maine was drawn into the fray of political criticism not, as Stephen was, to combat a philosophy of democracy, but to explode certain beliefs in regard to it.[32] Everywhere he saw uncritical enthusiasm lavished on democracy. It is thought, he says, that democracy is superior to every other form of government. Many believe that it advances with an irresistible and preordained movement. Many hold that it is of indefinitely long duration. Almost all the devotees of democracy are convinced that it means change and that democratic change will bring about infinite progress. These beliefs, which are largely the result of Rousseau's *a priori* speculations, cannot withstand inspection. If they are treated scientifically, if they are tested by the large body of facts that have in recent years accumulated on democracy, their extravagance will be revealed.

History, Maine points out, can give no support to the claim that democracy is irresistible. Though the Athenian and Roman republics contained popular elements, they were really special forms of aristocracy.[33] From the reign of Augustus Caesar to the establishment of the United States, democracy as a rule was always on the decline, nor was the decline arrested till the American federal government was founded.[34] Thus for seventeen centuries there was an all but universal movement toward kingship.[35]

Nor, he argues, does history show that modern democracy

[30] *Ibid.*, p. 50.
[31] M. E. Grant Duff, *Sir Henry Maine: A Brief Memoir of His Life,* p. 90.
[32] Maine's statement of his chief purpose in *Popular Government* is to be found not only in the Preface but in various statements throughout the work.
[33] *Popular Government,* pp. 42, 80.
[34] *Ibid.,* p. 81.   [35] *Ibid.,* p. 80.

is of indefinitely long duration. The introduction of political freedom in France, Spain, and the South American nations brought about great instability in those countries.[36] Putting aside the anomalous period from 1870 to 1885, France since 1789 has had forty-seven years of liberty and thirty-seven of stern dictatorship. Spain, since the first establishment of popular government in 1812, has had forty military risings of a serious nature. The upheaval that has characterized the South American republics is well illustrated by the case of Bolivia; of fourteen presidents thirteen have died assassinated or in exile. The only evidence worth mentioning for the duration of popular government is to be found in the British constitution during two centuries under special conditions and in the success of the American constitution during one century under conditions still more peculiar and more unlikely to recur.[37] Not only does Maine believe that the record of popular government shows it to be extremely fragile,[38] but he also holds that since the introduction of the principle of popular rule, governments everywhere have become more insecure: "Since the century during which the Roman Emperors were at the mercy of the Praetorian soldiery, there has been no such insecurity of government as the world has seen since the rulers became delegates to the community."[39]

Maine believed that not a little of this "singular modern loss of political equilibrium" was due to the growth of the military spirit and to irreconcilable bodies, especially to nationalists.[40] He attributed, however, the chief cause to what he called the difficulty of democratic government.[41] To him democracy was the most difficult of all forms of government.

If we are to understand Maine's charge, we must first see what he means by democracy. He accepted Austin's definition that democracy is simply and solely a form of government, and is distinguished from other forms only by a quantitative or

[36] *Popular Government*, pp. 14, 16, 19. [37] *Ibid.*, p. 54.
[38] *Ibid.*, p. 20. [39] *Ibid.*, p. 21.
[40] *Ibid.*, pp. 21–28. [41] *Ibid.*, p. 88.

Henry Maine

numerical difference.[42] As compared with monarchy and aristocracy, the other two main forms, democracy is government by the many instead of government by the one or by the few. In essence, he says, it does not differ from monarchy or aristocracy; like these governments, it must preserve the national existence and secure the national greatness and dignity, and internally it must secure obedience to law and maintain order.[43]

Acts of state, Maine holds, are determined by an exertion of the will. Democracy is the most difficult of all forms of government, for many minds must be consulted before an act of government is possible.[44] How, he asks, can a multitude come to a common agreement on any but the simplest questions? Increase the complexity of the question slightly, and an identical opinion can only be reached by trained minds, assisting themselves by demonstration more or less rigorous. On the complex questions of politics, which tax to the utmost all the powers of the strongest minds, the common determination of the multitude is a chimerical assumption.[45]

The most successful experiments in popular governments, Maine says, have recognized the difficulty of determining the popular will and have resorted to a representative system. The effect of this system was to diminish the difficulty of popular government in exact proportion to the diminution in the number of persons who had to decide public questions. But the representative system is now in decay. The caucus is turning the representative into a mere mouthpiece; he is less and less an unfettered representative and more and more an instructed delegate.[46]

The old Italian toxicologists are said to have arranged their discoveries in a series of three terms — first the poison, next the antidote, thirdly, the drug which neutralizes the antidote. The antidote to the fundamental infirmities of democracy was Representation, but the drug which defeats it has now been found in the Caucus.[47]

Maine also points out that the plebiscite and the referendum

[42] Ibid., p. 59.   [43] Ibid., pp. 61–62.   [44] Ibid., p. 88.
[46] Ibid., p. 89.   [46] Ibid., pp. 93–94.   [47] Ibid., p. 94.

Henry Maine

are experiments which, like representation, acknowledge the fundamental difficulty of democracy.[48]

He contends that democracy has fallen back upon other devices in an attempt to surmount its fundamental difficulty. Democracy, he says, could not work if it were not for the political party.[49] The party system consists in half the cleverest men in the country taking the utmost pains to prevent the other half from governing. Maine stresses the strong affinity of party with religion and observes that its discipline closely resembles military discipline.[50] He remarks that, historically speaking, party is probably nothing more than a survival and a consequence of the primitive combativeness of mankind.[51] But, he argues, even party would probably be unable to function if it were not for another political force — corruption:

> In a democracy, the fragment of political power falling to each man's share is so extremely small, that it would be hardly possible, without the aid of the Caucus, the Stump, and the Campaign newspaper, to rouse the interests of thousands or millions of men, if Party were not coupled with another political force. This, to speak plainly, is Corruption.[52]

In America, Andrew Jackson's principle "to the victors belong the spoils" has been one of the main stimulants to party action. Though England is the only nation that has turned over all patronage to the civil service, it must not be thought that we are safe from corruption.[53] Maine feared a different kind of bribery in England — the taking by legislative action of property from one class and transferring it to another.[54]

In addition to party and corruption a third expedient, Maine says, has been discovered in recent times for producing not, indeed, agreement, but the semblance of agreement. This is generalization.[55] All generalization is the product of abstraction; abstraction consists in dropping out of sight a certain number of particular facts and constructing a formula that will embrace the remainder. Men ambitious for political authority

[48] *Popular Government*, pp. 95–96.   [49] *Ibid.*, pp. 98–99.
[50] *Ibid.*, p. 100.   [51] *Ibid.*, p. 101.   [52] *Ibid.*, p. 102.
[53] *Ibid.*, p. 105.   [54] *Ibid.*, p. 106.   [55] *Ibid.*, pp. 106–07.

have found out the secret of manufacturing generalities in any number. Crowds of men can be got to assent to general statements, clothed in stiking language; and thus there is formed a sort of sham concurrence of opinion. Useful as it is to democracy, this levity of assent is one of the most enervating of national habits of mind. It has seriously enfeebled the French intellect and it is now affecting injuriously the mind of England.[56] Thus the principal means by which democracy would overcome its difficulty are injurious either to the morality or to the intellect of the governing multitude.[57]

More important than Maine's criticism of democracy on the ground of difficulty was his criticism of the democratic belief in progress. It was at once an attack on what he believed was the popular desire for change, on zeal for reform, and on the view that democracy will bring about infinite progress. Maine insisted that a relatively small portion of the human race will so much as tolerate a proposal or attempt to change its usages, laws, and institutions.[58] The Mohammedan world, he says, detests reform. The enormous mass of the Indian population hates and dreads change. The multitudes in Africa detest it. The millions upon millions in China loathe and despise it. An absolute intolerance of political change characterizes much the largest part of the human race, and has characterized the whole of it during the largest part of its history.

Maine argued that resistance to change was typical not only of the political thinking of men, but also of the whole field of habit, of manners, and of fashions.[59] He admitted that man had changed much in Western Europe, but added that it was singular how much of the savage there still was in him:

Like the savage, the Englishman, Frenchman, or American makes war; like the savage, he hunts; like the savage, he dances; like the savage, he indulges in endless deliberation; like the savage, he sets an extravagant value on rhetoric; like the savage, he is a man of party, with a newspaper for a totem, instead of a mark on his fore-

[56] *Ibid.*, p. 108.   [57] *Ibid.*
[58] *Ibid.*, pp. 132–36.   [59] *Ibid.*, pp. 136–42.

Henry Maine

head or arm; and, like a savage, he is apt to make of his totem his God.[60]

Maine concluded that the natural condition of mankind was not the progressive condition. This natural condition is, he said, one not of changeableness but of unchangeableness.[61] The immobility of society is the rule; its mobility is the exception.

Maine declared that enthusiasm for change was not only rare and extremely modern but also of a highly special kind, being exclusively for political change;[62] and that such change was not older than the free employment of legislation by popular governments.[63] He was convinced that enthusiasm for change was attributable largely to a group of words, phrases, maxims, and general propositions that have their root in the political theories of Rousseau and Bentham, especially of Rousseau.[64] He was certain that no belief was less warranted by experience than that a democratic republic is in the long run given to reforming legislation:[65]

The ancient republics hardly legislated at all; their democratic energy was expended upon war, diplomacy, and justice; but they put nearly insuperable obstacles in the way of a change of law. The Americans of the United States have hedged themselves round in exactly the same way. They only make laws within the limits of their Constitutions, and especially of the Federal Constitution; and judged by what has become the English standard, their legislation within these limits is almost trivial.[66]

If the whole, Maine observes, of the known history of the human race be examined, we shall see that the great authors of legislative change have been powerful monarchies.[67]

Nor does history in any way show that democracy leads to progress. Rather does it indicate that aristocracy is the mother of progress:

So far as the human race has experience, it is not by political societies in any way resembling those now called democracies that human improvement has been carried on. History said Strauss . . .

---

[60] *Popular Government*, p. 144.   [61] *Ibid.*, p. 170.
[62] *Ibid.*, p. 177.   [63] *Ibid.*, p. 134.   [64] *Ibid.*, pp. 136, 151–70.
[65] *Ibid.*, pp. 67, 135.   [66] *Ibid.*, p. 67.   [67] *Ibid.*, p. 65.

Henry Maine

is a sound aristocrat . . . the progress of mankind has hitherto been effected by the rise and fall of aristocracies . . . by the succession of one aristocracy to another. There have been so-called democracies, which have rendered services beyond price to mankind, but they were only peculiar forms of aristocracy.[68]

Maine's attack on the democratic faith in progress was not confined to an appeal to past history and anthropology. Equally if not more important was his analysis of the inherent nature of democracy, which he thought showed that democracy promised not progress but stagnant conservatism. He declared that it was one of the strangest of vulgar ideas that democracy would or could promote progress, new ideas, new inventions, and new arts of life. No doubt, he says, the immediate effect of a very wide suffrage would be the extensive destruction of existing institutions; but in the long run the chances are that it would produce a mischievous form of conservatism.[69] Universal suffrage would stamp upon law the average opinion of the community, which would bring about a tyranny of ignorance.[70]

Universal suffrage which today excludes Free Trade from the United States, would certainly have prohibited the spinning-jenny and the power-loom. It would certainly have prohibited the threshing machine.[71]

If for four centuries there had been a very widely extended franchise . . . there would have been no reformation of religion, no change of dynasty, no toleration of Dissent, not even an accurate calendar.[72]

Maine sees a marked antagonism between democratic opinion and science.

The central seat in all Political Economy was from the first occupied by the theory of Population. This theory has now been generalized by Mr. Darwin and his followers, and, stated as the principle of the survival of the fittest, it has become the central truth of all biological science. Yet it is evidently disliked by the multitude, and thrust into the background by those whom the multitude permits to lead it.[73]

[68] *Ibid.*, pp. 41–42.   [69] *Ibid.*, pp. 34–35.   [70] *Ibid.*, pp. 35, 36, 67.
[71] *Ibid.*, p. 36.   [72] *Ibid.*, p. 98.   [73] *Ibid.*, p. 37.

Henry Maine

Even in our day, vaccination is in the utmost danger, and we may say generally that the gradual establishment of the masses in power is of the blackest omen for all legislation founded on scientific opinion, which requires tension of mind to understand it and self-denial to submit to it.[74]

Thus Maine declares there is no grosser delusion than that democracy, when it has once had all things put under its feet, is a progressive form of government.[75]

The crux, he insists, of the whole matter is that most men do not know their own best interest.[76] Bentham's prodigious mistake was that he greatly overestimated the intelligence of the mass of men. Bentham's fundamental proposition, that if you place power in the hands of the multitude, they will use it for their own interest, turns against him when it is considered in the light of Machiavelli's realistic remark that "the world is made up of the vulgar." The fact is that the multitude includes too much ignorance to be capable of understanding its interest; and this furnishes the principal argument against democracy.[77]

Though Maine was convinced that democracy in the long run would probably bring about a stagnant conservatism, he feared that the immediate result of universal suffrage would be a period of destruction.[78] "The truth seems to be that the extreme forms of government, Monarchy and Democracy, have a peculiarity which is absent from the more tempered political systems founded on compromise, Constitutional Kingship and Aristocracy. When they are first established in absolute completeness, they are highly destructive." [79] Maine was well aware that democracy was the enemy of privilege, just as he was well aware that democracy would attack the inequality of property. He believed that such an attack could only end in chaos. He thought the assault would take the form of an attempt to re-divide the common stock of good things, which many believe to be unlimited in quantity.[80] Maine vividly described the process of redivision and its consequences when he said:

[74] *Popular Government*, p. 98.   [75] *Ibid.*, p. 97.   [76] *Ibid.*, pp. 86, 166.
[77] *Ibid.*, p. 86.   [78] *Ibid.*, pp. 45, 66.   [79] *Ibid.*, p. 66.   [80] *Ibid.*, pp. 43–45.

186

Henry Maine

. . . if the mass of mankind were to make an attempt at redividing the common stock of good things, they would resemble, not a number of claimants insisting on the fair division of a fund, but a mutinous crew, feasting on a ship's provisions, gorging themselves on the meat and intoxicating themselves with the liquors, but refusing to navigate the vessel to port.[81]

Maine also feared that there might be an exhaustion of the good things or a great decrease in their amount brought about by a subtler process.[82] Democracy, he suggested, through a program of heavy taxation for the most laudable philanthropic objects, might undermine the motives to labor and to save. These motives, to which the competitive system appeals, are basic to the production of wealth, and they infallibly entail inequality in its distribution: "They are the springs of action called into activity by the strenuous and never-ending struggle for existence, the beneficent private war which makes one man strive to climb on the shoulders of another and remain there through the law of the survival of the fittest." [83]

If Maine was fearful of the destruction democracy might bring about in the near future, he was hardly less concerned with the democratic demand that the House of Commons be the supreme governing authority of the state. He was convinced that the establishment of the popular chamber of unlimited power would mean the introduction of autocracy; yet he envisaged an autocracy not so much of the House of Commons as of the Cabinet, "drifting toward a type of government associated with terrible events—a single Assembly armed with full powers over the Constitution, which it may exercise at pleasure. It will be a theoretically all-powerful Convention, governed by a practically all-powerful secret Committee of Public Safety." [84]

Maine was not without hope that the destructive tendencies of democracy in England might be checked. He thought that "anarchy" might be avoided if the constitution was more difficult to change. He proposed two safeguards against change.

[81] *Ibid.*, p. 45.   [82] *Ibid.*, pp. 47–50.   [83] *Ibid.*, p. 50.   [84] *Ibid.*, p. 126.

Henry Maine

For one he turned to America; he held that the success of the American constitution appeared to result rather from skillfully applying the curb to popular impulses than from giving them rein.[85] In his eyes the great virtue of the American instrument was that it had drawn a distinction between constitutional and ordinary legislation, and had made the former difficult to enact through the provision of a complicated system of amendment.[86] Maine advocated that England should follow America and erect a similar safeguard against irresponsible majorities.[87] The other check he recommended was a House of Lords as strong as that of his own day if not stronger.[88] It is impossible, he affirms, to be sure that first chambers are always right; and in view of the increasing difficulty of democracy the doubt grows stronger that popularly elected legislatures are infallible.[89]

There appears to be no escaping from the fact that all such institutions as a Senate, a House of Lords, or a Second Chamber, are founded on a denial or a doubt of the proposition that the voice of the people is the voice of God . . . They are the fruit of the agnosticism of the political understanding.[90]

The function of a second chamber, he thinks, is not to act as a rival infallibility, nor as a mere revising body, but as an additional security.[91] The House of Lords is fitted to serve this function. An hereditary right to share in government is not, as some seem to think, absurd, for there is a greater chance that ability will be called to the direction of affairs under aristocracy than under alternative systems.[92]

V

No one can deny that Maine's criticism is impressive. The clarity of his style, the classical turn of his sentences, which are reminiscent of Burke, his gift for the telling phrase, and his technical knowledge, all carry a persuasive power that it is difficult to resist. Now and then he can unhinge our minds

[85] *Popular Government*, p. xi.   [86] *Ibid.*, pp. 120–24, 240–46.
[87] *Ibid.*, pp. 124–25.   [88] *Ibid.*, pp. 179–80, 187–88.   [89] *Ibid.*, p. 180.
[90] *Ibid.*, p. 179.   [91] *Ibid.*, p. 180.   [92] *Ibid.*, pp. 187–88.

from the present and make us see ourselves in something of a perspective. He can show us that our emancipation from the tyranny of custom is indeed but recent. He can show us that democracy is rare in the history of the world. And, whether he deals with the present or the past, he can convey to us a sense of the power of habit in political and social affairs.

Perhaps no one in England in the nineteenth century gave so searching a criticism of democracy as a method of government. This criticism, it may be observed, anticipates the fascists in holding that an inherent weakness of democracy is the difficulty it must encounter in making decisions. Maine's analysis of political parties was rather remarkable for its psychological penetration; it showed him to be of the twentieth rather than of the nineteenth century. As one writer has said, Maine suggests the psychological studies of Graham Wallas.[93] Maine was not without prophetic insight; the Great War and the years after have borne out his observation that "nationalism is full of the seeds of future civil convulsion." [94] The recent experience of Germany and Austria has shown the pertinence of his view that a modern army and a democracy are a contradiction in terms, and that the former may destroy the latter.[95]

In regard, however, to Maine's chief concern in *Popular Government,* the destruction of certain democratic beliefs, it cannot be said that he was very successful. His criticism of the belief that democracy is irresistible was his most convincing performance. Though he did not prove that the belief is wrong, he gave us reason to doubt that it is right. Maine's criticism was based on an appeal to past history — that from the time of the Roman Empire there has been an almost universal movement toward kingship. The argument from the past is never conclusive, for we do not know enough about past events to be able to say whether a political movement is irresistible or not. Perhaps Maine was a little too certain that democracy is not irresistible.

[93] K. B. Smellie, "Sir Henry Maine," *Economica,* 8:91 (March, 1928).
[94] *Popular Government,* p. 27.
[95] *Ibid.,* pp. 22–23.

But it must not be forgotten that when he wrote, many an intellectual considered history as capable of scientific results as astronomy, and consequently held that history could give positive answers to important questions.

Maine was unable to destroy the belief that democracy is of indefinitely long duration. That is to say, he has not persuaded us to accept his contention that the record of democracy in the modern world shows it to be characterized by great fragility. This contention was founded on the view that in France, Spain, and the South American countries, democracy has given birth to violence, revolution, and dictatorship. Yet in none of these countries, during the period that Maine considers, was there democracy or popular government in Maine's sense of the term, which we may accept as satisfactory for his purpose. According to Maine, popular government is the rule of the many as opposed to the rule of the one or the few; his criterion of popular government is that the rulers are the servants of the ruled. It can hardly be said that France enjoyed popular government from 1789 to 1870. How could the rulers be the servants of the ruled with the House of Bourbon or the House of Orleans at the head of the state, even though the upper middle class did for some time enjoy a technical franchise? How could there be a government of the many with Louis Napoleon on the throne, even though he did refer his power to a popular plebiscite? Not until 1870 could it be said that popular government or democracy was in any real sense the government of the French nation. Yet France was Maine's best example. Spain and the South American countries were even less of an approximation to popular government. As Lord Bryce said of the latter, whatever one might call them, they were certainly not democracies.[96]

Maine's argument that democracy has been characterized by fragility is of little weight. Whether democracy is fragile cannot possibly be ascertained empirically, for our experience with democracy has been very limited indeed; when Maine wrote, democracy in the sense of universal manhood suffrage had been

[96] James Bryce, *Modern Democracies* (2 vols., London, 1921), I, 210.

Henry Maine

in existence in the modern world about a half century. Maine's argument at best amounts to no more than that the coming of democracy has been attended by severe birth pains. It may be asked, what system of government has not in the process of its establishment been accompanied by disorder? Was the founding of monarchy and aristocracy attended by no disruption? Despite the many years that monarchy reigned in the West, it failed precisely because, as Morris Cohen says, it led to insurrection.[97] And one reason, it seems, why aristocracy failed is that it ultimately involved too much disorder. That all government, as Maine says, has become more unstable since the introduction of the principle of popular rule in the seventeenth century [98] is possibly a criticism of monarchy and aristocracy. Maine did not consider that perhaps the privileged orders were either too weak to withstand the pressure of new demands or refused to give way without a struggle to a system of government based upon broader principles of justice. Granted, however, that democracy has been associated with upheaval, the final question must be, has it been worth the price? Maine did not show that democracy involved more disruption than it was worth, for, among other things, he hardly took any account of its worth.

It may be remarked that whatever upheaval has accompanied and will accompany the establishment of democracy, of all systems of government it offers the most stability. Obviously, it is not immune against violence. Problems that touch men's deepest passions, like slavery in America in the last century, or like property in this, may very well be incapable of settlement by any kind of government. But this is an indictment of human nature

[97] Morris R. Cohen, *Law and the Social Order: Essays in Legal Philosophy* (1st ed., New York, 1933), p. 65.

[98] Maine fails to maintain a clear distinction between the introduction of the principle of popular government and the fact of its acceptance by the community. On pages 9 and 10 of *Popular Government* he says that popular government was established in principle in England in 1689, but that it was not accepted in fact until two centuries later. On page 54 he refers to two centuries of British experience as evidence for the duration of popular government. And on page 135 he says that for two centuries Englishmen have had a "nearly unqualified popular government."

rather than of democracy. Democracy offers the greatest stability because it stands for government by consent, and because it stands for discussion and criticism, and because it can hold its leaders responsible and change them when they have betrayed their trust; this gives reason a greater, and force a lesser, place in settling the differences of men. Democracy, to repeat the time-worn maxim, substitutes ballots for bullets.

Maine held that the chief cause of democracy's fragility was the difficulty of many ordinary minds arriving at a common conclusion on various problems, most of which are complex enough to tax the wits of experts. Though Maine hardly showed how the difficulty of democracy was connected with the record of its instability, the difficulty he posited is a real one. Maine's criticism rests on two propositions: first, there is great difficulty technically in obtaining common agreement from many minds holding various opinions; second, most men do not know what they want, let alone what constitutes their own interests.

Any critical student of government would agree with Maine that the franchise and the representative system are crude and rough instruments at best for determining the "will" or the interests of the community. But Maine overemphasized the numerical or quantitative aspect of the problem and underestimated the importance of interests. Nor did he consider the difficulty that monarchy and aristocracy can have in making up their minds; Louis XVI could not make up his mind and as a consequence lost his throne and his head, and the English aristocracy in 1832 could not come to a common mind on reform and averted a crisis by submitting to a will from without. Perhaps the best answer to Maine's doubt concerning the difficulty of democracy in making up its mind is the fact of the social service state, which was emerging in his day. That democracy had obtained in Maine's time such legislation as education and health acts, and since his time such services as unemployment insurance, shows that democracy has not found it an impossible task to come to some agreement on important problems. Of course there have been delays, serious delays, but these have been due less to the difficulty arising from numbers and the complexity of issues than to the resistance of privilege. Nevertheless this criticism of democracy, made by both Maine and the fascists, that it is inherently difficult for democracy to act, will have to be met in the near future. If democracy finds it impossible in the face of privilege to act effectively to alleviate distress and to attempt a solution of the problems of our age, it seems likely that dictatorship will, temporarily at any rate, supersede democracy.

To argue, as Maine did, that democracy is the most difficult form of government on the ground solely of one consideration, that of determining the governmental will, is hardly satisfactory. The problem, for example, of carrying out a governmental decision after it has once been made may be equally if not more difficult than the problem of arriving at that decision. Monarchy can come to a decision with celerity, yet this may be but the beginning of monarchy's difficulty. George III unquestionably arrived with ease at his decision that there shall be taxation without representation, but his attempt to execute that decision drove him to war and finally to surrender a great colony. An advantage of democracy over monarchy and aristocracy is that in a democracy there is a greater likelihood that laws will be effectively administered, because they rest upon a wider, more genuine, and better-informed basis of consent.

We said above that Maine's argument that democracy is the most difficult of all forms of government rested not only on the technical difficulty of consulting many minds, but also on the view that the mass of men are too ignorant to know their own interests. It would seem that plain men know their own interests sufficiently well, so that if they have political power their interests are to some extent served, whereas if they have not, their interests are less well served. The point is that when men who do know or might know the interests of the common man better than he does himself have been in power, in governments other than democratic, they have given little evidence of such knowledge. If ordinary men are not competent to judge their own interests, kings and aristocrats have shown themselves even less competent to judge them.

As is so often the case with the specialist or technical critic, Maine magnifies political problems as enough to perplex the wits of experts, and then proceeds to ask how a multitude of roughs and clowns can find a solution. His argument exaggerates the importance of technical knowledge in the problem of determining the "will" of the electorate. What is wanted from the common man is judgment of a general character in regard to party programs or the policy of a government. It is not necessary, though desirable, for the ordinary man to know the intricacies of the credit system in order to make democracy work. What is wanted from the common man is a judgment on whether the government has attempted to relieve him from starvation, or whether his son should have an opportunity to be educated. On such questions he is generally as capable of rendering a significant judgment as is the expert; occasionally he is even more capable. The great limitation of the expert is that all problems are expert problems to be solved exclusively in terms of the expert's own particular *expertise*. Where expert knowledge is especially needed in a democracy is in devising means of carrying out general policy and in the actual administration of it.

Let us, however, assume that democracy is more difficult than its alternatives. Does this necessarily discredit democracy? The democrat will argue that difficulty is a small price to pay for liberty and equality. He will argue that the difficulty of democracy is more than compensated for by the opportunity it provides for a more creative life for all, which is not secured, at least in the same degree, under monarchy and aristocracy. He will argue that most things worth while are difficult, that the very difficulty of democracy is the secret of its challenge, and that the finest fruits of a free life lived in common are obtainable only as men are able to meet this challenge. In order to make his argument decisive, Maine had to show that democracy is so difficult, either as such, or in connection with other defects, that it is less good than an alternative system of government. This he did not succeed in doing.

No one who has read Maine's criticism of the belief in progress can hold that belief without qualification. But Maine did not show that democracy is hostile to progress, which was his most important task. Maine argued that democracy must in the long run lead to a stagnant conservatism, but he marshaled little evidence in support of his contention. It is important to examine Maine's evidence in some detail, for he laid claim to a scientific treatment of politics. Maine's argument for the contention that democracy is hostile to progress or science consisted for the greater part in the assertion that "if there had been . . . there would have been." This is a historical speculation of what might have been had things been different. It presents no evidence for Maine's contention. He says that universal suffrage excluded free trade from America. But he does not establish this statement. All that can be said is that there was universal suffrage in America and that protection was found alongside of it. It might be—to give Maine the benefit of the doubt—that universal suffrage was a condition for bringing about protection, but that does not make it the cause of protection. Maine's fallacy is that he ascribes to a political mechanism a policy that was effected essentially by economic interests. Universal suffrage was no more than a mechanism through which vested interests, which dominated a party, registered the power of their wealth.

Maine also argued that democracy was hostile to the doctrine of the survival of the fittest, which was the central truth of all biological science.[99] If this was the case, democracy showed good sense. For the doctrine as stated is so general that it means almost nothing. And when it is applied, as it was by Maine, to

[99] Lord Morley said that he had not seen any evidence that the masses were hostile to the theory of population and the doctrine of the survival of the fittest. See his effective criticism of Maine in "Maine on Popular Government," in *Oracles on Man and Government*, pages 104–06. He also said that vaccination was not in danger. He pointed out, however, that compulsory vaccination was threatened, but indicated that the threat came from the middle class rather than from the lower. *Ibid.*, p. 102.

social affairs, it involves justifying the strong, it involves accepting that might makes right. But Maine might be answered more directly. Had the mass of men really been hostile to the doctrine of the survival of the fittest as applied to political, social, and economic affairs, they would never have permitted the rise of the capitalist, nor would so many ordinary men have attempted to become little capitalists. If, in his argument that the masses are hostile to progress, Maine had mentioned the destruction of looms by some of the handicraft workers during the early days of the industrial revolution, he might have improved his case. But the comment then would have been that these men were motivated to destroy not because they disliked science but because they disliked losing their jobs and their livelihood.

Maine's argument that democracy leads to stagnant conservatism was based on the conviction that the mass of men are ignorant and unintelligent. Clearly the mass of men are not distinguished for brilliance, but this does not mean that they therefore oppose science (or new ideas), any more than it means that they favor it. Whatever may be the ordinary man's want of knowledge and lack of tension of mind, he has either accepted science, at least its results, or remained indifferent to it. This is true even though scientific and technological developments have been responsible from time to time for throwing large numbers of men out of work.

Had all Maine's evidence of democracy's hostility to science been valid, still it would have been concerned with but a very small part indeed of the whole field of science. His evidence pertained at best to one or two ideas from biology, economics, engineering, and medicine. In regard to most of the ideas in these fields, as in the entire fields of mathematics, physics, astronomy, chemistry, zoology, botany, and geology, there seems to be no substantial evidence that the mass of men were or are hostile to science. On the contrary, from such various facts as the great extent to which science has been applied to daily life and the important place it has come to occupy in popular education, it would seem that science has been well received by the mass of men.[1]

It is certainly true, however, that the ordinary man is not schooled in scientific method, i. e., in the careful weighing of evidence, in close reasoning, in a realization of the assumptions of science. Nor, indeed, do many scientists seem to show a grasp of what scientific method means outside their own field. In fact, most scientists are unacquainted with the philosophical assumptions of their method. Little attempt has been made to educate men in the philosophy of science, and in its application, especially in the social sciences.

If Maine did not succeed in showing that democracy is hostile to progress, neither did he succeed in showing that aristocracy is of all governments the most friendly to progress, or that it is the form of government from which all improvements have hitherto sprung. Clearly improvement or progress springs essentially, not from a system of government, but from causes far outside its province. Maine held that progress consists in the production of new ideas. It is obvious that these are the result essentially of such factors as personal genius, cultural conditions, and accident, not of government. England produced Newton not because England was a monarchy or because English monarchy fostered genius in physics, but because Newton was Newton and cultural conditions were what they were, and because Galileo and Copernicus had gone before Newton. Yet if it is urged that one type of political organization is more friendly to new ideas than another, it would seem that that type is democracy. For doubt, criticism, and discussion are more native to democracy than to any other system of government, and doubt, criticism, and discussion are the very lifeblood of science.

[1] Godkin, in replying to Maine's argument that democracy is the enemy of science, said that never has there been a society in which new discoveries and new inventions have been received with so much readiness as in the United States, yet it is the country in which dominating opinion is most distinctly that of the multitude. E. L. Godkin, "An American View of Popular Government," *Nineteenth Century,* 19:180 (February, 1886).

Henry Maine

Though Maine believed that in the long run democracy would probably lead to a stagnant conservatism, in the near future he feared that it would bring about disorder. The masses, he thought, would attack private property and attempt to redivide the wealth of the community, which would result in "anarchy." Maine was right in holding, as the income and inheritance taxes show, that democracy will attack the privilege that is born of private property. And it seems likely that democracy will continue to attack the private property system until the holding of property is based on something like an idea of justice. But it is unlikely that such an attempt to alter property relations will incite workingmen to disorder. It is far more likely that it will incite middle-class men and men of property to fascist revolution, as it has done in Germany and in Italy, or incite military men and men of property to fascist rebellion, as it has done in Spain. If history is any guide in these matters, men who enjoy privilege generally refuse to surrender it without a struggle.

Maine's belief that democracy will probably plunge itself into an orgy of confiscation of property, bringing about "anarchy," is based on the view that the common man has in him a strong tendency to disorder. If the common man has such a tendency, it is shared by his "superiors." Moreover, what evidence there is points to the conclusion that capacity for disorder is not only shared by the common man's "superiors," but has been monopolized by them. Revolutions have been undertaken almost exclusively by the middle and upper classes; as H. G. Wells has acutely said, the class war is an old habit of the governing classes. It may be observed that no group has shown such patience with suffering as the lower class. If disruption results from democracy's drive toward a greater equality of property, a more likely cause than the common man's proclivity for disorder will be the willingness of those who derive benefits from the present property system to resort to force in order to protect them. This is one thing fascism illustrates, and fascism is revolution from the middle and the top.

Henry Maine

It is interesting to note that when Maine talks of property, the masses are ignorant and tend to riot, and when he talks of science they are merely ignorant. It may be asked whether if the masses have a tendency to disorder, it is likely that they will be content to settle down to a dead-level conservatism.

To sum up Maine's criticism of democratic beliefs, we may say that he discredited the claim that democracy is irresistible, but that he did not prove that democracy is fragile, or that it is hostile to progress, or that it necessarily threatens disorder. Though Maine has convinced us that there is no reason to believe that democracy is irresistible, it was not really important for him to do so. What was important for him to do was to show that democracy is not the best form of government or the form that ought to be. This he did not do.

Popular Government is a protest against a changing world. It is fundamentally a protest of a conservative view of human nature against a liberal view. No doubt many liberals in Maine's day were more hopeful of man's progress than the facts could justify. But it is equally true that Maine overemphasized the unchangeableness of human nature, that is, of attitudes, of ideas, and of interests. This is perhaps best seen in his fear and distrust of legislative change, and in his desire to restrict legislative action. No reasonable person will argue that legislative action can by itself accomplish anything; neither will any reasonable person deny that legislative action along with other factors has rendered important service. Maine did not seem to appreciate that remarkable improvements, such as those achieved in health and sanitation, can be made through legislative action.

In keeping with his view of human nature was the doctrine underlying his political philosophy, that institutions grow and are not made. Despite what truth there is in this doctrine, it represents at bottom a distrust of reason, for this doctrine says, "make little attempt to order, to guide, and to direct man's destiny, but let things grow more or less as they will." Such distrust underestimates the power of reason. In the political sphere it is only necessary to mention the creation of the American system of government and the governments of the British dominions to show what reason can accomplish. And in the field of law, as Dean Pound has pointed out, American judges made over seventeenth-century English law into American common law, and a whole body of law was taken over at one stroke in the reception of Roman law in Western Europe and in the reception of the French Civil Code in many different countries. Even admitting, however, that reason plays a small part in human affairs, that does not mean we should be fearful of using it. On the contrary, that is why we ought to make the most of it, and give it the largest place possible; for to rely upon the alternative, instinct, is to rely upon blindness.

The doctrine that institutions grow and are not made is opposed to the democratic philosophy, which emphasizes the possibilities of change. Democracy does not exalt the past; it does not place faith in countless generations merely because they are countless generations, but in the capacity of individuals to reason and will, and thereby to grow and to better their lives. This means that democracy accepts, not what the past has seen fit to impose on the present, but the ability of men to change their ideas and to mold the environment somewhat after their heart's desire. By its opposition to change, the doctrine that institutions grow and are not made tends to subject the present to the past; as Roscoe Pound has said, our continuity to the past is a necessity and not a duty.

Maine's approach to the present from the past — his deep belief in the doctrine that institutions grow and are not made — led him to idealize institutions that had outworn their usefulness. Maine did not see, as Matthew Arnold did, that though an aristocracy could be justified in a feudal world, it could not be justified in an industrial and democratic society. Maine, like Carlyle, Ruskin, and Stephen before him, did not seem to realize that the failure of governments by the few is that they rule for the few rather than for the community. Even if the argument from biology — the transmission of acquired characteristics—which Maine invoked to support his belief in aristocracy were true (and what knowledge we have indicates that it is not),[2] it would not greatly strengthen his position. For, as Lord Acton said, political power corrupts even the noblest; that is to say, no man nor any set of men is good enough or wise enough to rule for long the rest of men.

It is easy for one who approaches the present from the past to believe that what is established is the most desirable. Maine did not question the assumptions of the economic system of competition; he did not question, in particular, the assumption that competition and the opportunity to make a fortune are necessary to induce men to labor and to save. He did not seem to consider that many men work and save who have little chance of becoming rich, that many work and save who compete but little, and that great masses work without receiving enough to be able to save. As William James said, the instinct of man is that of the bee and the beaver. Maine did not ask whether the state might save. Nor did he consider that a system whose main productive energies were devoted, in the first instance, to providing the basic needs of men, rather than what can be made to pay, might permit and encourage more saving, if that is desirable.

Maine did not question the consequences of the competitive system. He seemed to agree that the scales must be weighted in favor of the economically strong as against the economically weak, irrespective of justice. Maine did not see, as Matthew Arnold did, that a society which permits great inequalities in the distribution of the goods of life, and which therefore denies

[2] It is a fallacy, H. S. Jennings says, that biology requires an aristocratic constitution of society; the maxim that like produces like, on which this notion rests, is largely fallacious. Superior parents by no means necessarily produce superior offspring, though they produce a larger proportion of superior children than do mediocre parents. From the great mass of mediocre parents, however, arise more superior offspring than from the few distinguished parents. "The classes do not perpetuate themselves as such. From the higher many lower are produced; from the lower, many higher. From the great mediocre group are produced more of the higher than the higher group itself produces; and more of the lower than the lower group itself produces." Herbert S. Jennings, *The Biological Basis of Human Nature* (1st ed., New York, 1930), pp. 218–48.

men equal social opportunity, is not truly civilized. Nor did he really see, as Aristotle did, and many political writers since Aristotle, that a society based upon a division into rich and poor is a society that is not likely to endure.

Maine justified the competitive system and its consequences, as is so frequently done, as the beneficent private war that makes for the survival of the fittest. He did not stop to ask, who are the fittest? and ought they to survive? Under economic individualism the fittest are too often the lion and the fox; too often the ruthless, the cunning, and the unscrupulous, rather than the intelligent, the wisest, and the best. As Thomas Henry Huxley pointed out, the application of the doctrine of the survival of the fittest to social relationships justifies the tiger ethic. Maine made the popular error of taking an observation from a field of inquiry, biology, which is in no way concerned with morality, and applying it to a field that is very much concerned with morality. And it goes without saying that unless man had capacity for moral action, society as we know it would be impossible.

So attached was Maine to the established institution of private property that he thought of it almost exclusively in terms of its protection. He seemed to be unaware of the broad implications of the safeguards he advocated. He evidently did not realize that the maintenance of abstract freedom of contract in a society where there were great inequalities in the distribution of economic power made for injustice. To say that workers, who generally have no economic reserve, are in a position to enter freely into a contract with their employers, who have economic reserve, is rather like saying that slaves are free to accept the commands of their masters. As Justice Holmes said, there can be no real freedom of contract unless there is equality of bargaining power.[3]

Maine did not hesitate to advocate a strong House of Lords even though the very existence of a House of Lords, whether

[3] Maine, it will be remembered, held that the modern progress of society is almost mysteriously dependent on the simplest freedom of contract. This view overestimates the value of a technical device, of a legal instrument, in civilization. The forces of

strong or weak (in the latter case, after the Act of 1911), is an obstacle to the realization of the popular will. Had his recommendation that England adopt the American system of constitutional amendment been accepted, social change would have been made still more difficult, and as a result privilege would have been still further entrenched.

The approach to the present by way of the past led Maine, as it had led Burke, to underestimate contemporary experience, perhaps just in the same degree as he overestimated the experience of the past. Like most conservatives, Maine forgot the remark of Bentham, "whatever *now* is established, *once* was innovation." He was unable to see that what he considered democracy's intemperate desire for change might in reality be the expression of wants unfulfilled or of needs long repressed. Had Maine been thoroughly aware of the necessity of approaching the present from the present, he would probably have placed less emphasis on the past and he might have been more sympathetic to newer ways of life.

Maine apparently did not realize that all history is a matter of inference — that every fact is a theory about a fact — and that every inference rests on a presupposition, and that this presupposition is formed by present experience.[4] Maine was not

which it is the expression, such as the spirit of private enterprise, are much more important in the explanation. If, however, it was admitted that abstract freedom of contract served society relatively well during the earlier stages of an industrial society, it would not necessarily follow that it is equally well fitted to serve a more advanced industrial civilization. The courts in the Western democracies have decided that there is more justice involved in the recognition of trade-unions, and the status which this implies, than in permitting a reign of abstract freedom of contract between employer and employee. Maine's strong belief in freedom of contract is at bottom Hegelian and metaphysical — that legal institutions show an ever greater realization of free, individual self-assertion. Maine was deeply influenced by Savigny and Savigny by Kant and Hegel. The end of law for Savigny is to bring about a maximum of individual self-assertion. In particular, says Roscoe Pound, the idea of contract is Savigny's will-theory projected back into Roman law as an instrument for organizing the law of the nineteenth century. The whole course of our law in the last generation, he continues, whether by legislation or by judicial decision, refutes Maine's generalization of progress from status to contract, unless indeed we have been progressing backwards. See Pound's brilliant criticism of Maine in his *Interpretations of Legal History* (Cambridge, Massachusetts, 1923), especially pp. 54ff., to which the above is indebted.

[4] See Francis H. Bradley's brilliant essay "The Presuppositions of Critical History," *Collected Essays* (2 vols., London, 1935).

Henry Maine

fully cognizant that his appeal to history was a partial appeal, an appeal to a very limited number of facts chosen by means of a presupposition which he thought the facts would bear out. Not realizing how very partial was his selection, it was easy for him to believe that the argument from history constituted proof. And it was easy for him to emphasize his main presupposition of history, that institutions grow and are not made, to the total exclusion almost of its opposite, as it was for all writers who followed in the footsteps of the historical school of Savigny and Maine. In view of his presupposition of slow growth, it is not surprising that he turned his attention to the periods of history in which men had great respect for custom and moved slowly; nor is it surprising that he avoided the dynamic periods. And it is not astonishing that when he dealt with Rousseau, a "radical" who wrote in a dynamic period, he ascribed a far greater influence to Rousseau's ideas than a more sober history can claim for them.

Maine, it will be remembered, set out to criticize democratic beliefs scientifically. That his view of scientific method was a crude empiricism somewhat weakened his criticism. His antipathy to *a priori* statements led him to attach more weight to historical fact and less weight to "values" than he should have done. In holding *a priori* statements (by which he meant statements that cannot be supported by the "facts"), especially those of Rousseau, in contempt, he implied that any proposition could be proved or disproved by an appeal to the "facts," which is not the case. He did not realize that all thinking must involve some *a priori* statements, which, technically speaking, are statements that cannot be shown to be true or false by any number of facts.[5] Science, as Morris Cohen points out, could not do without unproved assumptions.[6]

Maine's "scientific" definition of democracy could only impair his criticism. To hold that democracy is no more than a

[5] See Morris R. Cohen, *Reason and Nature: An Essay on the Meaning of Scientific Method* (1st ed., New York, 1931), pp. 140ff.
[6] *Ibid.*, p. 140.

mere form of government in which the many have ultimate political power, instead of the one or the few, must hinder the understanding of democracy and put a premium upon technical criticism. To think that a system of government can be understood simply by considering a distinguishing feature of its form is like thinking that a church can be understood merely by pointing out that it is distinguished from other buildings by a spire. The meaning of democracy cannot be grasped unless its spirit or its motivating ideas, which produce its form, are taken into account. There can be no fundamental criticism of a system of government, any more than of an institution, unless its purpose or its objectives are considered. Maine did not seem to understand that the impulse of democracy is happiness for ordinary men, and that democracy is strongly attached to liberty and equality.

His neglect of such characteristics led him to magnify the importance of democratic machinery and to exaggerate the significance of its defects. Thus the difficulty of determining the will of the electorate and the inadequacy of the devices for surmounting the difficulty — representative machinery, the caucus, party, corruption, and facile generalizations — become formidable evils. At the same time, the possible virtues of democratic machinery, or its philosophic purpose, are given little or no attention.

Maine did not distinguish clearly between a tendency to popular government and the fact of its acceptance.[7] He used faulty evidence; he assumed democracy to exist in France, Spain, and the South American countries when clearly it did not. Though he was deadly opposed to what he calls *a priori* statements and took Rousseau severely to task for them, he indulged more than once in generalizations that were either not self-evident or inadequately supported by the facts, as in the statement that democracy is hostile to science, or that aristocracy is the parent of progress. He assumed causal relationships to exist where there was no ground for so doing, as in his state-

[7] See above, p. 191n.

ment that universal suffrage was responsible for protection in
the United States.

Maine's violation of scientific method or of ordinary rules of
reasoning shows perhaps more than anything else the strength
of his conservatism. That strength can be well understood
when we reflect that science, in which Maine had so much
faith, stands for the supremacy of reason, while conservatism,
to which he subordinated science, stands rather for confidence
in instinct. It may be worth while to recall that through Maine's
conservatism spoke the philosophy of the historical school with
its aversion to change; through it spoke the autocratic spirit of
an Indian official; through it spoke the formalism of the
lawyer, and a scientific method whose assumptions had not yet
received a thoroughgoing criticism.

That *Popular Government* has shown a capacity to survive
(six editions appeared between 1885 and 1910) may be another
illustration of the fact that the social scientist in recent times
overestimates the value of the argument from history and the
argument from technical analysis, just as he underestimates the
importance of ethical and philosophical considerations.

WILLIAM LECKY

I

LECKY marks the close of the Victorian tradition of Burke.[1] His *Democracy and Liberty,* which was first published in 1896, is the last will and testament of an intellectual reaction that was founded largely on eighteenth-century ideas. Stephen and Maine had protested against the consolidation of political democracy; Lecky recognized its victory and turned to point out its disastrous consequences. Where Stephen and Maine had set their lance against democratic ideas, democratic dogma, and democratic confidence, Lecky set his against the implications of democracy. He saw political democracy moving toward an equalitarian state and beginning to direct its attack upon industrial privilege; he fully realized that it was turning from its triumph over aristocracy to an attack on the middle class. He wrote to warn Englishmen that the realization of universal

[1] William Hurrell Mallock was not in the tradition of Burke; he was not primarily a conservative in the basic sense of opposing change as such. He was a conservative in the sense of standing broadly for the arrangements of his own time; for economic individualism and the supremacy of the industrial oligarchy. Unlike most conservatives, he did not believe the common man was untrustworthy and irresponsible. He believed that the common man was endowed with the ordinary virtues, such as common sense and honesty, yet held that he was incompetent. He insisted that the common man without the leadership of the able few would produce no more than a subsistence living. Mallock's conservatism sprang from an individualism which held that all economic progress came from the brains of the few — the scientists, inventors, engineers, managers, and financiers of capitalism. He argued that inequality of reward, such as existed in his time, was essential if the élite were to make the most of their talents. Mallock is perhaps better placed in the twentieth than in the nineteenth century. It may be worth noting that about half of his writing on political and social matters was done during the first two decades of the present century.

William Lecky

suffrage would be the end of parliamentary government and the beginning of socialism.

Though Lecky set out to take stock of democracy in the modern world, he was actually far more interested in defending middle-class parliamentary government against the rule of common men. More concerned with legislation than Stephen and Maine, he presented more evidence to show that democracy was encroaching upon private property. Lecky was the leader of the attack on the democratic politician; he saw him as an agitator who fomented the assault on property; in his eyes the politician was ever ready to bargain away the savings of the thrifty for the sake of political office. Possessing a wider knowledge of practical affairs than most critics, he showed how political leaders could become the servants of organized minorities. More than anyone else, he called attention to the decline of parliamentary government, though his explanation of the decline was far from adequate. More than anyone else he showed how definitely England had by the nineties parted with the policy of laissez faire. Seeing that men were less able to do as they pleased with what was their own, he deduced that constitutional liberties had suffered a decline.

Lecky came to his task with the technical equipment of a historian. But his book is less a historical study than a polemic, and less a polemic than an imposing compilation of widely assorted facts, whose relations to one another are not always clear. He introduced materials as various and remote as the property system of the Hebrews and the fine points of Sabbatarian doctrine under the Stuarts. He elaborated his discourse in two heavy volumes, running to more than eleven hundred pages; and he delivered his message over and over again.

When he brightened his writing with critical comment, he did so for the greater part not in a spirit of detachment, but as one taking part in a conflict. Excited by the tendency of the democratic state to distribute more and more material benefits to the working classes, he made haste to defend property. He repeated old shibboleths in its honor; and he called up all

William Lecky

the eloquence of which he was capable to warn Englishmen of the evils of a socialist state. He was indignant that private ownership should be questioned; but his indignation, as well as his righteousness, carried a hollow ring. When defending the property system of his time, he wrote as a man who had taken his property for granted, and was now being challenged to show why he should not have it taken away; he wrote as a man stirred to anger by the threat of insecurity. Before he came to admonish his generation that democracy threatened property, he had made his name as a historian in English history; in *Democracy and Liberty* he established himself as an ardent partisan of the middle-class state. Seldom have value judgments thrust so sharply through the cloak of a scholar.

The main effort Lecky made met with little success; political democracy has continued to encroach upon private property, though not drastically, and the democratic state has entered more and more into the economic and social sphere. Though it is obviously too early to pass judgment on the ultimate implications of political democracy, it can hardly be said that universal suffrage has destroyed parliamentary government. Nor can it be said that universal suffrage has brought about a decline of liberty for the community as a whole; rather it has broadly made for liberty's enhancement. Lecky's *Democracy and Liberty* went through two editions but, unlike Stephen's *Liberty, Equality, Fraternity* and Maine's *Popular Government,* it apparently did not exert even a small influence. The *Quarterly Review,* which praised Maine's book, found little distinction in Lecky's, and Lord Morley gave *Democracy and Liberty* a scathing criticism. But neither the conservative *Quarterly Review* nor the liberal Lord Morley was in a position to see what was significant in Lecky's work. Their failure to see what was significant was not due to the prolixity of Lecky's writing, any more than it was to his pessimism. The *Quarterly Review* was too close to Lecky in its basic assumptions and Lord Morley was too close to Lecky in historical time to grasp the implications of what he had to say.

William Lecky

Democracy and Liberty foreshadows the struggle within the modern democratic state. It points to the struggle between the demand of the middle class to secure benefits under the private property order as the middle class have organized it and the demand of working-class men to increase their standard of life. Supporting the claims of the middle class, Lecky showed us its power to resist socialization. He revealed after the manner of a Marxist the extensive control the capitalists have over society in virtue of their control of the instruments of production. Yet he was aware, as few exponents of capitalism have been, of its insecurity; he was aware of its want of moral principle, just as he was aware that it was bringing about an ever deepening sense of injustice among workers. At the same time, he demonstrated the strength of middle-class beliefs; for, in spite of his admission that capitalism was morally inadequate and in spite of his feeling that the plutocracy developed by capitalism threatened social catastrophe, he tenaciously supported the capitalistic system. He showed as few political writers of his persuasion have done that constitutional liberty for middle-class men means above all freedom to do what they will with their own. In his observation that propertied groups of the middle class may be driven to the use of force in order to defend constitutional liberty, he hinted at a fundamental element in fascism. Lecky is a signpost to the twentieth century.

He stood at the end of the Victorian era; more than anyone else he reflected the mind of a class which was beginning to realize that political power was slowly slipping through its fingers. He reflected the resentment of a class that had seen the handwriting on the wall just as it had begun to settle down to the fruits of supremacy. Lecky represented conservatism on the defensive; in reality, private property seeking refuge from an attack on its privileged position, which had for some time been out of harmony with the needs of an industrial society. He represented a conservatism that was beginning to lose confidence in itself; a conservatism that was capable of little more than a protest against change; a conservatism that was falling back upon institutions, preparing to assert rather than to argue its claim to privilege.

II

Unlike Stephen, Lecky was not crucially affected by the religious views of his parents, nor was he, like Maine, crucially influenced by thinkers of a foreign country. His political ideas seemed to be determined more by the social and economic background in which he was brought up than by the thought of others. It was important, not that he was descended from Scottish, Irish, and English origins, but that he was from a family in Ireland of ample means. Lecky was first and last the product of the landowning class. That the most marked characteristic of the only considerable book he ever wrote dealing with the politics of the day, *Democracy and Liberty,* was an angry attack on those who sought to question the private property system is abundant testimony to his social inheritance.

In 1855 Lecky entered Trinity College, Dublin. It was his intention to prepare himself for the ministry. But contact with such various minds as Locke, Coleridge, Newman, Emerson, Pascal, Bossuet, Voltaire, and Rousseau, dissuaded him from a career in the church and interested him in history.[2] His first historical work, *The Religious Tendencies of the Age* (1860), signalized his change of heart; this book fell stillborn from the press, as did his other early work, *The Leaders of Public Opinion in Ireland* (1861). The latter was a study of the Irish patriots Swift, Flood, Grattan, and O'Connell. It breathed the spirit of Irish patriotism and showed that Grattan was a source of inspiration. As the great crusader against the Act of Union of 1800, Grattan epitomized for Lecky the meaning of Irish freedom. But Lecky's passion for Irish freedom was not destined to last; though he never failed to be attached to Ireland, he permitted his devotion to Irish independence to be overshadowed in later years by his devotion to the British Empire.

[2] See his "Formative Influence," *Historical and Political Essays* (New York, 1910), p. 96.

William Lecky

Despite the failure of his early writings, Lecky decided on history as a career, and was not long in showing that his decision had been well taken. His first important production, the *History of Rationalism* (1865), won immediate success, as did the work which followed, the *History of European Morals*. Lecky's most distinguished work, the *History of England in the Eighteenth Century* (1878-90), shows clearly the nature of his political ideas. Before pointing out its significance, it is necessary to call attention to the influence that was next in importance to Lecky's social background in the shaping of his political thought.

Burke was the chief intellectual force of Lecky's life. In an address he delivered at Trinity College, Dublin, in 1897, commemorating the centenary of Burke's death, Lecky said that there was perhaps no writer in all English literature to whom he was so deeply indebted.[3] But equally important was his remark that he had acquired Burke's *Reflections on the French Revolution* when he entered Trinity College, and that for many years this book had been his favorite pocket companion in long solitary walks in Ireland and Switzerland, and that he had marked and annotated almost every page. It is not surprising that while Lecky was at Trinity College he was untouched by Mill's thought, though Mill at that time was at the height of his fame. Nor is it surprising that *Democracy and Liberty* was an echo of the *Reflections*. Burke, it would appear, clarified for Lecky those vague thoughts and feelings which his social environment had stamped upon him; and in the process Burke provided him with a political philosophy for the defense of the class from which he sprang.

Lecky's *History of England in the Eighteenth Century* not only showed his political ideas in nearly final form, but it also showed how much he owed to Burke. In his discussion of Burke's political views, Lecky himself entered upon a discussion of first principles, and followed Burke on nearly all the

[3] Elizabeth van D. Lecky, *A Memoir of The Right Honourable William Edward Hartpole Lecky* (2d ed., London, 1910), p. 305.

fundamental points of his philosophy.[4] With Burke, he showed a deep veneration for the past and a profound fear of change. With Burke, he insisted that stability was indispensable to the life of the state, and was best reached by placing the chief political power in the hands of the propertied classes. Again with Burke, he held that democracy was extremely dangerous.

Nor was the guiding hand of Burke ever absent from Lecky's view of practical politics. When writing, in 1868, on the question of the disestablishment of the Irish Church, Lecky expressed the wish that such an organic change could be completed as rapidly as possible, for a long agitation, he said, meant the immense strengthening of the pure voluntaries in England and a contest between the people and the House of Lords which, with new constituencies and many revolutionary ideas in the air, was more likely than anything else to precipitate England into pure democracy.[5]

While at work on the *History,* Lecky became passionately excited over the Irish land problem. He championed the cause of the Irish landlords, claiming that the Land Act of 1881 had increased the insecurity of property.[6] But the event that fired his strongest feelings was the Home Rule controversy, which burst upon the country in 1886.[7] Lecky, who had always stood staunchly by Gladstone, now opposed him in his fight for Irish independence. The chief objection to Home Rule, he said, was that the party that demanded it was animated by two leading ideas—a desire to plunder the whole landed property of the country and an inveterate hatred of the English connection in every form.[8]

The Home Rule conflict, it has been said, made Lecky a politician and, in 1895, when it was revived, drove him into Parliament.[9] Lecky's elation in the same year over the advent

---

[4] *A History of England in the Eighteenth Century* (Cabinet Edition, 7 vols., London, 1925), III, 419–28.
[5] Elizabeth van D. Lecky, *A Memoir of William Lecky,* p. 56.
[6] *Ibid.,* p. 157.   [7] See *ibid.,* chaps. 8–12, inclusive.   [8] *Ibid.,* p. 186.
[9] George P. Gooch, *History and Historians in the Nineteenth Century* (London, 1913), p. 368.

to power of a large Conservative majority showed that at bottom his views were more in line with the Conservative than with the Liberal party. He spoke of the Conservative victory as showing beyond all possibility of doubt that on the Home Rule question the House of Lords represented the true sentiments of the democracy of the country.[10] Besides his almost fanatical aversion to the liberal movements favoring the lower classes in Ireland, Lecky was hostile to important economic and social reforms. In 1899, after sitting on a committee in Parliament dealing with old-age pensions, he could only discover that the scheme under consideration was one of the most dangerous of all forms of state socialism.[11]

It is of no little significance for the understanding of *Democracy and Liberty* that toward the end of his life Lecky fell, as did Maine, under the shadow of pessimism. Where Maine's appeared to be born of despondency, Lecky's seemed to spring from disillusionment. He took a gloomy view of the future, and in 1893 wrote that the world seems to have grown very old and very sad.[12] It was under this influence, says G. P. Gooch, that he wrote *Democracy and Liberty,* a passionate attack on the newer developments in the political and industrial world.[13] *Democracy and Liberty* was published in 1896, and was received without enthusiasm. The book, says Prothero, is a doubt, a protest, and a regret.[14]

III

Lecky's political philosophy, unlike Carlyle's, was not founded on a view of religion; nor, in contrast to Maine's, was it founded on any kind of philosophical view of history; it was built on a conception of the middle-class state. Though Lecky believed that the middle class ought to control the state, he nevertheless admired the aristocracy — landed property, be-

[10] Elizabeth van D. Lecky, *A Memoir of William Lecky,* p. 267.
[11] *Ibid.,* p. 328.   [12] *Ibid.,* p. 256.
[13] George P. Gooch, *History and Historians in the Nineteenth Century,* p. 368.
[14] George W. Prothero in the *Dictionary of National Biography,* Second Supplement, II, 439.

ing permanent and stationary, not fugitive and movable, was conducive, he thought, to virtue.[15] If he had been compelled to choose between the England of the Georges and the England of the last decade of Victoria's reign, he would doubtless have chosen the former. But his political ideas were firmly anchored to property as such, and industrial property was more important than landed in the English state of the nineteenth century. It was only natural for Lecky to think that the middle class should control the government and that aristocrats were eminently qualified to administer.

The government that was Lecky's ideal, and the standard by which he measured the tendencies and characteristics of democracy in his day, was the government that had been maintained in England between 1832 and 1867. Of this government he said:

It does not appear to me that the world has ever seen a better Constitution than England enjoyed between the Reform Bill of 1832 and the Reform Bill of 1867. Very few parliamentary governments have included more talent, or represented more faithfully the various interests and opinions of a great nation, or maintained under trying circumstances a higher level of political purity and patriotism.[16]

To Lecky the great virtue of the government between 1832 and 1867 was that it placed the chief controlling power in the hands of the middle class. He held with Aristotle that the middle class was the section of the community to which the chief power in government might be most wisely given:

It is not the class most susceptible to new ideas or most prone to great enterprises, but it is distinguished beyond all others for its political independence, its caution, its solid practical intelligence, its steady industry, its high moral average. It also, perhaps, feels more promptly and more acutely than any other class the effects of misgovernment . . .[17]

Though the Reform Bill of 1832, he pointed out, gave the chief controlling power to the middle class, all the old powers

[15] *Democracy and Liberty* (Cabinet Edition, 2 vols., London, 1899), I, 141; II, 500.
[16] *Ibid.*, I, 21.   [17] *Ibid.*, p. 20.

and influences were retained; only their proportionate weight was changed.[18] The House of Lords still remained an important element in the constitution. The landed interest was still powerful in the country constituencies. Property was specially and strongly represented, and the Reform Bill brought great masses of hitherto unrepresented property, as well as great centers of population, into the circle of the constitution. The active administration of affairs was chiefly in the hands of the upper and most cultivated class. At the same time, the suffrage was so arranged that it was, in some degree at least, within the reach of the skilled artisans — a great and intelligent class, who should have a distinct place in every well-ordered government.

The chief principle of Lecky's politics was respect for private property, the individualist view that there should be very little interference by the state with the property order. This principle explained why he argued that representation must be based mainly on property, and that property should be accorded special protection by a system of plural voting.[19] It was the reason for his conviction that the burden of taxation should rest on all alike;[20] that the graduated tax was for the most part a penalty on saving and industry, a premium offered to idleness and extravagance;[21] and that democracy weakened the relation between the voting and taxing power.[22] It lay behind the support he gave to the principle of freedom of contract. It cast considerable light on why he thought the lower classes were dangerous and why he believed that the realization of universal suffrage might bring about the breakup of society. Finally, respect for property explained why he could hold with Locke that society was chiefly a compact for securing to each man a peaceful possession of his property.[23]

Lecky's view of the mass of men in the lower classes — that they were ignorant, incompetent, and irresponsible — undoubtedly led him to fear democracy and to fear change. It is clear

[18] *Democracy and Liberty*, I, 20–21. [19] *Ibid.*, pp. 31, 276.
[20] *Ibid.*, pp. 157, 342. [21] *Ibid.*, pp. 346ff.
[22] *Ibid.*, pp. 32, 273–76; II, 377. [23] *Ibid.*, II, 501.

William Lecky

that Lecky's political ideas were quite like Burke's except that they had a middle-class instead of an aristocratic base. Like Burke he stressed the importance of property and the virtues of those who possessed it, and like Burke he had little respect for, and considerable fear of, the masses. Like Burke he attached great value to the brains and character of the few, though unlike Burke he identified the few with the middle class rather than with the aristocracy. Again like Burke, he emphasized the necessity of organic growth.

IV

One of Lecky's most important aims in *Democracy and Liberty* was to take stock of the effects of democracy on parliamentary government and liberty. Few things impressed him more than that democracy had brought about a deterioration in parliamentary government. He admitted that universal suffrage had been least dangerous in countries like Germany and the United States, where the powers of the representative body were greatly limited, or in new countries, which were inhabited by thinly scattered, prosperous, and self-reliant colonists, and where there were no old institutions to be destroyed.[24] But he insisted that in a number of countries there had been real deterioration; in some there had been extreme deterioration; in Mexico and in Spain there had been recurring alternations between anarchy and despotism.[25]

The type of deterioration he was for the most part concerned with was of a very different order and much less extreme; it was the tendency, as he would put it, of parliaments to break up more and more into small groups.[26] And the consequences of this, he held, were to enfeeble the executive, to give a disproportionate power to self-seeking minorities, to turn important branches of legislation into class bribery, and to lower the tone of public life. Lecky saw the tendency of parties to disintegrate exhibited in parliaments throughout the world; he believed it had gone farthest in Germany, Italy, and France,

[24] *Ibid.*, I, 35.   [25] *Ibid.*, p. 34.   [26] *Ibid.*, p. vi.

though only in the case of France did he discuss its consequences.[27]

One of the striking results of the multiparty system in France, he thinks, is the astonishing ministerial instability — between 1870 and 1893 France had thirty-two ministries — which makes for a weak executive and impairs the continuity of policy.[28] A still more striking result in Lecky's view is class bribery. It is conspicuous, he says, in enormous and wasteful expenditures on public works; such expenditures, which are extended to every department, almost to every commune, are for the purpose of conciliating the working classes or are a reward for supporting the government.[29] Though Lecky believes that the disintegration of parties has not gone as far in England as it has in France, Germany, and Italy, England is the country in which the tendency alarms him. He sees the Cabinet losing its old commanding and controlling authority over Parliament; he fears that without a homogeneous majority in Parliament, a coalition or a minority may at any time overthrow the Government.[30] He declares that this evil is greatly accentuated by the discovery that the multiplication of parties is exceedingly conducive to the triumph of strongly organized minorities.[31] The action of the Irish Home Rule party seems above all to have impressed this upon his mind.

If Lecky was disturbed by the threat of a weakened executive and parliamentary system, he was excited by what he calls the growing tendency of class legislation. Irish land legislation especially aroused his indignation; he spoke of it as the "most evident instance of confiscatory violation of contract in modern legislation." [32] Not only did Lecky argue that there had been a tendency to class legislation since the extension of the franchise to the lower classes in 1867, but also that there had been a marked tendency to class bribery. The Liberal party, he said, in 1886 purchased votes by adopting the policy of the National

[27] *Democracy and Liberty*, I, 150.
[28] *Ibid.*, pp. 45, 60.   [29] *Ibid.*, pp. 55–57; II, 400.
[30] *Ibid.*, I, 151; cf. p. xi.
[31] *Ibid.*, pp. 151–52.   [32] *Ibid.*, p. xix.

William Lecky

League.[33] Gladstone in 1874 dissolved Parliament when there was no necessity, and went to the country on a program to abolish the income tax.[34] Though Lecky realized that this instance of class bribery was not one of a democratic character, nevertheless it was class bribery, and another illustration of political immorality, which he observed was greatly increasing in his day. In the existing state of parliamentary representation, he declared, it is necessary to seek for a popular cry, which generally means some organic and destructive change in the constitution.[35] Since Disraeli, and the passing of the Reform Bill of 1867, which was one of the most discreditable episodes in our modern history, not one but two parties bid for popular support: "there is no longer a party whose business it is to initiate and a party whose business it is to restrain. Within wide limits the two parties move on the same lines, and are more like competitors in a race than adversaries in the field." [36]

Experience showed Lecky that parliamentary government had worked well where it had been mainly directed by the educated and propertied classes. In all the instances, he remarked, where parliamentary government has been conspicuously successful, the representative body was returned not on a purely democratic basis, but on a restricted suffrage, which is an essentially different thing. This is manifestly true of the British parliaments of the past; of the Italian parliaments after the war of 1859 and after the death of Cavour; of the Austrian parliaments, which transformed a despotism into one of the best governed countries of Europe; of the Belgian parliaments, which maintained constitutional government without organic change for sixty years; and of the Dutch parliaments, where self-government has long been as perfectly attained as in any portion of the globe.[37]

The main reason in Lecky's mind for the deterioration of parliamentary government was the admission of the lower classes to the suffrage. After the franchise act of 1867, Parlia-

[33] *Ibid.*, pp. 197, 228.   [34] *Ibid.*, p. 160.   [35] *Ibid.*, p. 153.
[36] *Ibid.*, pp. xii–xiii.   [37] *Ibid.*, pp. 33–34.

William Lecky

ment, according to him, no longer represented the best elements of the nation. Great uniform masses, he insists, of ignorant and influenced voters threaten to swamp the varieties of genuine opinion.[88] Great numbers will vote at the bidding of other men; the landlord, the clergyman or the dissenting minister or the priest, the local agitator, or the public-house keeper will direct the votes of many. Still more will be won by appeals to class cupidities, jealousies, and antipathies. Another large group, chiefly found in towns, is composed of those who have failed in the race of life, and who hang loosely on the verge of the criminal classes. Without knowledge and without character, their instinct will be to use their power for predatory and anarchic purposes; to break up society, to obtain a new deal in the good things of life, will be their object.

As for the ignorant classes who have opinions of their own, they will be of the vaguest and most childlike nature. A man will vote blue or yellow as his father did before him, and large numbers will vote on the "turn-about-system." When such voters do attempt to judge, how can it be expected that men as ignorant as children will have an intelligent view on foreign affairs, finance, or constitutional changes? The evil of evils of present-day politics is that the constituencies can no longer be fully trusted.[39] Lecky concluded that unless the government of mankind is essentially different from every other form of human enterprise, it must inevitably deteriorate if placed under the direct control of the most unintelligent classes:

Nothing in ancient alchemy was more irrational than the notion that increased ignorance in the elective body will be converted into increased capacity for good government in the representative body; that the best way to improve the world and secure rational progress is to place government more and more under the control of the least enlightened classes.[40]

Lecky believed that democracy had brought about not only a deterioration of parliamentary government, but also a decline of liberty. The constant tendency of democracy, he argued, is

[88] *Democracy and Liberty*, I, 21–25.   [39] *Ibid.*, p. 25.   [40] *Ibid.*, p. 26.

to impair the efficiency and authority of parliaments, which have hitherto proved the chief organs of political liberty.[41] Lecky was deeply impressed with what he called democracy's love for authoritative regulation. Democracy, he said, is like the church and the guild of the Middle Ages; it has a conspicuous desire to regulate.[42] Freedom of contract and free trade have been discredited; the majority of the democracies of the world are frankly protectionist. Though he believed that a considerable amount of interference was desirable, as in the case of factory acts and health regulation, he also held that a great deal of it was not. He held that public elementary education was indispensable if England was to compete successfully with modern nations in the economic and political sphere; yet he entertained some doubts of public education. He thought that it made many workers discontented with their lot, and he feared that if public education was extended to the secondary field, parental responsibility would be impaired, and a "grinding weight of taxation" would be placed upon some of the most struggling classes of the community.[43]

Needless to say, he looked upon the trend of increasing interference and regulation by the state with distrust and hostility; in his mind it was opposed to liberty, above all, it was opposed to the liberty of property owners.[44] The multiplication of the functions of the state resulted in an increase of taxation, which he considered a restriction of the liberty of property. Not only did he think that taxation under a democracy was likely to take forms which were particularly hostile to liberty, such as in the graduated tax,[45] but also that it threatened the propertied classes:

It is obvious that taxation is more and more employed for objects that are not common interests of the whole community, and that there is a growing tendency to look upon it as a possible means of confiscation; to make use of it to break down the power, influence, and wealth of particular classes; to form a new social type . . .[46]

[41] *Ibid.*, p. 257. [42] *Ibid.*
[43] *Ibid.*, p. 322. [44] *Ibid.*, pp. 256ff.
[45] *Ibid.*, p. 258. [46] *Ibid.*, p. 259.

William Lecky

Just as Lecky believed that the grant of power to the working classes was the fundamental cause of the decadence of parliamentary government, so was he convinced that it was the great factor endangering liberty. He believed that it was doubtful whether liberty in other forms was likely to be very secure if power was placed mainly in the hands of men who, in their own sphere, valued it so little.[47] He thought that the emphasis trade-unions placed upon regulation was an illustration of how little workingmen valued liberty. A school, he says, has arisen among popular working-class leaders which no longer desires that superior skill, or industry, or providence should reap extraordinary rewards. Their ideal is to restrict by the strongest trade-union regulations the amount of work, and to introduce legal compulsion into every branch of industry; to give the trade-union an absolute coercive power over its members.[48] In all countries and ages it is the upper and middle classes who have chiefly valued constitutional liberty, and those classes it is the work of democracy to dethrone.[49] Lecky grimly suggests that democracy may yet produce despotism:

The instability and insecurity of democratic politics; the spectacle of dishonest and predatory adventurers climbing by popular suffrage into positions of great power in the State; the alarm which attacks on property seldom fail to produce among those who have something to lose, may easily scare to the side of despotism large classes who, under other circumstances, would have been steady supporters of liberty.[50]

Lecky was not without suggestions for mitigating the evils that he believed democracy had produced in the English parliamentary system. He recommended that the number of Irish seats in the House of Commons be reduced, and that there be a rearrangement of the basis of representation in Ireland, giving greater weight to property.[51] He recommended that the Hare system of proportional representation be adopted,[52] and he thought that plural voting based on property and education ought to be established, though he realized that this was hardly

[47] *Democracy and Liberty*, I, 258.   [48] *Ibid.*, p. 257.   [49] *Ibid.*, p. 259.
[50] *Ibid.*   [51] *Ibid.*, p. 263.   [52] *Ibid.*, pp. 267–69.

feasible in his time.[53] Lecky saw in the referendum a real instrument for checking unbridled democracy; he advocated its use chiefly for constitutional issues involving changes in the disposition of power in the state.[54] The great merit of the referendum in Lecky's mind was that it would introduce into England that distinction between constitutional and ordinary legislation which he thought, just as Maine before him had thought, was a great factor making for stability and the protection of property in America.[55] It is true, he says, that the referendum would have the effect of lowering the authority of the House of Commons; but this would be one of its great merits.[56] The old saying of Burghley that "England can never be ruined but by her Parliament" was never more true than at the present time. The uncontrolled, unbalanced authority of a single representative body constituted like England's is one of the gravest dangers of the empire.

Perhaps Lecky's most important suggestion as a remedy for the ills of democracy was that the House of Lords should be given greater power; like Maine, he believed that a strong second chamber might bar the path to sudden organic change. He looked at the problem in the light of American experience: America possessed a second chamber of considerable authority; England needed a House of Lords whose veto should at least extend over one Parliament.[57] He argued, in fact, that England should have a law providing that no measure should be carried against the resistance of the upper house unless it had been adopted by two successive Houses of Commons, and by majorities of at least two-thirds.[58] This, he commented, would diminish in theory the present powers of the House of Lords, but in practice it would considerably increase them.

Lecky's survey of democracy extended beyond his inquiry into its effect upon parliamentary government and liberty. He was hardly less interested in the relation between democracy and various other subjects like militarism, foreign policy, and

[53] Ibid., p. 276.   [54] Ibid., pp. 286–93.   [55] Ibid., p. 286.
[56] Ibid., p. 291.   [57] Ibid., p. 465.   [58] Ibid., p. 466.

the "spoils" system. He found in France, England, and the United States materials for gauging still further the tendencies and characteristics of democratic government.

Alarmed by the gigantic increase in military expenditures and a great strengthening of the military system since the middle of the century in Europe, Lecky feared the danger of a European war.[59] Never, he says, in the history of mankind have explosive elements of such tremendous potency been accumulated in Europe, and, with all our boasted democracy, the issues of peace or war have seldom rested so largely with three or four men. If universal compulsory military training is furnishing governments with tremendous engines of repression, it is also preparing the time when every revolutionary movement will be made by men who have the knowledge and experience of military life.

A great military Power continually augmenting its army in hopes of repressing anarchy presents a spectacle much like that which may be seen at a Spanish bullfight when the banderilla has been planted by a skilful hand, and when every bound by which the infuriated animal seeks to shake off the barb that is lacerating its flesh only deepens and exasperates the wound.[60]

After admitting all the values of military training, he finds that the shadows of the picture remain very marked. It is impossible, he says, to turn Europe into a military camp without in some degree reviving the ideals and standards of a military age. Military training sterilizes the finer types of individuals; among such men, it is difficult to overestimate the waste and ruin of high talent, or the amount of acute and useless suffering that it produces. To democracies these things are of little moment, and they seem lost in the splendor and pageantry of military life.[61]

Lecky agrees with Maine that military conscription is the natural brother of universal suffrage. The leveling and intermingling of classes it produces renders it congenial to a democratic age; yet, he argues, it is in many respects difficult to think

---

[59] *Democracy and Liberty*, I, 313–14. [60] *Ibid.*, p. 314. [61] *Ibid.*, pp. 314–15.

of a greater contrast in spirit and organization; the military system substitutes for majority rule and liberty the strictest despotism and subordination.[62] Will the present relation between democracy and the military system last? Will eagles always be governed by parrots? Though Lecky deplores the growth of militarism, he apparently sees nothing inconsistent in his stand for an English fleet of overwhelming power, which, he says, is the first and most vital condition of the security of the English nation.[63] Lecky suggests that the great growth of militarism in the latter half of the nineteenth century has contributed largely, though indirectly, to the prevailing tendency to aggrandize the powers of government and to seek social reforms in strong, coercive organizations of society.[64]

The foreign policy of France under democracy, observes Lecky, has not served the forces of liberalism but those of reaction. Few sadder spectacles have been witnessed in our time than the declaration of France in 1883, in a transport of enthusiasm, that her foreign policy was now identified with Russia's — the union of the chief democracy of Europe with its one great persecuting despotism.[65] In discussing English foreign policy, Lecky does not apologize for English imperialism, which he frankly recognizes and supports with the typical imperialist arguments. He believes that the great amount of territory which England annexed in the last half of the nineteenth century was absolutely necessary because England needed markets for her industries. He says that though much of the annexation was due to commercial enterprise, a great deal of it was due to "the necessity which often compels a civilized power as a mere measure of police and self-defence to extend its frontier into the uncivilized world."[66] He observes that the foreign policy of the United States is in striking contrast to that of the nations of Europe; escaping the militarism that is corroding the greatest powers of Europe, its gigantic energies have been steadily directed in the paths of peace.[67]

[62] *Ibid.*, pp. 315–16.   [63] *Ibid.*, pp. 306–07.   [64] *Ibid.*, p. 316.
[65] *Ibid.*, p. 63.   [66] *Ibid.*, p. 308.   [67] *Ibid.*, p. 127.

William Lecky

Not the least serious defect, Lecky thinks, of modern democracy is that it fails to draw the able men of the community into political service. The record of France since 1870 has not been a brilliant one; for French governments have produced or attracted little talent.[68] America even more clearly than France illustrates the truth, which is seen again and again, that pure democracy is one of the least representative of governments; in hardly any other country does the best life and energy of the nation flow so habitually apart from politics.[69] Yet Lecky seems to believe that the development of a permanent civil service is democracy's outstanding contribution to government. The introduction, he says, of competitive examination realized, on the whole more perfectly than any other system, the ideal of the Revolution: "La carrière ouverte aux talents."[70] In England the Civil Service has maintained a high standard of professional honor and competence;[71] and in France the permanent service includes men greatly above the average, whom universal suffrage has brought to the front.[72]

Though Lecky is convinced that democracy has brought about a decline in parliamentary government in England, he defends the suffrage in local government. The introduction, he says, of the elective system in local government in England may be a valuable corrective to the old regime, which was corruptly administered for the benefit of the few. Moreover, local government forms one of the best training grounds for politicians; and the elective system stimulates interest in public affairs; it furnishes a security that the wants of all classes will be brought to light; and it infuses new strength and energy into local administration.[73]

Lecky finds that corruption is the great defect of the American democracy. Corruption, he says, is largely the product of the spoils system — the treating of all the smaller posts and offices under the federal and state governments as rewards for party services, and the changing of occupants with every change

[68] Democracy and Liberty, I, 43. [69] Ibid., p. 114. [70] Ibid., p. 245.
[71] Ibid., p. 243. [72] Ibid., p. 45. [73] Ibid., p. 239.

of political power.[74] This system is very distinctly a product of democracy; it is defended on the ground that it opens the ranks of official life to the greatest possible number of people.[75] Yet this system, Bryce says, successfully excludes the more respectable class from political life, and throws its whole management into the hands of the professional politician and the "machine." [76] Politics, Bryce continues, has now become a gainful profession, like advocacy, stockbroking, the dry-goods trade, or the getting up of companies. People go into it to live by it, primarily for the sake of the salaries attached to the places they count on getting, secondarily for incidental, and sometimes illegitimate, gains.[77] The main evil of the spoils system, according to Sterne, is not so much that it brings incompetent men into office and wastes public money as that it demoralizes both parties, and makes contests which should be for principle mainly for plunder.[78]

Lecky himself observes that one very natural result of the American spoils system is that while there is no country in the world in which party contests are fought with more energy and tenacity, there is no country in which the motives that inspire them are more abjectly sordid.[79] Great unselfish causes are not the true reasons for party divisions. In other countries this is not so. Selfish and corrupt motives no doubt abound; but in the contests between Liberals and Conservatives in England, or in the quarrels between clericalism and anticlericalism or capital and labor that divide parties on the Continent, there is always some real principle at issue, some powerful element of unselfish enthusiasm. Lecky suggests that this difference between America and European countries is partly due to the absence of great issues in a country which has few serious relations with other countries, which has almost wholly disconnected the interests of church and religion from national politics, and in

[74] *Ibid.*, p. 78.   [75] *Ibid.*, p. 83.
[76] *Ibid.*   [77] *Ibid.*, p. 86.
[78] *Ibid.*, p. 83. Lecky's reference is to Simon Sterne, *Constitutional History and Political Development of the United States* (New York [1882]), pp. 227–31.
[79] *Democracy and Liberty*, I, 85.

which the constitution imposes insuperable obstacles to organic change.[80]

There is one thing, Lecky argues, that is worse than corruption; it is acquiescence in corruption. No feature of American government strikes a stranger so powerfully as the extraordinary indifference, partly cynicism and partly good nature, with which notorious frauds and corruption in the sphere of politics are viewed by American public opinion.[81] There is nothing altogether like this to be found in any other great country. This corruption would not be acquiesced in if it were not that an admirable written constitution, enforced by a powerful and vigilant Supreme Court, had restricted to small limits the possibilities of misgovernment.[82] All the rights that men value most are placed beyond the reach of a tyrannical majority.

Lecky observed that organized minorities were playing an increasingly greater part in the American democracy, just as they were in the parliamentary democracies of Europe. The power of party organizations over nomination, he thought, was even greater than the power of such bodies in England; but the managers of the machine had to take nonpolitical opinion into account in the more important elections.[83] The drive of minorities to attain private ends was not limited to political spoilsmen and their party machines; it was also to be found in a vicious degree in American industry, and among the veterans of the Civil War. The policy of protection, he says, which began with the Woolen Act of 1867 and ended in the McKinley tariff includes as much purely class legislation, intended to support class interests and carried by corrupt means, as can be found in the most effete monarchy in Europe.[84] A war pension list has been created in the United States that far exceeds in magnitude any other known in history, including pensioners totally unconnected with the War of 1812 and the Mexican War; yet it would not have been so if the protectionist interest had not found it necessary to maintain and expend an enormous sur-

[80] *Democracy and Liberty*, I, 85–86.   [81] *Ibid.*, p. 113.
[82] *Ibid.*, p. 116.   [83] *Ibid.*, p. 106.   [84] *Ibid.*, p. 134.

plus.[85] No other country could have borne such an expenditure for pensions, and certainly public opinion in no other country would have tolerated it.

In spite of the corruption and the class legislation in America, Lecky believes that its general legislation ranks very high,[86] and that federal and state administration is not sensibly inferior to the administrations of European countries.[87] But, though American civilization is supremely great industrially, little can be said for its intellectual and aesthetic achievements.[88] Tocqueville believed that there was no country with less intellectual independence, less real liberty of discussion, or where the expression of unpopular opinion was more bitterly resented. Modern democracy is not favorable to the higher forms of intellectual life; democracy levels down as well as up. The belief in the equality of man, the total absence of the spirit of reverence, the apotheosis of the average judgment, the fever and the haste, the advertising and sensational spirit that American life so abundantly generates, are all little favorable to the production of great works of beauty or of thought.[89]

He holds that the American experiment in democracy carries with it as much of warning as of encouragement. He holds with Maine that America shows that a written constitution, which protects private property and makes fundamental change difficult, is essential to democracy if it is to attain stability.

. . . all the best observers in America, whether they admire or dislike democracy seem agreed . . . that it is absolutely essential to its safe-working that there should be a written constitution, securing property and contract, placing serious obstacles in the way of organic changes, restricting the power of majorities, and preventing outbursts of mere temporary discontent and mere casual coalitions from overthrowing the main pillars of the State. In America, such safeguards are largely and skilfully provided, and to this fact America largely owes her stability.[90]

Lecky not only looked at the recent record of democracy, he also considered its future. He saw dark clouds gathering on the

[85] *Ibid.*   [86] *Ibid.*, p. 121.   [87] *Ibid.*, p. 111.
[88] *Ibid.*, pp. 127–31.   [89] *Ibid.*, p. 131.   [90] *Ibid.*, p. 136.

horizon; middle-class parliamentary democracy was threatened by the ultimate implications of universal suffrage, and by the abuse of wealth. It was his deep-seated fear that universal suffrage would ultimately lead to socialism. Shuddering at the thought that socialism had so many supporters in the modern world,[91] he argued strenuously against it. He referred to the socialization plans of Hyndman, Webb, Bernard Shaw, and Hobhouse as insane and grotesque. Any approach to them, he says, would blast as in an hour the whole prosperity of the nations; capital would leave England, great unemployment would follow, and famine would then seize upon the country.[92] If England turned socialist, the poor would become still poorer not only as a result of losing their jobs, but also as a result of losing their savings and the benefits created for them. Public debts and landed property are the forms of property which it is the special object of socialists to plunder. To plunder these would mean that the savings bank of the poor man would sink in the same boat as the fortune of the millionaire. It would mean that most of the funds of benefit and insurance societies and of charities, which are invested in government funds or are a first charge upon the land, would be destroyed.[93]

Even if a flight of capital could be avoided, socialism is impossible to achieve. Government organization may be applied with some success to such industrial undertakings as can be managed on the system of strict routine, and by rigid and inflexible rules.[94] The state administers the post office and the telegraph services very efficiently, and in some countries it manages the means of transport, or the supply of a few commodities of great public necessity, such as gas and water. But in all those departments of industry which are not susceptible of this kind of management it is certain to fail.[95] It is utterly unfit to undertake on a large scale the duties of a landowner. The state could not be turned into a gigantic shopkeeper or manufacturer, providing for the vast and ever changing human wants and tastes.

[91] *Democracy and Liberty*, II, 351.   [92] *Ibid.*, pp. 393–94.
[93] *Ibid.*, p. 472.   [94] *Ibid.*, p. 400.   [95] *Ibid.*, pp. 400–01.

William Lecky

Its form of administration represses the qualities that are needed for success in these fields: tact and foresight which anticipate changes, promptitude that seizes the happy moment for action — all the qualities that are found in exceptional individuals, acting under the strong impulse of personal interest. The rare combination of daring, caution, and insight, which is essential to the success of a great industry, will never be found in routine-ridden government officials. And if the disciplined action of the government is relaxed, if the hard and fast rules are abandoned, there will be the imminent danger of jobbery and favoritism.

The first condition of success of a socialist community is complete isolation; socialism is essentially opposed to free trade and international commerce. Socialism is conceivable in a remote island of the Pacific, where the whole population might be organized into one great cooperative society, in which each member filled an assigned part and discharged an assigned duty in obedience to the authority of the whole. But this organization must be kept stereotyped; it must be kept separate, drilled and disciplined like a regiment of soldiers. Such a society is absolutely inconceivable where there is a vast, fluctuating, highly locomotive population, deriving its subsistence from many distant countries, bound to them by the closest commercial ties, continually sending out vast streams of emigrants, continually absorbing alien populations.[96]

Lecky admits that there is some truth in the socialist charge of waste and overproduction under the competitive order, and he thinks that most of the future industrial progress will probably consist in cooperative schemes for mitigating these evils.[97] He also anticipates profound changes in the incidence of taxation, in the part which government will play in initiating, directing, and subsidizing industry, and in providing for the old, the impoverished, and the unemployed.[98] But, he says, the socialist remedies could only bring far greater evils than any that they could prevent. Under their system there would be no mo-

[96] *Ibid.*, p. 368.   [97] *Ibid.*, p. 367.   [98] *Ibid.*, p. 364.

William Lecky

tive for saving.[99] Under their system there would be no adequate motives to stimulate production; there would be no longer the desire of each man to improve his circumstances, to reap the full reward of superior talent, energy, or thrift.[1] Yet these desires are the very mainspring of the production of the world. The organization of a people in the framework of a socialist state can never succeed, for it conflicts with the fundamental laws and elements of human nature.

The sense of right and wrong, which is the basis of the respect for property and for the obligation of contract; the feeling of family affection, on which the continuity of society depends, and out of which the system of heredity grows; the essential difference of men in aptitudes, capacities, and character, are things that never can be changed, and all schemes and policies that ignore them are doomed to failure.[2]

Lecky's final word on socialism is that a system which preaches the most wholesale and undisguised robbery will never approve itself to the mass of men, unless all the foundations and sanctions of morality have been effectually destroyed.[3]

Though Lecky is a vigorous defender of the capitalist order, he is uneasy over the new property. Though he believes that most wealth is honestly made, he is often impressed by the evils of the acquisitive system. America stands out to him as the country in which the worst abuses occur. There is no country, he says, where the struggle for wealth is fiercer or more unscrupulous, or where vast sums have been more frequently or more rapidly accumulated by evil means.[4] In a country where there is no rank, and where political eminence gives little or no dignity, the thirst for wealth acquires a maddening power.[5] Corrupt political organizations come in constant contact with great railway and industrial corporations, and each can do much to assist and to demoralize the other.[6] Speaking of the railway kings, he says that in no other country has this class of men been so prominent, and in no other country has their power been more hideously abused.[7] He believes that the irresponsibility of American wealth, which is a factor bringing

[99] *Democracy and Liberty*, II, 368. [1] *Ibid.*, p. 367. [2] *Ibid.*, p. 369. [3] *Ibid.*, p. 350. [4] *Ibid.*, p. 362. [5] *Ibid.*, I, 126. [6] *Ibid.* [7] *Ibid.*, p. 124; II, 363.

about a decline in political morality, must one day lead to retribution: "The colossal fortunes built up by the railway-wrecker, by the railway-monopoliser, by the fraudulent manipulator of municipal taxation, by unjust favours extorted from bribed legislators, by great commercial frauds and commercial monopolies under the names of trusts and syndicates, must one day bring a terrible Nemesis." [8] Lecky notes that American industrialism contributes to lowering the political plane by diverting from it the best energies of the country.[9]

He sees the new property developing a class of parasites who live only for luxury and ostentation. He observes that all the more dissipated capitals and watering places of Europe and America are full of men living lives of absolute frivolity, dissociated from all serious interests, ever seeking with feverish eagerness for new forms of pleasure. Such men, he insists, depress the moral tone of the society in which they live; for rich men will always contribute largely to setting the tone of society, to forming the tastes, habits, ideals, and aspirations of other classes.[10] Wealth, he says, which brings with it no ties and is obtained with no effort is to most men a temptation and a snare.

Lecky is impressed with the great inequality and false standards to which the new property has given rise. In America pauperism has appeared and spread widely through the cities, while the unoccupied land, which was once a safety valve for dangerous energies, is fast contracting.[11] In the immediate neighborhood, he says, of the wretched slums of England's great cities there are to be found societies where dignity is mainly measured by wealth, irrespective of the sources from which it is derived and the purposes to which it is applied.[12] In the mad race of ostentation men lavish sums on the pleasures of a single night that might bring comfort to a hundred families. In the words of one of the most popular of the socialist writers, "Jay Gould, the financier, got more pay and

[8] *Ibid.,* II, 362. [9] *Ibid.,* I, 68. [10] *Ibid.,* pp. 358–59.
[11] *Ibid.,* II, 362. [12] *Ibid.,* p. 502.

William Lecky

held more wealth than Gladstone, and Carlyle, and Darwin, and Koch, and Galileo, and Columbus, and Cromwell, and Caxton, and Stephenson, and Washington, and Raphael, and Mozart, and Shakespeare, and Socrates, and Jesus Christ ever got amongst them."[13] Lecky holds that in the light of such injustice it is not surprising that feelings should strengthen and that opinions should grow that portend great convulsions in the state.[14] No one, he says, who peruses modern socialist literature, no one who observes the current of feeling among the masses in the great towns, can fail to perceive their deep, growing, and not unreasonable sense of the profound injustices of life.

Lecky reflects that inequalities of fortune are undoubtedly more keenly felt than in the past.[15] The agglomeration of men in great towns, he says, and the sharp division into quarters of the rich and quarters of the poor, bring into salient relief the contrasts between extravagant luxury and struggling misery. Education has strengthened among the poor the sense of the disparities of life; and by increasing self-respect and by multiplying wants, it raises the standard of what are deemed its necessaries. Well-being has greatly increased, but it has not increased as rapidly as have desires. The breaking up of religious beliefs has given additional impulse to the restlessness of society; when there is no longer the hope of a future world for consolation amidst the miseries of life, it is not surprising that the desire to obtain the best things of this world should attain a passionate force.

Lecky harbors the very evident fear that the development of plutocracy, with its lack of social responsibility, may undermine the state:

It is not the existence of inherited wealth, even on a very large scale, that is likely to shake seriously the respect for property: it is the many examples which the conditions of modern society present of vast wealth acquired by shameful means, employed for shameful

[13] Robert Blatchford, *Merrie England: A Plain Exposition of Socialism* (New York, 1895), p. 139.
[14] *Democracy and Liberty*, II, 502.   [15] *Ibid.*, pp. 496–97.

purposes, and exercising an altogether undue influence in society and in the State. When triumphant robbery is found among the rich, subversive doctrines will grow among the poor. When democracy turns, as it often does, into a corrupt plutocracy, both national decadence and social revolution are being prepared.[16]

His principal suggestion for mitigating the danger is a wider diffusion of property among industrial labor by means of profit-sharing schemes and cooperatives, and among agricultural workers by means of a greater subdivision of the land.[17]

v

If *Democracy and Liberty* received little attention in its day, part of the explanation lies in Lecky's treatment of his material. He seldom pulls his views together, there is little pattern, and there are many dreary pages. His book lacks, as Lord Morley says, Maine's sinewy and athletic style, and the severe simplicity of his argumentative method. When, however, his discussion is critical, he never leaves us in doubt as to what he thinks; unlike Maine, he always states his own position clearly. Two motives contend in *Democracy and Liberty;* the motive to describe and the motive to declare a scheme of values.

But, with all the defects of its writing, *Democracy and Liberty* hardly deserves to be so soon forgotten. If Lecky saw nothing more than selfishness or passion in the activity of pressure groups, he showed that they could bend the state to their will. That the principle of majority rule does not always work on the majority principle is being more and more widely recognized.

It was well that Lecky emphasized the evils of the spoils system in American life, though this had already been done by Bryce. But if Lecky saw the connection between big business and the spoils system more clearly than Bryce, he did not see, any more than Bryce did, the connection in terms of an owning class, which could commandeer the services of politicians. He saw that spoils were morally reprehensible in the sense that

[16] *Ibid.*, pp. 501–02.   [17] *Ibid.*, pp. 470ff., 484–85.

William Lecky

they reflected dishonesty, but he did not really perceive their deep injustice in the sense of class privilege. It was useful that he followed Bryce and called attention to the fact that ability turned away from political life in America, and that the nation was more concerned with economic development than with perfecting its political institutions. It was timely, too, that he pointed out that in no country was the race for wealth more fierce and more unscrupulous. And if he repeated Tocqueville in remarking that democracy in America did not encourage intellectual effort of the highest order, it was interesting that another critic should have come to the same conclusion.

It was well that he called attention to the fact that the rich set the tone of a society. His observation that the mass of men were more keen to feel injustice than ever before and the reasons he adduced for this fact were not less valuable. His warning that the rich may turn against democracy and look to autocracy for salvation will have to be heeded in the democratic states which have so far escaped being undermined; for capitalists in Germany and in Italy helped to bring fascism to power, and capitalists are now trying to bring fascism to power in Spain.

Lecky's warning that the growth of militarism and the great increase in armaments in an atmosphere of nationalism threatened war was not idle, any more than the similar warnings of Ruskin and Maine. Though militarism was not the main cause bringing about the destruction of democracy in Italy, in Germany, and in Austria, it nevertheless was an important one; and it is an all-important cause in the present attempt on the life of the Spanish democracy.

Lecky's criticism of democracy on the ground that it made for instability in parliamentary government was only partly true in the case of France, which was his best example. Universal suffrage as such was hardly the cause of the multiparty system and of the ministerial instability that resulted from this system. The principles by which the French parliament and representative system were organized and French individualism were surely the chief causes. Though there was some evidence toward the end of the nineteenth century for believing that England might develop the multiparty system, he exaggerated its significance. Lecky gave greater weight to the part played by the Irish party than the facts will bear out; he misjudged the particularity of its character. He did not see that the action of the Irish party was a reflection, not of party disintegration in England, but of English misgovernment in Ireland. And the Home Rule bloc of the Liberal party and the Unionist bloc of the Conservative party had the same origin.

Lecky's fundamental criticism of democracy, that it threatened to undermine private property, was a criticism that could not hope to have any validity save from a narrow middle-class point of view. Lecky exaggerated the power of the franchise under capitalism; he did not seem to realize that so long as economic power remains in the hands of the middle class, it is unlikely that universal suffrage will be able to make any thoroughgoing alteration in the property system. His fear that democracy would attack private property was based very largely on the Irish land acts, especially the act of 1886; but those acts were not only just, they were also necessary. His fear that democracy would attack property was based, too, in part on the increasing popularity of the graduated income tax; in opposing this tax, Lecky placed the interests of property above equity, for those who enjoy large incomes are more able to pay; and he failed to take account of the fact that large incomes are very much a social product, made possible in part by withholding from the worker a fair return for his labor, and acquired in many cases by inheritance, or in other words, by accident.

Though there has been some alteration in property relations as organized under capitalism, it can hardly be said that democracy has basically changed them; democracy has done little more than soften them. In the light of recent experience in Italy, Germany, Austria, and Spain, the question is not whether democracy will rob property owners of their property, but whether propertied interests will rob common men of their chief weapon of defense against exploitation, democracy.

Lecky's criticism of democracy on the ground that it was hostile to liberty was valid only on the assumption of his individualist view of liberty. On the assumption that there should be as wide a field as possible for individual action, democracy with its increasing social services was interfering more and more with liberty. But the individualist view of liberty is a narrow view; it tends to make unrestrained action an end in itself; it neglects very largely conditions in which actions take place. In this view, a great many workers possess liberty when in fact they are something like slaves. To say that a man possesses liberty who is born in a slum under conditions of grinding poverty and is compelled to work long hours every day is to make liberty all but meaningless. If the ideal of liberty is not absence of restraint, but opportunity to act creatively, or as Graham Wallas put it, opportunity for continuous initiative, then Lecky's case against democracy falls down. Surely a society is freer in which employers are forbidden to sweat their workers than one in which this is not the case.

The liberty for which Lecky stood was the liberty of property owners to do as they please; as Ruskin showed, such liberty involved exploitation of the worker. Lecky followed the middle-class tradition in holding that the main purpose of the state was to protect property; he argued with Locke that society was a compact chiefly for securing property. At best this view made a material condition that is necessary to the good life the main purpose of the state itself, which is a confusion of values. It may be worth while to call attention to Lecky's view that trade-unions were autocratic and therefore hostile to liberty. It is true that at times trade-unions act autocratically and restrict talent, yet it hardly need be said that on the whole they increase liberty by protecting the worker against the encroachment of the employer. What is important to remark is that Lecky did not see that industry is far more authoritarian than trade-unions. Trade-unions are governed broadly on the democratic principle, whereas industry is governed broadly on the autocratic principle. It is significant that industrialists in Germany and Italy helped to bring fascism to power. The autocratic tendency of a governing class under capitalism is reflected in Lecky's remark that attacks on property may easily scare to the side of despotism large classes who, under other circumstances, would have been steady supporters of liberty.

Lecky found democracy bringing about the decline of parliamentary government and interfering with property and liberty mainly because the common man was not fit to participate in political power; in his view the common man was ignorant and inclined to plunder.[18] Lecky repeated the stock argument of every group in power — that those who are knocking at the gate are somehow without qualification. The same argument had been made against the middle class by aristocrats, and against aristocrats by kings, and against aristocrats and kings by priests. If the stock argument directed against the working class seemed to carry some weight when Stephen and Maine were writing, it could carry hardly any weight when Lecky wrote. When *Democracy and Liberty* appeared it was clear that men who share in power share in benefits; it was not accidental that there was a wider spread of advantages for the lower classes after the franchise acts of 1867 and 1884–85.

Following the capitalist view of human nature, that men are chiefly motivated by self-interest, Lecky held that the workingman, who had little property, would be likely under democracy to plunder the wealthy. So far, workingmen have made no serious attack on wealth; on the contrary, workingmen in the great democracies have been content to suffer immense inequalities. Lecky's view that the common man threatened property was based on fear rather than sober analysis. Men who spend the day in hard toil trying to make a living have little time and less means — especially since the invention of the machine gun — to destroy property, unless, indeed, they are driven by great suffering or unbearable exploitation. Moreover, if a

[18] For further discussion of this point see the chapter on Maine, page 198.

poor man should contemplate plunder, he would probably, crisis apart, be more impressed with the chances of failure, of increased poverty, or of death, than with success. The workingman is the most insecure of all; if his insecurity does not produce fear and timidity, it is more apt to produce hopelessness than courage. Apart from a severe social crisis, what little security the workingman has undoubtedly looms very large in his eyes. It is not true, as is often said, that a man of little income has nothing to lose and everything to gain if he should attempt to divide the spoils; he might lose what he has and he might lose his head.

Lecky believed that it was well to make the workingman conscious of paying taxes in order to develop a sense of civic responsibility, for the ultimate purpose apparently of providing a brake on heavy governmental expenditure. How, it may be asked, can workingmen develop a sense of responsibility by paying more taxes than they should (in view of the relatively lighter burdens of those who have the capacity to pay) on incomes that are hardly enough to keep body and soul together? The view that workingmen should bear a disproportionate tax burden in order to develop a sense of civic responsibility is largely a moralizing on the part of middle-class men against a more equitable distribution of property. Paying taxes under capitalistic democracy develops, as the rich testify, a sense of responsibility to property rather than to government.

It is true, as Lecky says, that the middle and upper classes have been the chief defenders of liberty, for they have been in a position in which liberty could mean something; they have had power and some leisure. The remedy for the ignorance of the workingman is education, and the remedy for what Lecky believed was his irresponsibility is a just industrial and agricultural system.

To Lecky a truly representative system was one that gave first claims to property. To be sure, he held that it was important to represent intelligence, but to him intelligence was generally the natural accompaniment of property. He conceded that "numbers," that is, the propertyless, should be given some representation; but it was not as a matter of right, but of grace, that he conceded this. Lecky did not consider that every man, in virtue of his humanity, is equally concerned with the action of the state. He did not consider that the purpose of the franchise is to voice the needs of the individual in the totality of his interests, and not merely in the interests of his property. It is significant that Lecky found democracy to be successful in local government, though not in Parliament; in local government the problem of property was not crucially affected.

Though Lecky is aware of many of the social and moral defects of capitalism, these are relatively unimportant in his scale of values compared to the great service rendered by private property under capitalism. The conceptions that have been developed to explain and to justify capitalism are to him a final teleology. No conception is more valid in his eyes than the view of human nature assumed by capitalism; yet the truth of this view is no greater than that found in the view of human nature assumed by other philosophies that have dominated men's minds for considerable periods. The puritan view, which was in the ascendant in the seventeenth century, held that man was a sinner; there is a sense in which man is a sinner — in the sense that he is capable of wrong actions. The thought of the Enlightenment, which was triumphant in the eighteenth century, assumed that man was rational; to some extent man is rational, but to a much smaller extent than rationalism supposed. Capitalism in the nineteenth and twentieth centuries assumes that man is a creature of self-interest motivated above all by the desire of material reward; there is some truth in this view, but not as much as the capitalists would like to believe.

In the capitalist view of things, the appeal of superior reward for superior work, as Lecky puts it, is the mainspring of production. This appeal has little significance for the mass of men who do the producing. Workingmen in large-scale industry have little chance to display superior ability, for most jobs are on a basis of routine; and where this is not the case, the appeal of superior reward still cannot operate very effectively, for the chance of the ordinary workman to become a foreman is very small, and the reward of the foreman is hardly superior. Moreover, the great work of the world, as Ruskin said, was done not for pay but for nothing; it is commonly recognized by scientific writers that the great discoveries in science and the great technical inventions which lie at the foundation of the machine age were made in most instances not because scientists and inventors had hopes of superior reward, but because they liked discovering and inventing.

In his discussion of socialism Lecky showed the strength of his middle-class assumptions rather than a flexible mind. Though he admitted that government could manage the postal service, he was convinced that it could never be trusted with an economic function in which enterprise and efficiency were essential. Experience not only in Russia but also in Germany, England, and America, to mention only a few of the larger countries, shows that it is possible for government to run successfully economic institutions that are not of the routine type.

Lecky asserted that socialism is opposed to the principle of superior reward for superior work. Many socialists, however, believe in inequality of reward within limits; what they do not believe in is inequality of such a magnitude as will impair the rights of men. Had Lecky been more fully acquainted with Marx he would have found that Marx did not exclude the possibility of unequal rewards. Russia has constructed a form of the socialist state in which the government not only owns the means of production, but has also adopted the principle of unequal reward. Such a state, which was inconceivable to Lecky except in a remote island of the Pacific, increased its rate of production, according to some estimates, as much as ten per cent in one year, whereas no capitalist nation has apparently exceeded four per cent. That Lecky fell back upon the argument that socialism was contrary to human nature and would destroy morality and the family shows that at bottom socialism was for him a subject more for emotion than reason.

William Lecky

Lecky's remedy for the ills of Parliament and the dangerous tendency of democracy was, as in the case of Maine, "machinery." His chief concern was the protection of private property, hence his chief remedy was, as with Maine, to strengthen the House of Lords so that a brake might be put upon the House of Commons. Lecky assumes that the House of Commons tends to act hastily; yet an examination of the history of important legislation, such as the Education Act of 1870 or the achievement of Irish Home Rule, shows that the House of Commons does not in general act hastily. Such legislation is usually the product of discussion for some twenty to thirty years in and out of the House of Commons. It is significant that the House of Lords only comes to life when there is a Liberal or Labour party in power;[19] and it comes to life not to discover whether the policy of the House of Commons is a true expression of the majority will, but to oppose that policy, whatever will it expresses. The House of Lords is inert except when it believes that property may be interfered with; yet Lecky could say that it was representative of the opinion of the nation.

Democracy and Liberty is more important for our time than for Lecky's; it brings out the incompatibility of democracy and capitalism. Lecky's work showed conclusively that middle-class liberalism was not prepared to follow the logic implicit in its theories; though it believed in the suffrage, it did not believe in making it effective for the working class. In rejecting economic democracy, liberalism rejected the means that would make political democracy truly significant.

[19] See A. L. Rowse, "The House of Lords and Legislation: A Historical Survey," *Political Quarterly*, 4:385–402 (July, 1933). Cf. Harold J. Laski, *The Problem of Second Chambers* (Fabian Tract No. 213, London, 1925) and Lewis Rockow, "Bentham on the Theory of Second Chambers," *American Political Science Review*, 22: 576–90 (August, 1928).

THE INTELLECTUAL PROTEST

I

In the eyes of the critics of democracy Victorian society was in danger of disruption. It was, they held, a society without unity; it was divided against itself, divided into opposing classes of rich and poor. It was a society without guidance; the aristocracy failed to lead, and the middle class was giving way to the anarchy of democracy. The aristocracy no longer commanded respect; men no longer admitted that the virtue of the few entitled the few to rule. Nor, in the eyes of these critics, were the mass of men impressed with the middle-class claim to govern; even Stephen, Maine, and Lecky, who were attached to property, were aware that power based upon property so far from inspiring loyalty often inspired discontent.

The critics, with the exception of Arnold, were convinced that the coming of democracy must mean disintegration. If, in their view, democracy did not promise the rule of ignorance and an impoverished culture, it promised dissolution of the social fabric. If the injustice of capitalist democracy, with its freedom to exploit and its freedom to be exploited, did not drive workingmen to revolt, the covetous nature of these men would tempt them to rebel and to destroy the private property order. And if, in their view, democracy led neither to stagnation nor to anarchy, it led rather to what was equally undesirable, to socialism.

In order to combat democracy and its threat of anarchy the critics championed authority and the title of the few to rule.

The Intellectual Protest

Carlyle and Ruskin looked to authority and to the few for the purpose of combating competitive capitalism as well as democracy. Though Arnold did not surrender to the ideas of a past world and recommend an aristocracy of the military type, he looked to a remnant of the truly civilized to set standards that would curb the excesses of laissez-faire individualism and abolish, through persuasion, the inequality of property. Stephen, Maine, and Lecky, however, did not advocate authority for social ends, but for the purpose of stemming the rising tide of democracy; they looked to authority to maintain middle-class capitalism.

II

The anti-democratic and authoritarian ideas of the intellectuals failed to make any impression on their age; that is to say, the anti-democratic and authoritarian ideas of Carlyle and Ruskin failed to make any impression. For Arnold, Stephen, Maine, and Lecky did not count in the matter of influence. It is not surprising that Carlyle and Ruskin persuaded very few, if any, to accept their anti-democratic and authoritarian ideas, for these ideas were for the most part in direct opposition to the political ideas of the middle class, which formed the main part of their reading public.

In speaking of the political ideas of the middle class, we do not imply a rigid line separating classes, or that all members of the middle class held identically the same views. We imply that, though many members obviously held ideas which other members did not hold, and though the same ideas were held with different intensity, there was a sufficiently common outlook to enable us to characterize their views in general. In order to show the opposition between Carlyle and Ruskin and the thought of the middle class, we will state the ideas of the latter in a more definite and extreme form than that in which most men in this group probably held them. Our only contention is that the ideas of the middle class were opposed to those of the prophets to such an extent that the middle class, when they

245

gave serious consideration to the views of the prophets, could hardly be convinced by them.

It is obvious that there was some common ground between Carlyle and Ruskin and the middle class. The middle class could agree with Carlyle and Ruskin that something should be done to alleviate the suffering of the workers. And if Carlyle and Ruskin did a little something to persuade the more enlightened members of the middle class to modify their views on laissez faire and to support state interference for humanitarian ends, for example, by passing factory acts, they were not able to persuade them to believe in authority for any more thoroughgoing purposes. The plea that the prophets made on behalf of the common man seems to have engendered more interest in, than well-wishing for him, more pity than genuine respect.

The liberals in the middle class who favored the franchise for workingmen and who helped to promote its realization could have only contempt for the prophets' view that the common man was inferior. The proposal of Carlyle and Ruskin for the regimentation of society, directed by an aristocracy of captains of industry or by an aristocracy of birth, could only be repellent to the middle class. The middle-class view of liberty was profoundly opposed to an emphasis on authority in the political sphere. Traditional English individualism, which the middle class had done so much to foster, could accept almost anything but an authoritarian state. A class that had fought for religious freedom against an overweening authority in the seventeenth century and had established its right to worship as it pleased, a class that still had to fight against religious discrimination at the universities in the nineteenth century, could not believe in giving government extensive power. A class that had been considerably hampered in the eighteenth and in the first half of the nineteenth century by government restrictions against freedom of trade must needs be suspicious of an authoritarian system of government. Moreover, the middle class had become what they were and had risen to power on the theory of as little government as possible, letting each man do as he likes, and

The Intellectual Protest

letting him be the judge of his own interests. The middle class, then, had found life at its best when they could follow the creed of individualism, the creed of a minimized state. This creed was directly opposed to political authoritarianism, which meant having to do what one was told.

Though the middle class admired the aristocracy and undoubtedly believed that it was the best that the world had ever seen, they could hardly desire to be governed by it or by anything similar to it. It could hardly be expected that a class that had struggled for at least a century and a half against the aristocracy before winning political ascendancy over it would be interested, within a few decades of its victory, in turning the government back to the aristocracy. A class that had witnessed the triumph of its own abilities over a class whose star had set could scarcely think that those whom they had superseded were better fitted to govern. The middle class had seen the aristocracy rule and they had felt the effects of its policy; they denied that rule by a hereditary class was the best way of selecting governors. They could not discern an extraordinary gift for governing in men who accepted privilege irrespective of merit, who permitted a rotten borough system to exist, and who stood out for protection when the interests of the nation clearly demanded free trade. They could not idealize the virtues of the few when the few were identified with privileges from which they were excluded.

Moreover, the middle class believed that they were better qualified to rule than the aristocracy; the nation had made truly great progress under their leadership. Furthermore, the interests of the nation were identified with the middle class rather than with the aristocracy; the nation was primarily industrial, not agricultural; the aristocracy could not know the needs of industry as well as the middle class. And the interests of the middle class itself were better served when they directed the state; not only were their economic interests better secured, but so also their liberties. And to surrender power to the aristocracy would mean a sacrifice of self-respect that the middle class was not prepared to make, especially in virtue of their success.

The middle class, as is shown above, was not convinced that democracy in the sense of universal suffrage would bring about the destruction of society; and they could not take seriously the idea of an authoritarian state ruled by an aristocracy. Neither was the middle class prepared to accept the charge of the prophets that the materialism of Victorian society and the exploitation of the laborer by capitalism threatened to bring about revolution. It is true of this charge, as of the anti-democratic and authoritarian ideas we discussed above, that many who read the prophets were stimulated and went their way, and that others rejected their charge as fantastic. It is also true that many who read their charge sincerely attempted, within the limits of their own way of thought, to see whether or not they could agree with it. It is our contention that the majority of these men of good will could not take the charge of materialism and of exploitation seriously, for it was in profound conflict with their economic and social philosophy.

Again, let it be said that when we refer to the middle class or to their ideas, we speak in general terms. In order to make our argument clear, we will present their positon, as we did above, in what is undoubtedly an exaggerated form as regards any single member of the class. For any member of the middle class who admitted the charge of materialism and of exploitation would have to change fundamentally his conception of the private property order. He would have to agree that profit (monopoly profit, the getting of something for nothing) should not be the chief incentive of work; that there should be a principle of justice explaining reward in terms of need, effort, and the quality of effort; and that the application of this principle would involve a great spreading of benefits to the lower classes, to the whole community.

To begin with, we may say that the middle class recognized to some extent the charge of materialism and of exploitation; they realized, for example, that limiting the working hours of women and children was necessary; but they did not recognize the charge in any fundamental way. It could hardly have been otherwise, for a fundamental recognition of the charge would have implied a rejection of their whole background and their social philosophy. The middle class had risen to power by means of industry and commerce organized under an almost unfettered system of private property. Men are not easily persuaded to reject the property order under which they have risen to the chief place in the state. Men who have become accustomed to power and the benefits it confers are not willing to part with it easily; certainly few are willing to part with it simply because they are admonished to do so by intellectuals. The middle class had great admiration for the social position of the aristocracy, and many aspired to the ranks of the aristocracy as a final crown of success. Wealth was the key that could unlock the gate; to reject the property system that made possible social distinction was not possible to men who would become aristocrats.

The middle class had risen to power under a private property system organized on the profit motive. To admit the charge of materialism and of exploitation was to admit that profit ought not to be the chief incentive to the acquisition of property; and to admit that was to give up the principle that had been at the very heart of their whole activity. It could hardly be expected that a class at the height of its power would surrender a principle that was so fundamental to its success.

The charge of the prophets was fundamentally opposed not only to the philosophy of economic individualism, but also to the spirit of materialism, which was so strong at the time the prophets were most widely read — from the sixties through the nineties. By the eighties the evangelists in religion could no longer appeal to the imagination of the middle class; where Wesley had been received as a prophet, General Booth was received with contempt. It was significant that missionaries left England to save souls. With capitalism at its zenith, the charge of materialism could hardly impress many minds.

The Intellectual Protest

Despite appearances to the contrary, humanitarianism aided fundamentally not in opening, but in closing, the minds of the middle class to the charge of exploitation. True enough, it played an important part in making for such needed reforms as the factory acts, prison reform, and the abolition of slavery in the West Indies. But these were minor, not major, reforms. When it came to the latter, humanitarianism acted as a hindrance.

Humanitarianism fortified the conscience against the recognition of vital social obligation, such as was implicit in the charge of exploitation. That the middle class had recognized part of their obligations to those below left them with a sense of having discharged their duty. The fundamental reason for this was that humanitarianism is based not on an idea of justice, but on a feeling of pity. Thus the minor concessions were acts of charity, acts of philanthropy; that is, they were done because the middle class had pity for the lower class, not because they recognized the injustice of the conditions under which the lower class lived, not because they recognized any genuine moral obligation to the lower class. To do that which the middle class believed they were not morally required to do demonstrated their virtue; and they were righteous for having done whatever they had done. Thus the little things done were as worthy as the big things left undone. The extent to which the middle class felt virtuous — and it was not small — measured the extent to which they were immune to the idea of right; measured, that is, the extent to which real obligation to society had been whittled away.

The very fact that humanitarianism was based on a feeling of pity instead of on an idea of justice, on what was so largely emotional instead of on what was rational, tended to dissociate it from reason. This fact tended to make humanitarianism unsympathetic to intellectual inquiry, unsympathetic to a search into the causes of the economic and social conditions that made for suffering among the workers and that made humanitarianism possible. And the very fact that humanitarianism was based on a feeling so personal in character as the feeling of pity meant, as it must do, that it lent itself easily to personal indulgence; very frequently the feeling of pity was held sentimentally, that is, it was held for its own sake. This made for a special concern with feeling, and for a lack of interest in reason. Very frequently, too, humanitarianism was accepted merely because it was fashionable or respectable; to accept anything merely because it is given and merely because it carries prestige is to abandon reason.

With humanitarianism, then, so little a matter of justice and so much a matter of feeling, and so little informed by reason, it is no wonder that it led to a preoccupation with the tangible, immediate, and obvious social evils. Nor, for the same reasons, is it any wonder that humanitarianism was concerned with remedies rather than with cure and prevention. To remove the minor, and to leave undisturbed the major, social and economic diseases is to remove the minor but temporarily. To be concerned with remedies, not with cure and prevention, is to perpetuate the need for basic reform. In fact, it is not too much to say that humanitarianism in a very real sense produces the need for reform, and is an obstacle to its own abolition. The philosophy that lay behind the charge of the prophets was hardly in sympathy with perpetuating reform for the sake of humanitarians.

Humanitarianism, lastly, inhibited the recognition of vital social obligation from another angle. Nothing is more important for the recognition of real social obligation than respect for personality, or for the potential intrinsic worth of the individual; yet humanitarianism made for disrespect of personality, especially in the case of propertyless men. The very condition essential to the existence of humanitarianism is an unequal society; humanitarianism is a function of inequality. If the middle class is to have pity for the many below, the many must be below. Because humanitarianism implies a superior and an inferior, it breeds disrespect among those better off for those less well off. The fundamental reason for this is not that there is a difference as such between the middle and lower classes, nor that there is a difference based on property, but that there is a difference based on an unjust property system.

When men do not have to justify what they own, they tend to justify whatever they possess. And those who own soon come to develop disrespect for those who do not, for those who own soon come to believe that the accumulation of property is a sign of character and ability, and they are easily persuaded that those without property are also without character and ability. Thus in the eyes of the middle class, those below did not really deserve even the minor benefits, like the factory acts, for they were men of little worth. The final comment on humanitarianism is that it enabled the middle class to keep their property and to claim their humanity.

Puritanism, the characteristic religion of the middle class, did little to open their minds to the charge of materialism and of exploitation; on the contrary, it worked to close them. What mattered fundamentally for the puritan was the communion of his soul with God; his religion was personal, not social, in essence. The emphasis the puritan placed on the individual character of his religion meant, as R. H. Tawney has pointed out, that religion entered relatively little into his social life. Less important for the puritan than the relation of his soul to God was his relation to his fellow human beings; what was important was the perfection of his spirit, not social justice. Puritanism, then, left the social life of the individual untenanted by any fundamental ethical principle; it left his social life open to an easy acceptance of the materialistic ideas of capitalism. In fact, puritanism lived with little difficulty side by side with capitalism, and came in a very real sense to sanction it. Wilhelm Dibelius, an acute observer of English life, has said: "Religion permitted, nay encouraged the massing of money. . . . The Christian altar was in perilous proximity to the Golden Calf." [1] Puritanism tended to set a seal of approval on the pursuit of private gain; God's chosen were those whom He was pleased

[1] Wilhelm Dibelius, *England: Her Character and Genius* (London, 1930), p. 125.

to favor with success in this lower world. Surely to permit the accumulation of a fortune was a sign of His blessing.

It is clear that the charge of materialism and of exploitation fell for the most part on deaf ears. If a few were convinced of the justice of the charge, very few indeed were prepared to act in order to mitigate it. Most of these few must have thought it impracticable to act in the face of the overwhelming power of the middle class, which stood for property and materialism, and permitted exploitation. However this may be, most men resolve to act, not as a result of reading the books of intellectuals, but as a result of their own experience. Moreover, it is rare that a man transcends the ideas of the class in which he is brought up, and is able to see its defects and to find himself in fundamental disagreement with it. It is still rarer that, because of his fundamental disagreement, he acts in order to remove the defects. To act with a view to mitigating the charge of materialism and of exploitation must mean a great change in the individual's thought and way of life, a far greater change than is possible for most men to make, certainly during a period of prosperity and contentment like that of the Victorian era.

III

The protest of the prophets, Carlyle, Ruskin, and Arnold, and of the technical critics, Stephen, Maine, and Lecky, against democracy was a protest against the rise of the common man. The democratic movement in England in the nineteenth century, as Arnold observed, was above all a movement of expansion on something like a communal scale. With the middle class receiving the franchise in 1832, and universal manhood suffrage all but achieved by 1885, it is clear that the democratic movement meant that the ordinary man was beginning to assert himself. And the social legislation that followed his participation in political power meant that the ordinary man was beginning to assert himself in order to better his lot. That he achieved from time to time somewhat better conditions of life partly satisfied and partly stimulated his craving for freedom, for an opportunity to express himself and to make something of his powers. Along with his desire to explore his personality went the desire for equality; unless opportunities were open to all, the fruits of a free life would not be enjoyed by common men, but would remain the privilege of the few.

The intellectual critics opposed democracy fundamentally because it gave common men too much freedom; to give common men power, they thought, would bring about disorder, a disintegration of society. If Carlyle and Ruskin believed that disorder would come in part from the freedom that democracy gave men, they believed that it would come still more from the fact that common men were incapable of governing. Arnold harbored fears of democracy on the ground that mediocrity might triumph, and perhaps even brutality find a place in affairs; he doubted whether the common man was sufficiently developed to exercise political power creatively.

The technical critics saw democracy threatening society not because it was impotent to act, but because it aggrandized authority too much and was too eager to act. Though Stephen believed that democracy lacked consistent purpose, power of unified action, and a sense of direction, he held that the philosophy of liberty, equality, fraternity was a far greater evil; if this philosophy were put into practice, it would, he feared, loosen all the bonds that held society together. Though Maine insisted on the difficulty and on the fragility of democracy, he was more concerned with arguing that democracy threatened economic disruption; the desire of common men to feast on milk and honey would bring about an attack on property. Though Lecky held that parliamentary government was becoming an institution for satisfying the greed of special interest groups, he held far more strongly that democracy endangered capitalism, on the ground that the common man wanted his share of the good things and would plunder in order to get them.

Although the prophet and the technical critic were broadly in agreement that democracy led to disorder because the common man was incapable of taking part in government, they came to this conclusion from somewhat different conceptions of the common man. Carlyle and Ruskin held that the ordinary individual was wanting in rational and moral ability to seek a way out by himself; and Arnold held that, though the ordinary individual had great potentialities for the future, and should be admitted to power, he was still insufficiently developed to make the most of it. The technical critics feared not that the common man was helpless or insufficiently developed; they feared that he was too assertive, that he was too selfish and too greedy, that he was too irrational and too rash. It is significant that the prophet-critics were critical of the organization of private property in their day, while the technical critics strongly supported it.

IV

What was the basis of the contention of the intellectual critics that the common man was not really capable of exercising political power? The critics would undoubtedly have replied that it was direct observation. They cited a number of facts and illustrations to support their view that the common man was inferior, and there can be no dispute that some of their facts do show this very thing. Given the conditions in which the upper classes permitted the lower to live, given the slums and the squalor, given a few riots, the revolutions of 1848 and the Paris Commune — given such facts, it was easy for the critics to conceive of the common man as deficient in mind and character. It was easy, however, on one condition, namely, that they thought that the common man was deficient before they looked for the facts; else they could never have found the facts. Since facts must be selected, a notion of what to select must precede the the act of selection. The question is, what was the source of the critics' notion of the common man's inferiority? What factors shaped the basic notion of the critics' political philosophy?

The intellectual protest against the rise of the common man was, so far as ideas were concerned, first and foremost a protest of puritanism. Carlyle, Ruskin, Arnold, and Stephen were brought up in puritan households and all were imbued with puritan ideas. They could hardly have escaped the view in some form or other that the mass of men were sinners. All the critics, though Lecky perhaps above all, were undoubtedly affected by the view current in the middle class of the common man's inferiority. If this view, which was given typical expression by Macaulay, was inherited in part from the aristocracy, it also came from middle-class sources; it came very much from the puritan conception of the depravity of human nature, and it came from the natural disposition of men in power to look upon those without as somehow inferior.

The other sources of the notion of the common man's inferiority are best seen in relation to the sources of the doctrine of aristocracy and the doctrine of authority. The special title of the few to rule, which the critics urged against the rule of common men, seems to derive in part from the puritan notion that only the few are elected, and that they are the salt of the earth. It also seems to derive from middle-class ideas of power: the industrial and commercial enterprises of the nation were the pride of the middle class; as of necessity they were managed by the few. There was common agreement in the middle class that these concerns were well managed. A class that set great store upon competition and believed in the survival of the fittest must have respect for the few who survive. Respect for the virtues of the few must also have come to some extent from the very fact that these critics lived in a class that admired aristocracy.

The stand taken for authority by Carlyle, Ruskin, and Stephen, and the lesser stand taken by Arnold, may be traced in part to puritanism. Force has always attracted the puritan mind as an effective weapon for stamping out sin; when God is a stern judge enforcing justice, coercion appears to be the most direct and tangible method of fulfilling the Law against the disobedient. Another source of the emphasis on authority, which may have more bearing on Stephen, Maine, and Lecky than on the prophets, is the respect of the middle class for authority in the economic sphere. In spite of the antagonism of the middle class to an authoritarian state, this class was an exponent of authority in the sphere of industry and commerce. The everyday experience of a great many in the middle class was to exercise authority or to live under it; industrial and commercial institutions were managed on the autocratic principle, however benevolent, of government.

If puritanism and middle-class ideas of power were the main sources, so far as ideas were concerned, of the three leading doctrines of the critics — the common man's inferiority, the title of the few to rule, and authority — if these were the main sources, they were not the only ones. Classical education, to which the critics were subjected in their youth, is a source that cannot be overlooked. The above doctrines were most perfectly represented in Plato's *Republic,* and the tone of classical education has rather implied Plato's view of these doctrines. And classical history, which showed the populace turning to disorder in Athens and in Rome, could support the view that the common man was inferior.

If Maine was chiefly indebted to the German historical school and to India for his appreciation of the three doctrines, Stephen was indebted to India and a little to Bentham. Carlyle's appreciation of the three doctrines was undoubtedly reinforced by Fichte, Goethe, and Novalis; Ruskin's by Carlyle and Plato; Arnold's to some extent by Plato and Burke; and Lecky's by Burke. It is not unlikely that respect for the special virtues of the few and respect for authority were strengthened a little by the very fact that the critics were members of the upper circles of society; and by the fact that they were themselves among the élite who were expected to give guidance.

The three doctrines of the critics were developed very largely in authoritarian periods, like the Reformation, or in epochs of concentration, like England in the eighteenth century; they were developed by writers like Calvin, and by writers like Burke and Hume. The doctrines of the common man's inferiority, of the special virtue of the few, and of authority were asserted when a few men or a part of the community claimed the title to govern. Those who ruled, whether they were churchmen, aristocrats, or middle-class men, found that the common man's inferiority was proof of their own special virtue and of their right to govern; and they were convinced that they could not deal with the common man and prevent civil disobedience unless they had considerable authority. The protest of the critics of democracy was a protest of the past against the present.

Ernest Barker has said that the literary man in politics is essentially a Platonist.[2] When a mind trained in letters turns from its own world to the social world, it seeks in the latter, as it does in the former, the beauty of order and the charm of definition. Not finding these, but finding disorder, it naturally looks to authority as a corrective. The technical critics as well as the prophets were probably influenced by the conditions under which a writer must work, by the necessity of ordering knowledge and of arranging ideas.

The intellectual critics may have been influenced by another condition necessary to their activity; an undisturbed atmosphere is essential to continuous thinking. That the atmosphere of the nineteenth century was, for the intellectual, not calm, but disturbed, perhaps especially by the growth of the democratic movement, may have augmented their hostility to democracy. Intellectuals do not like to be interrupted in the pursuit of their business any more than do businessmen or administrators in theirs. Security and orderly life are desirable for sustained thought.

The fact, too, that the critics were specialists who went outside their specialties to criticize in the field of social science, where they had not been trained, is undoubtedly significant in explaining their aversion to democracy. The specialist is always impressed with the complexity of his own field, and is easily led to believe that all problems are equally complex; and, in turn,

[2] Ernest Barker, *Political Thought in England, 1848 to 1914* (rev. ed., London, 1928), p. 203.

that only the few who are specialists can hope to understand the life of the world. Not only does the specialist tend naturally to be anti-democratic with contempt for common opinion, but he also tends naturally to be skeptical of change. He is impressed with the sinfulness of error, and he fears to tread in the province of the unverified, where change always lies, for the possibility of error, he thinks, is overwhelming. To him novelty is dangerous; change should not be attempted unless there is certainty of a correct result, that is to say, change should not be attempted. The specialist, then, from the very nature of his activity, tends to be unsympathetic to democracy, because, at bottom, he forgets that problems are simple as well as complex, else life as it is lived by the mass of men, and by intellectuals when they are not specialists, could not be lived as we know it.

Again, the fact that the critics were specialists in ideas is perhaps not without some bearing upon their authoritarianism. Men who deal with ideas and men who become exponents of a point of view are prone to assume the cloak of authority. The consciousness that their minds are trained and that they have knowledge easily leads them to indulge in oracular pronouncement. They tend to believe that a trained mind, whatever its training, is entitled to an impressive hearing. Nor is it irrelevant to say that the success of these men in their own pursuits tended to make them a little authoritarian; men who achieve distinction tend to lay down the law. Perhaps this is especially true of intellectuals.

That Carlyle, Ruskin, and Arnold were men of letters, that Stephen was a judge and Maine a lawyer and Lecky a historian, that these men were engaged in professions more or less removed from life, could only strengthen their belief in the three doctrines. That these men lived very largely apart from the world meant that they had little opportunity of testing and correcting the ideas and attitudes that they had acquired in their youth. Their anti-democratic and authoritarian ideas, which they had learned from their parents and taken from their class and from the environment of their class, were never subject, except in the case of Arnold and to some extent in the case of Stephen, to the modifying influence of practical activity.

That they lived in their ivory towers meant more than this; it meant that the three doctrines were held as if they represented ultimate truth. This is not difficult to understand. These critics thought continually with the same assumptions, assumptions which they acquired in their youth, and they found nothing in their own experience to contradict them; thus their assumptions became part of themselves and part of the permanent order of things. Since their life was their thought, their thought was reality; the democratic movement in the world outside, which ran counter to their thought, was the appearance that was false. That their basic ideas remained unaltered in a world of flux made them more certain of their reality; what was permanent was true, and what was changing untrue. As the democratic movement gained momentum and the contradiction between what the critics thought and external events became greater, it did not occur to them to question what they thought. On the contrary, the doctrines of the inferiority of the common man, of the special virtue of the few, and of authority became more vivid in their minds.

That Arnold was much less hostile to democracy and much less authoritarian than the other critics was in part due to his participation in practical affairs. He presents a striking contrast to Carlyle, Ruskin, Stephen, Maine, and Lecky, and stands in relation to these men as the natural law jurists of the seventeenth and eighteenth centuries stood in relation to the historical jurists of the nineteenth. Arnold had a career in the everyday world, and the natural law jurists had careers wholly in that world; the writings of the latter were a by-product of their practical activity. Arnold believed in the possibilities of democratic change, and the natural law jurists had confidence in reason, taught principles of constructive legislation, and believed in action. Carlyle, Ruskin, Stephen, Maine, and Lecky opposed democratic change, and placed their faith in an aristocratic or middle-class utopia of an authoritarian nature; and the jurists of the historical school who had academic careers distrusted legislative change and were averse to action.[3]

Arnold, unlike the other critics, came into vital contact with the lower classes; as an inspector of elementary schools, he saw that human beings come from the slums as well as from Mayfair. His study of the structure, the administration, and the working of English and foreign schools kept him in touch with actual affairs; Arnold's practical activity helped to keep him human. His work as an inspector put him in touch with the life of the community and made him more sympathetic to those who were trying to find themselves. It seems that it is essential for an intellectual to take some active part in the world if he is to retain a sense of the present and its importance, and if he is to understand what the community is thinking and doing.

The source, however, of the three doctrines lies not only in the early family training and social background of the critics, and in the nature and conditions of intellectual work, but also in their temperaments. The egoistical, assertive, and absolutistic temper of Carlyle, Ruskin, and Stephen was probably a main source of their belief in authority and in the superior virtues of the few. Arnold's temperament was also a source of his authoritarian strain. These men had in them the urge of the prophet. Carlyle, Ruskin, and Stephen possessed in a high degree the combative spirit; they were fighters who found their antagonists in the realm of ideas. In argument these men were convinced of the moral rightness of their own views and of the wrongness of their opponents; they asked and gave no quarter. Carlyle and Ruskin were so certain of their inspiration that they could brook no opposition. If Lord Acton is correct, there was in Maine behind his academic calm a tendency to Caesarism. That Lecky stood less strongly for authority than Carlyle, Ruskin, and Stephen was due in part to his more open and

[3] Dean Pound says that it was significant that the historical jurists Savigny, Puchta, Maine, Ames, Thayer, and Bigelow were academic men and were opposed to legislative change and to action, while the natural law jurists Burlamaqui, Montesquieu, Blackstone, Kent, and Story had practical careers and believed in reason and change. *Interpretations of Legal History* (Cambridge, Massachusetts, 1923), p. 17.

more tolerant temperament. Though he could become in his own way as indignant as any of these men, he usually took account of the views of his opponents.

That Arnold could harbor doubts concerning the common man and emphasize authority and the special virtues of the few, and, at the same time, retain his belief in democracy was very largely due to his temperament. His friendliness and his gaiety, his grace and his wit, his ability to see himself in a humorous light, his flexibility and resilience, his refusal to make seriousness a cardinal virtue, his attempt to understand his opponents, his sensitiveness to those subtle attitudes that make the great differences, all these characteristics enabled him to get the upper hand of his tendency to egoism and his tendency to the pontifical manner. In spite of his aristocratic and authoritarian traits, he could identify himself with his fellows, whether they were in the upper or in the lower classes; that is to say, he could see the importance of liberty and equality and maintain a democratic spirit. The importance of temperament as a source of the three doctrines may be illustrated by saying that though Stephen, Maine, and Lecky were men who emphasized the importance of fact and careful reasoning, though they were historians, they asserted their prejudices more strongly than Arnold, and on occasion they gave way to statements as extreme in expression for them as any of Carlyle's were for him. Though Arnold never inquired into the "facts" with such pertinacity as the technical critics, he gave reason and temperate judgment a greater place in his views on contemporary politics than they did in their views. And though Maine set out purposely to apply scientific method to politics, even Carlyle, who stood for intuition, hardly violated it more than he.

As the critics grew older, the liberal strain that was in their temperament tended, except in the case of Ruskin, to disappear. Carlyle, in his early years, was deeply sympathetic with the working class; in his later years he found the working class disobedient. Arnold, in his later years, could find in the common man a tendency to disorder, and could attach no little importance to the virtue of the few and to the doctrine of authority. In the latter part of his life, Stephen's Calvinism dominated the liberal strain he acquired from Bentham. As a young man, Maine supported democracy in France and stood for some elements of socialism; toward the end of his life he distrusted democracy and looked back to aristocracy. Ruskin's liberal side never altered except perhaps to become more liberal; that is to say, his denunciations of the exploitation of the worker increased in his later years.

Finally, it is probably true that the dyspepsia from which Carlyle suffered, the brain fever with which Ruskin was afflicted, the depression that came over Maine and Lecky, had the effect of increasing the distrust these critics felt for the democratic movement.

V

Any criticism of the intellectual protest must begin by attacking it at the base; the critics' view of the common man must in its essentials be rejected. Their attack on democracy was based at bottom on the view that the common man was too inferior to be entrusted with power. It is our contention that the intellectuals were mistaken in holding that the common man monopolized the defects of human nature. The defects of the common man, his want of mind and of character, are not limited to the economic lower classes, but are to be found in all classes. All kinds of individuals and types, H. S. Jennings says, are to be found in any section of society.[4] And he points out that "if one means by democracy such a constitution of society that any part of the mass can in time supply individuals fitted for all its functions — in that sense the biological situation is that of democracy." The intellectual critics, we suggest, distorted the nature of the common man: they emphasized his weaker side and neglected his stronger side; they emphasized his defects and neglected his virtues.

[4] Herbert S. Jennings, *The Biological Basis of Human Nature* (1st ed., New York, 1930), pp. 220-21. Cf. p. 201 above.

The Intellectual Protest

At the same time, the intellectual critics overemphasized the importance, so far as politics is concerned, of the superiorities of the few. Admitting the great value of unusual qualities of mind and character, and admitting that they are rare, they are not so unusual that it would be safe to entrust them with the sole governing authority. A government of the wisest and best, of Plato's philosopher-kings, might be efficient, but never safe. The problem of government is not only a problem of intelligence and character, but also a problem of will and sentiment. The mass of men must be consulted if rulers are to be reasonably certain of the continuous execution of their orders.

Moreover, to withhold political power from the mass of men is to give privilege to the few. Men who are excluded from power are excluded from benefits. Not that the few are wanting in good intentions; they are merely unable to translate them in terms other than their own experience. And their own experience generally leads them to believe that the interests of the community are best served by advancing the interests of their class. Moreover, to leave the mass of men politically inert is to leave the few to become corrupted by their own privilege and the mass of men to suffer from the disadvantage of inferiority.

Since the intellectuals had little respect for the lower classes, they had little understanding of the need of that class for freedom. They did not appreciate that a prime condition of human development is the opportunity of taking a significant part in directing one's own life, for only by taking such a part can men hope to live creatively. It is obviously true that there can be no freedom without authority; freedom for all is impossible without restraints for all, and authority is necessary in maintaining restraints. But the intellectuals put too much emphasis on authority, and too little on freedom. They did not see that the democratic system, which they opposed, is the very best system for achieving their end; they did not see that the best way to make men responsible is to give them some responsibility, and that the best way to humanize them is to educate them.

Index

INDEX

Index

Index

Index

Index

posed by Maine, 185, 192; in America, 195, 206, 217; effect on parliamentary government, 208, 209, 230, 236, 237; for labor, 216, 243, 246; results, 217, 218, 219; act of *1867*, 219, 239; Lecky's view, 224, 226; act of *1885*, 239, 253; attitude of middle class, 248
Fraternity, Stephen's view, 3, 135, 155. *See also* Democracy, Equality, Liberty
Frederick the Great, history by Carlyle, 27, 29, 31
Freedom, *see* Liberty
Freedom of contract, Maine's view, 202; Lecky's view, 216, 221
French Revolution, of *1789*: influence on Carlyle, 24, 29, Arnold's view of, 103, 104; of *1848*: Stephen's attitude toward, 138
Froude, James A., 23, 27

German historical school, 171; influence on Maine, 170, 174, 257
German literature, influence on Carlyle, 21–23
Germany, effect of militarism, 189; fascism, 198, 236
Gibbon, Edward, 21
Gladstone, William E., 51, 142, 219; quoted, 14; on Irish independence, 213
Godkin, E. L., 197n
Goethe, Johann Wolfgang, 98, 257; influence on Carlyle, 21–23
Gooch, G. P., 214
Government, Arnold's theory, 2, 102, 103, 110, 119–29; Carlyle's theory, 12, 18, 27, 33, 45; Ruskin's theory, 56, 57, 58, 64, 65, 67, 79, 80, 82, 84, 88, 90; Stephen's theory, 136, 141, 143, 144, 156–58, 159; Maine's view, 175, 176, 180, 181, 186; relation to progress, 197; Lecky's theory, 215, 224–26, 230, 241, 242; requirement for permanence, 264. *See also* Aristocracy, Cabinet, Democracy, Monarchy, Parliament, Parliamentary government
Grattan, Henry, 211
Gray, Thomas, 100
Green, T. H., 5
Guild Socialist Movement, 4, 59
Guilds, proposed by Ruskin, 81, 82

Hare system of proportional representation, 222
Harrison, Frederick, 66, 133, 164; quoted, 93
Hedonism, opposed by Carlyle, 31. *See also* Utilitarianism
Hegel, Georg, 203n
High Church movement, 120; protests against economic distress, 12
History, Carlyle's view, 22, 25, 39; view of Eichhorn and Savigny, 171; Maine's view, 172, 173, 177, 189, 203, 204
Hitler, Adolf, 4, 18, 47, 48, 51
Hobbes, Thomas, 136, 137, 139, 164
Holmes, Oliver Wendell, Justice, 202
Home Rule, *see* Ireland
House of Commons, *see* Commons, House of
House of Lords, *see* Lords, House of
Humanitarianism, relation to Carlyle, 9, 13, 26, 39; analysis of, 246, 250–52
Hume, David, influence on Carlyle, 21
Huxley, Thomas Henry, 140, 202

Imperialism, 9; Stephen on, 142; and industry, 163; English, 225
India, influence on Stephen, 140–42, 164, 165, 257; caste system, 155; influence on Maine, 175, 176, 257
Individualism, of Carlyle, 7, 14, 15; relation to anarchy, 53; Arnold's view, 115, 116, 117, 245; Benthamite, 143; of Manchester school, 143; of Lecky, 216, 238; of middle class, 246, 247. *See also* Property
Industrialism, *see* Capitalism
Inequality, Carlyle's belief in, 14; Plato's view, 68; Ruskin on, 75, 88; Arnold on, 96, 106, 126, 127, 130, 132; Stephen's view, 151, 154, 155, 161; relation to humanitarianism, 251. *See also* Aristocracy, Common man, Equality, Leadership
Ireland, Arnold's attitude, 103, 104, 106, 107, 108, 109, 133; Home Rule controversy, 165, 213, 214, 237, 243; Lecky's attitude, 211, 213, 218, 237
Italy, *see* Fascism

Jackson, Andrew, 182
Jamaica Committee, 140
James, Henry, 28

271

Index

Index

toward aristocracy, 169, 173, 177, 186, 188; attitude toward property, 169, 172, 178, 186, 198, 202, 244; influence of German school, 170, 257; in journalism, 170; antipathy to Rousseau, 172, 173; belief in scientific method, 173, 185; individualism, 173; legal instinct, 174; influenced by India, 175, 176, 257; illnesses, 176; temperament, 176, 261, 262; defends economic competition, 178, 187, 201, 202, 245; defends freedom of contract, 179; conception of democracy, 180, 191n, 204; doctrine of change, 183, 200, 204; attitude toward suffrage, 185, 186; evaluation, 188–206, 263; style, 188; analysis of political parties, 189; on civilization and contract, 202n; lack of scientific method, 204, 206; compared with Lecky, 207, 208, 209, 211, 214, 223, 224, 229, 235, 236, 243; socialistic tendency, 263. WORKS: *Popular Government*, 168, 174, 175, 177, 189, 199, 206; *Ancient Law*, 171, 172; *Village Communities*, 171; *Early History of Institutions*, 171; *Dissertations on Early Law and Customs*, 171

Mallet, Sir Louis, 177

Mallock, William Hurrell, political and economic theory, 207n

Marriage, Ruskin's theory, 79; Stephen's view, 152, 160

Martineau, Harriet, quoted, 7

Marx, Karl, 2, 6, 54, 81, 89, 95, 210, 242; criticism of political economy, 55

Materialism, Arnold's attitude, 2, 94, 113, 127, 132; condemned by Carlyle, 7, 21, 31–34, 46, 47; Ruskin's attitude, 54, 56, 68–74, 86, 90. *See also* Mechanism

Mazzini, Giuseppe, 26, 58

Mechanism, criticized by Carlyle, 31; importance to society, 32, 33; attacked by Ruskin, 68, 86. *See also* Materialism

Middle class, power, 1; Carlyle's attitude, 12, 58; Ruskin's attitude, 58, 63; Arnold's attitude, 94, 95, 99, 102, 103, 104, 106, 107, 119–29; attitude toward aristocracy, 169; capacity for disorder, 198; Lecky's attitude, 210, 215, 222; attitude toward property, 237, 238, 240, 249, 253; political ideas,

245; attitude toward working class, 246; in government, 247; attitude toward franchise, 248, 249, 252; humanitarianism, 250–52; puritanism, 252; respect for economic authority, 257

Militarism, relation to fascism, 4, 47; Lecky's attitude, 224, 225, 236

Mill, John Stuart, 1, 5, 6, 21, 24, 103, 128, 130, 131, 134, 135, 139, 167, 168, 212; association with Carlyle, 25; on Jamaica Committee, 140; doctrines analyzed by Stephen, 144–56, 159; attitude toward common man, 144; doctrine of liberty, 144–52, 159, 163, 166; view of taxation, 145; plea for tolerance, 150; theory of equality, 152–55, 160, 161; on equality of women, 152, 163; attitude toward force, 153, 154, 160; doctrine of fraternity, 155

Mirabeau, Honoré, Count de, 22

Monarchy, Stephen's view, 158, 165; Maine's view, 179, 181, 186, 189; Cohen's view, 191; compared with democracy, 193, 194

Morley, John, Lord, 133, 136, 195n, 209, 235; quoted, 176

Morris, William, 59, 61

Mussolini, Benito, 4, 18, 47, 48, 51

Nationalism, 189

Newman, John Henry, Cardinal, 7, 98, 211

Nonconformity, Arnold's criticism, 104, 105, 118, 123, 129

Novalis, influence on Carlyle, 22, 23, 257

Oxford University, 59, 60, 61, 102, 122, 129; influence on Arnold, 97

Parliament, Carlyle's attitude, 8, 25, 27, 37, 38, 43, 51; Arnold's attitude, 122; Lecky's attitude, 223. *See also* Commons, House of; Lords, House of

Parliamentary government, Carlyle's attitude, 47, 50; Stephen's attitude, 141, 148, 156, 158, 165; Lecky's attitude, 208, 217–24, 226, 230, 236, 239; effect of franchise, 209

Index

Index

Index

Taine, H. A., 169

Tawney, R. H., 4, 252

Taxation, Ruskin's view, 72; Mill's view, 145; Stephen's view, 150, 156; on income, 198, 219, 237; on inheritance, 198; Lecky's view, 216, 221, 231, 240

Tennyson, Alfred, Lord, 65; influence of Carlyle, 26

Thackeray, William M., 26, 64

Tocqueville, Alexis Charles de, 103, 126, 229, 236

Tractarian Movement, 98

Trade-unions, 12, 81, 203n; under fascism, 47; Lecky's view, 222, 238

Trinity College (Dublin), 211, 212

Unemployment, Carlyle's discussion, 25, 44–46

Unions, see Trade-unions

United States, democracy in, 39, 77, 107, 108, 147, 150, 154, 159, 179, 224, 226; Senate, 108; inheritance tradition, 132; Civil War, 160; constitution, 177, 178, 180, 184, 188, 203, 229; spoils system, 182, 226, 227, 235; suffrage, 195, 206, 217; reception of science in, 197n; government, 200; stability, 223; foreign policy, 225; lack of political leaders, 226, 235; corruption in, 228; civilization, 229; wealth in, 232; industrialism, 233

Universal suffrage, see Franchise

University of London, 139

Utilitarianism, 46; relation to common man, 13; opposed by Carlyle, 31; influence on Stephen, 135, 136, 139,

143, 145, 152, 161, 163, 164. See also Bentham, Mill

Value, Ruskin's theory of: 54, 68, 81, 88, criticism of economists, 55, 58, 76

Victorian Age, liberalism, 1, 27, 137, 167, 168, 258; reaction to Carlyle, 6, 17, 18, 45, 46; Carlyle's opinion of, 29; reaction to Ruskin, 57, 61, 64, 65, 66; reaction to Arnold, 93; social structure, 95; progress, 110; prosperity, 167; in eyes of critics, 244; materialism, 248, 253

Vinogradoff, Paul, 172, 173

Voltaire, François Arouet de, 6, 211

Wages, Ruskin's view of: effect of competition, 70, under capitalism, 72, effect of demand and supply, 75, 76, fixed wage plan, 79

Wallas, Graham, 189, 238

War, Ruskin's view of: 92, in relation to capitalism, 55, 72, 77, 87; effect on progress, 163; Maine's prophecy, 189; feared by Lecky, 224; result of militarism, 236

Wealth, Ruskin's view of: 58, 87, on origin, 65, 69, as source of power, 70, 71, 86, 87, abuse, 77, 78; Arnold's attitude, 96, 114, 117, 118; Lecky's view, 230, 232, 233, 234, 239; importance to middle class, 249. See also Property

Welsh, Jane, 23

Whig party, 24, 28, 97

Xenophon, 58, 61; Economist, 60

Date Due